TEACHER'S GUIDE

GRADE 4

READING AND WRITING Sourcebook

Authors

Ruth Nathan
Laura Robb

Great Source Education Group

a Houghton Mifflin Company
Wilmington, Massachusetts
www.greatsource.com

Authors

Ruth Nathan, one of the authors of *Writers Express* and *Write Away*, is the author of many professional books and articles on literacy. She earned a Ph.D. in reading from Oakland University in Rochester, Michigan, where she co-headed their reading research laboratory for several years. She currently teaches in third grade, as well as consults with numerous schools and organizations on reading.

Laura Robb, author of *Reading Strategies That Work* and *Teaching Reading in the Middle School*, has taught language arts at Powhatan School in Boyce, Virginia, for more than thirty years. She also mentors and coaches teachers in Virginia public schools and speaks at conferences throughout the country.

Great Source® is a registered trademark of Houghton Mifflin Company.

Printed in the United States of America.

International Standard Book Number: 0-669-48442-3

2 3 4 5 6 7 8 9 10 POO 06 05 04 03 02

Readers and Reviewers

Judy Backlund
Mt. Stuart School
Ellensburg, WA

Diane Brown
Island Lake School
New Brighton, MN

Nan Bryant
Winchester, VA

Janel DeBoer
Stonewall Magnet School
Nicholasville, KY

Helen Dorothy
Little Village Academy
Chicago, IL

Lois Johnson
Panama City, FL

Diane Kraft
Apple Creek School
Bismark, ND

Judith McAllister
Bath, ME

Kim Prater
Lynn Haven, FL

Sheri Sayers
LA Unified School District
Westchester, CA

Janet Thompson
Great Falls, MT

Table of Contents

Table of Contents

Lesson Resources

LEXILE / GRADE LEVEL

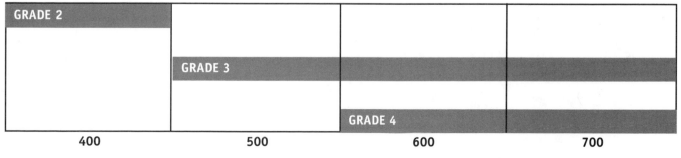

GRADE 2

GRADE 3

GRADE 4

400   500   600   700

PUPIL'S EDITION SKILLS AND STRATEGIES

The chart below identifies the strategies for each part of each pupil's edition lesson.

Selection	I. Prereading	II. Response Notes	Comprehension	Word Work
1. Booker T. Washington (nonfiction)	predict	question	directed reading	compound words
2. Gloria's Way (fiction)	think-pair-and-share	connect	double-entry journal	silent *e*
3. Train to Somewhere (nonfiction)	anticipation guide	make clear	directed reading	homophones
4. First Flight (fiction)	word web	draw	double-entry journal	contractions
5. A Drop of Blood (nonfiction)	preview	draw	directed reading	building words from prefixes and suffixes
6. A River Dream (fiction)	word web	connect	directed reading	words with more than one meaning
7. How We Learned the Earth Is Round (nonfiction)	K-W-L	make clear	directed reading	prefixes and suffixes
8. I Am Rosa Parks (nonfiction)	preview	question	cause and effect chart	consonants and consonant clusters
9. Germs Make Me Sick! (nonfiction)	think-pair-and-share	make clear	retell	compound words
10. The Skirt (fiction)	preview	connect	directed reading	words with "auto"
11. Through Grandpa's Eyes (fiction)	predict	draw	retell	syllables
12. Me and My Shadow (nonfiction)	think-pair-and-share	question	directed reading	compound words
13. Follow That Trash! (nonfiction)	think-pair-and-share	make clear	double-entry journal	suffixes of words that end in "y"
14. Otherwise Known as Sheila the Great (fiction)	predict	connect	story chart	adding suffixes to one-syllable words
15. "Hawk, I'm Your Brother" (narrative poem)	think-pair-and-share	connect	retell	contractions
16. "Fun" and "By Myself" (poetry)	web	draw	double-entry journal	consonants and consonant clusters

III. Prewriting	IV. Writing	Grammar/Usage	V. Assessment
brainstorm	letter	capitalization	enjoyment
word web	journal entry	spelling	ease
narrowing a topic	expository paragraph	homophones	meaning
5 Ws chart	news story	apostrophes	understanding
a) brainstorm b) organize details	descriptive paragraph	commas	ease
a) story string b) opening sentence	narrative paragraph	spelling	enjoyment
main idea and details	expository paragraph	end punctuation	understanding
web	letter	commas	meaning
5 Ws chart	expository paragraph	fragments	understanding
story chart	narrative paragraph	capitalization	enjoyment
sensory details web	descriptive paragraph	homophones	understanding
main idea and details	poem	capitalization	ease
opinion and supporting details chart	paragraph of opinion	capitalization	meaning
character map	narrative paragraph	apostrophes	ease
word web	descriptive paragraph	apostrophes	meaning
brainstorm	poem	apostrophes	understanding

TEACHER'S GUIDE SKILLS AND STRATEGIES

The chart below identifies the strategies for each part of each teacher's guide lesson.

Selection	Vocabulary	Prereading	Comprehension
1. Booker T. Washington (nonfiction)	context clues	a) prediction b) picture walk	stop and think
2. Gloria's Way (fiction)	synonyms	a) think-pair-and-share b) graphic organizer	double-entry journal
3. Train to Somewhere (nonfiction)	context clues	a) anticipation guide b) think-pair-and-share	stop and think
4. First Flight (fiction)	context clues	a) word web b) brainstorm	double-entry journal
5. A Drop of Blood (nonfiction)	context clues	a) preview b) K-W-L	stop and think
6. A River Dream (fiction)	context clues	a) word web b) preview	stop and think
7. How We Learned the Earth Is Round (nonfiction)	context clues	a) K-W-L b) quickwrite	stop and think
8. I Am Rosa Parks (nonfiction)	context clues	a) preview b) skim	cause-effect chart
9. Germs Make Me Sick! (nonfiction)	context clues	a) think-pair-and-share b) cluster	retell
10. The Skirt (fiction)	suffixes	a) preview b) think-pair-and-share	stop and think
11. Through Grandpa's Eyes (fiction)	context clues	a) anticipation guide b) prediction	retell
12. Me and My Shadow (nonfiction)	context clues	a) anticipation guide b) sketch	organize
13. Follow That Trash! (nonfiction)	synonyms	a) think-pair-and-share b) graphic organizer	double-entry journal
14. Otherwise Known as Sheila the Great (fiction)	context clues	a) prediction b) anticipation guide	story chart
15. "Hawk, I'm Your Brother" (narrative poem)	context clues	a) preview b) K-W-L	retell
16. "Fun" and "By Myself" (poetry)	pronunciation	a) word web b) graphic organizer	double-entry journal

Questions	Prewriting	Assessment
a) comprehension b) critical thinking	brainstorm	multiple-choice test
a) comprehension b) critical thinking	word web	multiple-choice test
a) comprehension b) critical thinking	topic sentence and details	multiple-choice test
a) comprehension b) critical thinking	5 Ws chart	multiple-choice test
a) comprehension b) critical thinking	topic sentence and details	multiple-choice test
a) comprehension b) critical thinking	storyboard	multiple-choice test
a) comprehension b) critical thinking	main idea and supporting details	multiple-choice test
a) comprehension b) critical thinking	character web	multiple-choice test
a) comprehension b) critical thinking	5 Ws chart	multiple-choice test
a) comprehension b) critical thinking	story chart	multiple-choice test
a) comprehension b) critical thinking	word web	multiple-choice test
a) comprehension b) critical thinking	main idea and supporting details	multiple-choice test
a) comprehension b) critical thinking	opinion and supporting details	multiple-choice test
a) comprehension b) critical thinking	character map and story chart	multiple-choice test
a) comprehension b) critical thinking	word web	multiple-choice test
a) comprehension b) critical thinking	brainstorm	multiple-choice test

CORRELATION TO *WRITERS EXPRESS* AND *WRITE ON TRACK*

Like the *Writers Express* and *Write on Track* handbooks, the *Sourcebook* will appeal to teachers who believe that writing is a way of learning. This *Sourcebook*, like *Writers Express*, is a book to "grow in." Here students read a series of carefully sequenced selections and respond to them. They jot notes, create organizers, plan and brainstorm compositions, and write drafts of their work. The *Sourcebook* is one way for students to read and write weekly if not daily.

After students write, they are asked to look again at their compositions in a feature called **Writers' Checklist**. This feature in **Part IV Write** highlights two or three key points of Grammar, Usage, and Mechanics. These features are brief mini-lessons. They invite students to look back at their writing and apply some aspect of Grammar, Usage, or Mechanics to it.

In the *Sourcebooks*, both the kinds of writing and the mini-lessons on Grammar, Usage, and Mechanics afford the best opportunities to use the *Writers Express* or *Write on Track* handbooks as a reference. To make this convenient, the writing activities are correlated to the handbooks below, and the mini-lessons are correlated on the following page.

Selection Title	Writing Activity	Writers Express ©2000 (pages)	Write on Track ©1996 (pages)
1. Booker T. Washington	letter	144–149	122–129, 297
2. Gloria's Way	journal entry	134–135	65–67, 77–81
3. Train to Somewhere	expository paragraph	80	55–63
4. First Flight	news story	156-165	110–115
5. A Drop of Blood	descriptive paragraph	78	55–63
6. A River Dream	narrative paragraph	79	55–63
7. How We Learned the Earth Is Round	expository paragraph	80	55–63
8. I Am Rosa Parks	letter	144–149	92–95, 122–129, 297
9. Germs Make Me Sick!	expository paragraph	80	55–63
10. The Skirt	narrative paragraph	79	55–63, 96–99
11. Through Grandpa's Eyes	descriptive paragraph	78	55–63, 159–163
12. Me and My Shadow	poem	243–245	177–189
13. Follow That Trash!	paragraph of opinion	347	55–63
14. Otherwise Known as Sheila the Great	narrative paragraph	79	55–63, 96–99
15. "Hawk, I'm Your Brother"	descriptive paragraph	78	55–63
16. "Fun" and "By Myself"	poem	243–245	177–189

CORRELATION TO *WRITERS EXPRESS* AND *WRITE ON TRACK*

For Writing Mini-Lesson

Selection Title	Writing Activity	Writers Express ©2000 (pages)	Write on Track ©1996 (pages)
1. Booker T. Washington	capitalization	389–392	307–309
2. Gloria's Way	spelling	306–309	224–227, 314–317
3. Train to Somewhere	homophones	406	318–323
4. First Flight	apostrophes	384	301
5. A Drop of Blood	commas	379–381	297–299
6. A River Dream	spelling	306–309	224–227, 314–317
7. How We Learned the Earth Is Round	end punctuation	377–388	295–296, 303–304
8. I Am Rosa Parks	commas	379–381	297–299
9. Germs Make Me Sick!	sentence fragments	115	274
10. The Skirt	capitalization	389–392	307–309
11. Through Grandpa's Eyes	homophones	406	318–323
12. Me and My Shadow	capitalization	389–392	307–309
13. Follow That Trash!	capitalization	389–392	307–309
14. Otherwise Known as Sheila the Great	apostrophes	384	301
15. "Hawk, I'm Your Brother"	apostrophes	384	301
16. "Fun" and "By Myself"	apostrophes	384	301

OVERVIEW

This **Sourcebook** targets struggling readers. In grades 3–5, these students need to be matched with quality literature that they can actually read. They need to be motivated, and they need good instruction in strategies that will help them learn how to transform sentences into a comprehensible text. They also need help with getting ready to write, help with grammar, usage, and mechanics; and they need help with writing different kinds of texts—letters, journal entries, descriptive paragraphs, and so forth.

A Comprehensive Approach

Because struggling readers have so many different needs, they often receive a number of small, separate activities—work on main idea and details, a list of spelling rules, some word work on prefixes, practice writing a topic sentence, and comma rules. But it seldom adds up to a coherent whole for students.

That's where this **Sourcebook** comes in. The **Sourcebook** takes a holistic approach, not a piecemeal one. Through a comprehensive 5-part lesson, each **Sourcebook** lesson walks the students through the steps needed to read a text at their reading level and write about it. The lessons pull it all together for students, weaving together many different skills into a coherent whole.

The 5-part lesson plan is:

I. **BEFORE YOU READ** (prereading)

II. **READ** (active reading and comprehension)

III. **GET READY TO WRITE** (prewriting)

IV. **WRITE** (writing; revising; grammar, usage, and mechanics)

V. **LOOK BACK** (reflecting and self-assessment)

With this comprehensive approach, students can see the whole process of reading and writing. By following a consistent pattern, students can internalize key aspects of the reading and the writing process. These patterns will help students build the habits they need to become successful readers and writers. See also the Book and Lesson Organization overviews on pages 18–23.

A Strategy-Intensive Approach

The **Sourcebook** also uses a strategy-intensive approach. Each **Sourcebook** builds students' repertoire of reading strategies in at least three areas:

1. To build motivation and background, prereading strategies are used to get students ready to read and to help them see the prior knowledge they already bring to their reading experiences.

2. To build active readers, each **Sourcebook** begins with an overview called "Be an Active Reader," showing students ways to mark up texts and respond to them. Then, at least one of these strategies is used in each lesson.

3. To build comprehension, each **Sourcebook** uses 3–5 different comprehension strategies, such as double-entry journals, retelling, graphic organizers, and so on. By embedding these strategies in the literature, the **Sourcebook** shows students exactly which strategies to use and when to use them, building the habits of good readers. Then, after students finish reading, they are directed to go back and reread.

A Literature-Based Approach

Above all, the *Sourcebook* takes a literature-based approach. It presents 16 selections of quality literature of various genres by a wide range of authors. These selections are leveled in difficulty, starting with the easiest selection and progressing to more difficult ones. This leveling of the selections makes it easy to match students to literature they can actually read.

An Interactive Approach

The *Sourcebook* is an interactive book. It is intended to be a journal for students, in which they can write out their ideas about selections, plan and write out compositions, and record their progress throughout the year. Students should "own" their *Sourcebooks*, carrying them, reading in them, marking in them, and writing in them. The *Sourcebooks* should become a record of students' progress and accomplishments. Students will take pride in "their" *Sourcebook*.

Lesson Planning

A single *Sourcebook* lesson can be taught in approximately 8–10 class periods, whether that is over two, three, or even four weeks.

DAY 1 Build background and discuss the selection.

DAY 2 Read the introduction. Do the prereading activity.

DAY 3 Introduce the selection. Discuss how to respond to the selection and the example. Then read the selection the first time.

DAY 4 Finish reading the selection. Then, encourage students to read the selection again, this time writing in the Response Notes.

DAY 5 Finish reading. Reread the selection again, as necessary, and respond to the comprehension activities in the selection.

DAY 6 Do Word Work and point out the Reading Reminder.

DAY 7 Begin Get Ready to Write.

DAY 8 Begin Writing Activity.

DAY 9 Finish writing. Talk about the Writers' Checklist mini-lesson, and revise writing.

DAY 10 Reflect on the selection and what was learned.

Assessment

Each *Sourcebook* lesson includes a multiple-choice test for assessment, as well as a more holistic self-assessment in the pupil's book in **Part V Look Back**. Both are useful gauges of student progress. Teachers need to demonstrate the progress their students have made throughout the year. The best measure of that progress will be a student's marked-up *Sourcebook* and the greater confidence and fluency with which students will be reading by the end of the year. For additional assessment ideas, see the **Strategy Handbook** in this *Teacher's Guide*.

MATCHING READERS WITH SELECTIONS

Probably one of the greatest challenges nowadays for teachers is matching readers with the right texts. The range of reading abilities in classrooms often spans four or even five grade levels. Some students read two grade levels below, and some read two or more grade levels above, grade level. The teacher's job is to match each of his or her students (usually 25 to 35 children) to the exact reading level, day in and day out. It is a large order.

What Level Is It?

To help match students to the appropriate books, educators have relied on "readability formulas" and levels. None of these measures is perfectly reliable. They are crucial, however, because you cannot read every book before matching it to each student in class.

The solution adopted in the *Sourcebooks* for grades 3–5 has been to begin with selections approximately two years below the students' actual grade level. That means that *Sourcebook*, grade 4, begins with what are normally considered grade 2 selections. Then, by the end of each book, the last few selections are approximately on grade level.

How Are Selections Leveled?

The selections in each *Sourcebook* are leveled, starting with the easiest and progressing to the most difficult. The measure relied upon to order them in the *Sourcebooks* is the Lexile level. This is a readability measurement that places readings on a common scale, beginning at 100 and going up to 1700. Reading programs, reading specialists, and the authors of this series all have used this readability measurement and found it useful. For the purposes of the *Sourcebooks*, the Lexile Framework provided a standard way to assess the relative difficulty of selections and a convenient measure to gauge which selections might be appropriate for students who are reading two or more years below their grade level.

How Does This Help?

Because the selections in each *Sourcebook* are leveled, you can start groups of students at the beginning, middle, or end of the book. Begin with selections that are easy for students to build their confidence. Then, gradually work toward more challenging ones.

At the same time, use the additional books by the author and those on the same theme suggested in this *Teacher's Guide*. Each *Sourcebook* lesson begins with recommendations of more books that are at or around the same Lexile level as the selection in the *Sourcebook*. The benefit of this plan is that it helps you quickly locate a lot of books you can use. You can also keep better track when students begin to read harder books, challenging and also supporting them.

The *Sourcebooks* will help you spend more time guiding students' learning, and less searching for the appropriate books. That part, at least, has already been done.

HOW TO USE THIS BOOK

Guiding Struggling Learners

Frequently schools have classes with students of all ability levels, from a few grade levels below to one or two grade levels above. Moreover, "average" students in one school district vary greatly from "average" students in a neighboring one. The *Sourcebook* series aims at those students who consistently rank in the lower 50 percent of test scores and national averages.

The *Sourcebook* offers a comprehensive program of student-appropriate literature, strategy-building, writing, revising, and reflecting. The approach is a holistic one. Rather than assigning a worksheet to attack a specific problem—say, comprehension—the *Sourcebook* addresses the broader problems as well.

Each *Sourcebook* weaves together a comprehensive network of skills (see pages 6–9) that brings together the appropriate literature, reading strategies for that literature, and prewriting, writing, and revising activities. Students who work through even two or three entire selections will benefit greatly by seeing the whole picture of reading actively and writing about the text. They will also benefit from the sense of accomplishment that comes through completion of a whole task and that results in creative, original work of their own— perhaps some of the first they have accomplished.

Working with Students in Groups

Students who are reading at the same level are often grouped together. Some students may be pulled out for special tutoring with trained reading tutors. Those students reading below grade level are placed in one group, those reading on level in another group, and those reading above level in one or more other groups. For you as the teacher, the effort becomes how to juggle the various groups and keep them all on task.

That's where the *Sourcebook* comes in. Each lesson presents a sustained, meaningful assignment that can be targeted at specific groups in your class. Students show reluctance to read when a selection is too difficult or frustrating for them to read independently. With the *Sourcebook*, you can match the group to a selection at a Lexile level that is just right. Then you have a sustained, meaningful lesson to guide them through as well as a number of additional books for the group to read at the same level.

Integrating Lessons with Other Activities

Because *Sourcebook* lessons are comprehensive, you can integrate read-alouds; strategy lessons on comprehension; word work on prefixes, suffixes, and base words; and writing mini-lessons. Each lesson affords you any number of opportunities to intervene at the right moment to guide students' learning.

Students can read selections silently to themselves and then work independently in one group while you are giving a strategy lesson to another group. Or, students may be reading independently any number of books on the same subject or theme.

Pulling Everything Together

The benefit of the *Sourcebook* comes in having everything pulled together in one place—for you and the student. You have 16 integrated units to choose from. Students have a book of their own, one they "own," that keeps them on track, guiding their learning and recording their progress. So, if you have interruptions because of holidays or field trips, or simply scheduling challenges, the *Sourcebook* holds the lesson together, allowing you and the students to double back if necessary and remember where they have been, and where they are going.

Summary

The *Sourcebook* will not fix every learning problem for every student, but it will be helpful for struggling readers, especially those who are reading one or two years below their academic grade. Reading and writing deficits are hard, almost intractable problems for students and require a great amount of effort—on the part of the teacher and the student— before any real improvement is made. The *Sourcebook* is one helpful tool in helping you create better readers and writers.

FREQUENTLY ASKED QUESTIONS

Because the *Sourcebooks* were extensively reviewed by teachers, a number of commonly asked questions have surfaced already, and the answers to them might be helpful in using the program.

1. Why is it called a *Sourcebook*?

The word *Sourcebook* captures a number of connotations and associations that seemed just right. For one, it is published by Great Source Education. The word *source* also had the right connotation of "place to go for a real, complete solution," as opposed to other products that help in only a limited area, such as "main idea" or "analogies." And, lastly, the term *Sourcebook* fit nicely alongside *Daybook*, another series also published by Great Source that targets better readers and writers who need help in critical reading, as opposed to this series, which targets struggling readers.

2. Can students write in the *Sourcebook*?

Absolutely. Only by physically marking up the text will students become truly active readers. To interact with a text and truly read as an active reader, students must write in the *Sourcebook*. The immediacy of reading and responding right there on the page is integral to the whole idea of the *Sourcebook*. By writing in the text, students build a sense of ownership about their work that is impossible to match through worksheets handed out week after week. The *Sourcebook* also serves, in a sense, like the student's portfolio and can become one of the most tangible ways of demonstrating a student's progress throughout the year.

3. Can I photocopy these lessons?

No, you cannot. Each page of the pupil's book carries a notice that explicitly states "copying is prohibited." To copy pages illegally infringes on the rights of the authors of the selections and the publishers of the book. Writers such as Patricia McKissack, Arthur Dorros, Byrd Baylor, and others have granted permission to use their work in the *Sourcebook*, but not the right to copy it.

You can, however, copy the blackline masters in this *Teacher's Guide.* These pages are intended for you to photocopy and use in the classroom and are marked clearly on each page.

4. Can I skip around in the *Sourcebook*?

Teachers will often want to skip around and adjust the *Sourcebook* to their curriculum. But, in *Sourcebooks* 3–5, the selections are sequenced in the order of the reading difficulty. Selections in grade 4 progress from a Lexile reading level of 400 to 600. A similar progression exists at the other grade levels. The benefit comes in having selections you know will be appropriate for students and in having skills that are carefully sequenced. The writing expected of students progresses in difficulty, just as the readability does, moving from easiest to hardest. Further, the Word Work skills build off one another, so that terms such as "base word" and "consonant cluster" are assumed in later lessons after being introduced in earlier ones.

5. Where did the strategies used throughout the book come from?

Most of the reading strategies used are commonplace in elementary classrooms throughout the country. Reading textbooks as well as teacher resource books and in-services all describe the prereading and comprehension strategies used in the *Sourcebooks*. What is unusual in the *Sourcebooks* is the way these strategies have been woven together and applied to high-quality, appropriate literature.

6. Why do you direct students to read and reread the selection?

One suggestion from reviewers was to help struggling readers by asking them to do one thing at a time. Teachers suggested it was easier to read a selection once just to get a sense of it, a second time to respond to it in the Response Notes, and a third time to respond to the comprehension activities embedded in the selection. Rather than ask students to do three things at once, the lessons progress in manageable steps. It reduces frustration and increases chances of success. Plus, additional readings of a selection increase reading fluency and help improve comprehension.

7. Why do the *Sourcebooks* rely on Lexile measurements of readability?

The benefit of Lexile measurements is that they provide small increments of readability—say, from 220 to 240—and they are in wide use. The Lexile Framework for Reading has an easily accessed website (www.lexile.com) that allows you to search for authors and titles at specific readability levels. The website already has measured a huge selection of books and lexiled them. As a result, this measurement provided a public standard by which to assess readability and an ongoing tool for teachers.

8. How were the selections chosen and what is their readability?

Each selection in the *Sourcebooks* met numerous criteria: quality of the selection, readability, balance of fiction vs. nonfiction, as well as of gender and ethnicity of the authors.

None of the criteria mattered if the selection did not hold the interest of students and didn't seem to be on a worthwhile subject or topic. But it is worth noting that nearly 50 percent of the selections in the *Sourcebooks* are nonfiction, at the request of teachers who wanted more help with this genre.

9. How can I know if my students can read this literature?

You have a number of ways to know how well your students can read the selections. First, you can simply try out a lesson or two with students.

Second, you can use a 10- or 15-word vocabulary pretest as a quick indicator. Choose 10 words randomly from each selection. Ask students to circle the ones they know and underline the ones they don't know. If students know only 1–5 words, then the selection will probably be frustrating for them. Spend some time preteaching the key vocabulary.

Third, ask students to read a selection aloud. By listening to the kind of miscues students make, you can gauge whether a selection is at, below, or above their reading level.

10. What if my students need even more help than what's in the *Sourcebook*?

This *Teacher's Guide* has been designed as the next level of support. Extra activities and blackline masters on vocabulary, comprehension, prewriting, and assessment are included here so that they can be used at the teacher's discretion. These aids can help scaffold individual parts of lessons, giving more help with Vocabulary, Word Work, or Prewriting. But let students work through the lessons. Even if they make mistakes, they still may be making progress and may need only a little patience and encouragement. The *Sourcebooks* offer a good foundation for your curriculum.

ORGANIZATION

Book Organization

Each **Sourcebook** has 16 selections organized sequentially from the easiest readability to the hardest. The first lesson begins with a selection at approximately two grade levels below the academic level. That is, **Sourcebook**, grade 4 begins with a selection at Lexile 400, which is approximately the end of second grade.

Lesson Organization

Each lesson in the **Sourcebook** starts with an introduction that draws students into the selection, often by asking a provocative question or making a strong statement. The purpose of this introduction is to stimulate students' prior knowledge and build interest.

Opener

- Each selection begins with an introduction to create motivation for reading.

I. Before You Read

- Each lesson has five parts.

- The prereading step—the critical first step—builds background and further helps students access prior knowledge. Among the prereading strategies included in **Part I** of this **Sourcebook** are:

  - Think-Pair-and-Share
  - Anticipation Guide
  - Previewing
  - Word Web
  - K-W-L

Booker T. Washington

What do you think of when you hear the word *freedom*? How would your life be different if you could not go to school, ride in a bus, or get paid for doing a job? Booker T. Washington was not a free person, but his life was soon to change.

BEFORE YOU READ

Have you ever tried to figure out what will happen next? When you do this, you are using clues in the story and what you know to make a prediction.
1. Read the 4 sentences from *Booker T. Washington*.
2. Tell what you think the reading will be about.

- "Booker and his family lived on a large Virginia plantation."
- "A fireplace warmed the cabin."
- "One day Booker passed by a school."
- "In 1863, President Abraham Lincoln freed all slaves in the South."

My prediction:

MY PURPOSE
Who was Booker T. Washington, and what was his life like?

11

12

II. Read

The reading step begins by telling students what they are about to read and then details how they are to read the selection. The first step tells students how to mark the text. The second step reminds them to write their reactions or responses in the Response Notes. An example of an acceptable response is always provided.

II. READ

Read this part of the biography of Booker T. Washington.
1. On the first reading, underline parts of the story that make you wonder what Booker's life was like.
2. On the next reading, write in the Notes the **questions** that popped into your head.

Booker T. Washington
by Patricia and Fredrick McKissack

Booker Taliaferro Washington never knew his birthday. He was born a slave, and the dates of slave births were not always written down. It is believed he was born sometime in 1856.

Booker and his family lived on a large Virginia plantation. Their one-room shack had a dirt floor. The door didn't shut well. The windows had no glass. There were cracks in the walls.

Booker didn't even have a bed. He slept on the floor next to his brother John and his sister Amanda. A fireplace warmed the cabin. But it was always too hot or too cold in their home.

plantation (plan•ta•tion)—large farm where slaves would often live and work.
shack—small, poorly-built cabin.

Response Notes

EXAMPLE:

How many people lived there?

What was Booker T. Washington's home like?

STOP AND THINK   STOP AND THINK   STOP AND THINK

Response Notes

BOOKER T. WASHINGTON (continued)

When Booker was five years old, his master put him to work. Booker fanned flies away from his master's table at mealtimes.

When he got older, he was given a new job. Every week he went to the mill with a load of corn. The corn was ground into meal there.

stop and think

What 2 jobs did Booker T. Washington have?

ground—crushed into powder.
meal—ground corn that people eat.

- The selection follows, with the challenging vocabulary highlighted throughout the selection. Vocabulary is defined at the bottom of the page. Each word is broken into syllables to make it easier for students to pronounce, with the stressed syllable highlighted in bold.

- Then, within each selection, a powerful comprehension strategy is embedded to help build in students the habits of good readers. Among the comprehension strategies included in **Part II** of this *Sourcebook* are the following:

  - Stop and Think (directed reading)

  - Graphic Organizer

  - Double-entry Journal

  - Retell

At the end of each selection, students take time for Word Work to develop their word attack skills. Students who struggle to read in the early grades need help in breaking apart words to improve their reading fluency. The purpose of these activities is to help students know how to handle longer words. Among the Word Work activities in this *Sourcebook* are the following:

- consonant clusters
- prefixes and suffixes
- compound words
- syllables
- contractions
- word parts
- homographs

WORD WORK

You can make a long word by joining 2 small words. The long word is called a **compound word**. Look at these examples:

out + side = *outside*   friend + ship = *friendship*

1. Skim *Booker T. Washington*. Find 4 compound words.
2. Write the compound words and small words below in the chart. One example has been done for you.

Compound Word	Small Word	Small Word
sometime	some	time
1.		
2.		
3.		
4.		

READING REMINDER
Predicting before you read and asking questions while you read can help you understand the story better.

16

At the bottom of the page, students will see a "Reading Reminder" that gives a critical reading tip. The reminders attempt to make explicit the strategies good readers use.

III. Get Ready to Write

The prewriting step helps students prepare to write. Through one or two carefully sequenced activities, the prewriting step helps students prepare to write. Students generate ideas, choose and narrow a subject, and locate supporting details. Often the prewriting activities will include one or more models. Among the prewriting activities are these:

- Main Idea and Supporting Details
- Brainstorming
- Writing a Topic Sentence
- Word Web
- Character Map
- Story Chart
- Narrowing a Topic

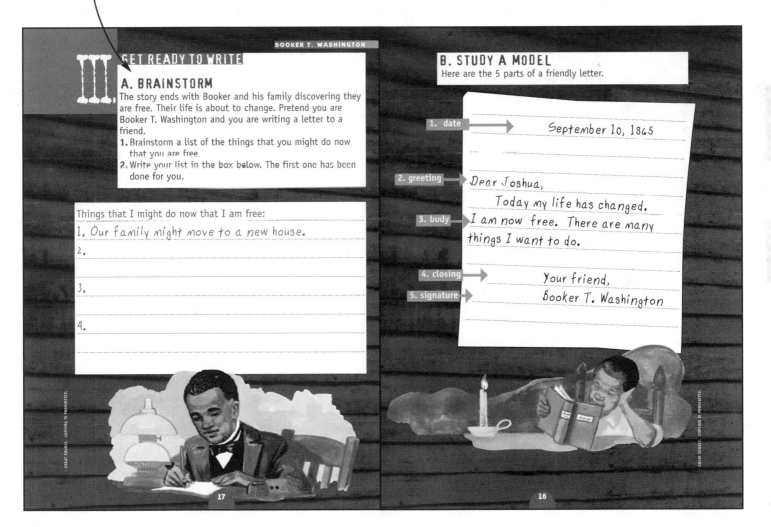

BOOKER T. WASHINGTON

III GET READY TO WRITE

A. BRAINSTORM

The story ends with Booker and his family discovering they are free. Their life is about to change. Pretend you are Booker T. Washington and you are writing a letter to a friend.
1. Brainstorm a list of the things that you might do now that you are free.
2. Write your list in the box below. The first one has been done for you.

Things that I might do now that I am free:
1. Our family might move to a new house.
2.
3.
4.

17

B. STUDY A MODEL
Here are the 5 parts of a friendly letter.

1. date → September 10, 1865

2. greeting → Dear Joshua,

3. body → Today my life has changed. I am now free. There are many things I want to do.

4. closing → Your friend,

5. signature → Booker T. Washington

18

IV. Write

The writing step begins with step-by-step instructions for building a writing assignment. Taken together, these instructions form the writing rubric for students to use in completing the assignment. Among the writing assignments included are the following:

- Poem
- Narrative paragraph
- Expository paragraph
- Journal entry
- Descriptive paragraph
- Letter
- News story

Each **Part IV Write** also includes a **Writers' Checklist**. Each one is a brief mini-lesson on a relevant aspect of grammar, usage, or mechanics. The intent of the **Writers' Checklist** is to ask students appropriate questions after they write, instilling in them the habit of going back into their work to revise, edit, and proofread. The **Writers' Checklist** also affords teachers the opportunity to teach relevant grammar, usage, and mechanics skills at a teachable moment.

BOOKER T. WASHINGTON

IV. WRITE

Now you are ready to write your own **letter**. Pretend to be Booker T. Washington and tell your friend the things you might do now that you are free.
1. Check the 3 ideas from your brainstorming list that you want to include.
2. Review the friendly letter model on page 18.
3. Use the Writers' Checklist to edit your letter.

Continue writing on the next page.

19

Continue your letter.

WRITERS' CHECKLIST

Capitalization

☐ **Did all of your sentences begin with capital letters?**
EXAMPLE: *School will be wonderful.*

V. Look Back

The last step of each lesson asks students to monitor their own reading and reflect. Students are asked a question about their reading and writing experience from the **Readers' Checklist**. This "looking back" is intended to help students see what they learned in the lesson. They are intentionally asked more than simply, "Did you understand?"

For good readers, reading is much, much more than "Did you get it?" Good readers read for pleasure, for information, for the pure enjoyment of reading artfully written material, for personal curiosity, for a desire to learn more, and countless other reasons. For students to see that reading is worthwhile to them, they need to believe the payoff is more than "Did you get it?" on a five-question multiple-choice test.

The *Sourcebook* attempts with **Part V Look Back** to help students ask the questions good readers ask of themselves when they read. It attempts to broaden the reasons for reading by asking students to consider four reasons for reading:

- Enjoyment
- Understanding
- Ease
- Meaning

Continue your letter.

WRITERS' CHECKLIST

Capitalization

☐ Did all of your sentences begin with capital letters?
EXAMPLE: *School will be wonderful.*

V. LOOK BACK

What part of Booker T. Washington's life did you enjoy reading about? Why? Write your answer below.

Think about Your Reading

READERS' CHECKLIST

Enjoyment

■ Did you like the reading?
■ Would you recommend the reading to a friend?

20

The *Sourcebook* is color coded for both aesthetic and organizational purposes. The color red is used for instructions. Black indicates literature, footnotes, and examples. Blue means the student will complete an activity.

How to Read a Lesson

Here are 3 easy steps to help you get the most out of the readings in this book.

1. For each reading, **read it once** and just circle or underline the important parts.

2. Then **read it again**. On the second reading, write questions or comments in the Notes.

3. Then, at the end of each reading, you will find a part called **Reread**. This part asks you to go back one more time and be sure you have answered all the questions.

Red=Follow Directions

Blue=Write Here

Black=Read This

READ

Read this part of the biography of Booker T. Washington.
1. On the first reading, underline parts of the story that make you wonder what Booker's life was like.
2. On the next reading, write in the Notes the **questions** that popped into your head.

Booker T. Washington
by Patricia and Fredrick McKissack

Booker Taliaferro Washington never knew his birthday. He was born a slave, and the dates of slave births were not always written down. It is believed he was born sometime in 1856.

Booker and his family lived on a large Virginia plantation. Their one-room shack had a dirt floor. The door didn't shut well. The windows had no glass. There were cracks in the walls.

Booker didn't even have a bed. He slept on the floor next to his brother John and his sister Amanda. A fireplace warmed the cabin. But it was always too hot or too cold in their home.

plantation (plan•ta•tion)—large farm where slaves would often live and work.
shack—small, poorly-built cabin.

Response Notes

EXAMPLE:
How many people lived there?

13

By reading and rereading, you will do what good readers do.

reread

Reread *Booker T. Washington* one more time. As you do, look for answers to the questions you wrote in the Notes. Be sure you have answered all of the **Stop and Think** questions.

10

Organization

TEACHER'S LESSON PLANS

Each lesson plan for the teacher of the *Sourcebook* has **twelve** pages:

PAGE 1 **Background and Bibliography**

- The lesson begins with background on the author and selection, and gives at least three additional titles by this author or on this same subject.

- The additional titles in the bibliography are included both for read-alongs and as independent reading, giving you ways to introduce the author, selection, and general subject.

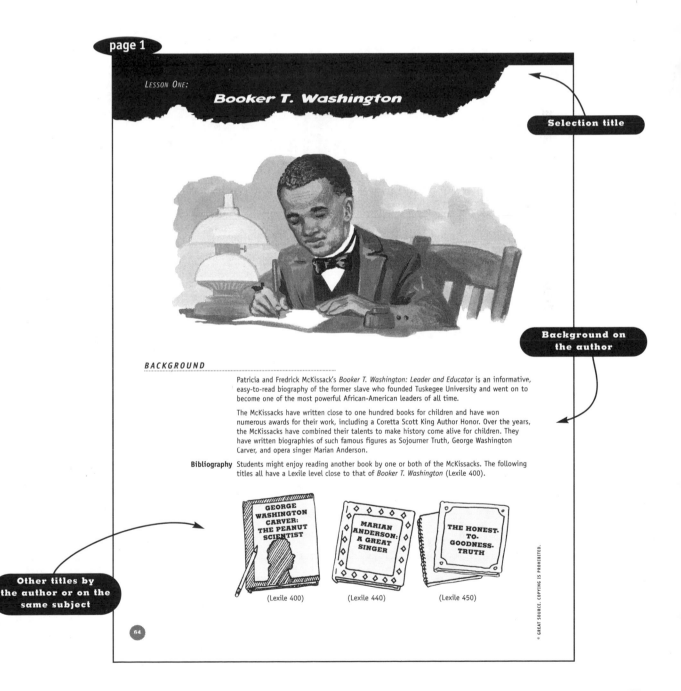

page 1

LESSON ONE:

Booker T. Washington

Selection title

Background on the author

BACKGROUND

Patricia and Fredrick McKissack's *Booker T. Washington: Leader and Educator* is an informative, easy-to-read biography of the former slave who founded Tuskegee University and went on to become one of the most powerful African-American leaders of all time.

The McKissacks have written close to one hundred books for children and have won numerous awards for their work, including a Coretta Scott King Author Honor. Over the years, the McKissacks have combined their talents to make history come alive for children. They have written biographies of such famous figures as Sojourner Truth, George Washington Carver, and opera singer Marian Anderson.

Bibliography Students might enjoy reading another book by one or both of the McKissacks. The following titles all have a Lexile level close to that of *Booker T. Washington* (Lexile 400).

Other titles by the author or on the same subject

GEORGE WASHINGTON CARVER: THE PEANUT SCIENTIST

(Lexile 400)

MARIAN ANDERSON: A GREAT SINGER

(Lexile 440)

THE HONEST-TO-GOODNESS-TRUTH

(Lexile 450)

64

PAGE 2 **How to Introduce the Reading**

- The next page of the teacher's plan introduces the selection and gives teachers a way to motivate students to read. In most cases, the introduction serves as a way to create a sense of expectation in students and to provide some initial background for the reading.

Other Reading

- Three more titles written at the same readability level are included in "Other Reading." The purpose is to suggest to teachers titles at this same reading level, so students can go beyond the selection in the text to other appropriate titles.

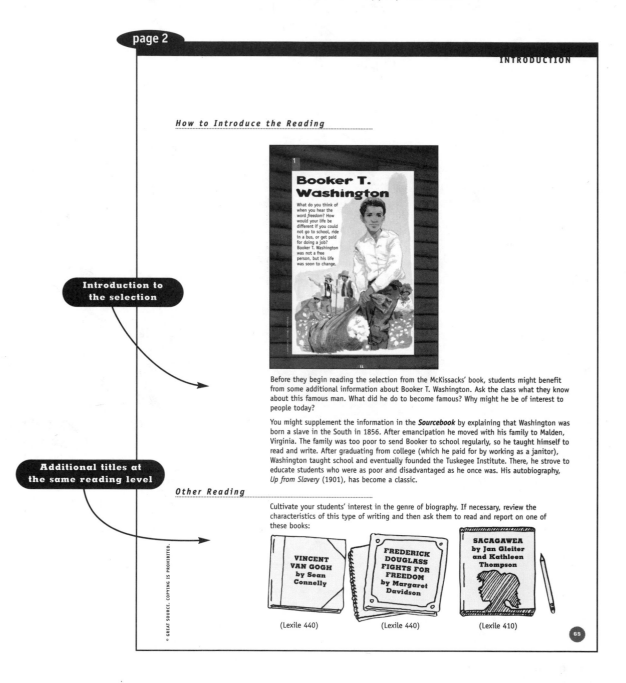

page 2

INTRODUCTION

How to Introduce the Reading

Booker T. Washington

What do you think of when you hear the word *freedom*? How would your life be different if you could not go to school, ride in a bus, or get paid for doing a job? Booker T. Washington was not a free person, but his life was soon to change.

Introduction to the selection

Before they begin reading the selection from the McKissacks' book, students might benefit from some additional information about Booker T. Washington. Ask the class what they know about this famous man. What did he do to become famous? Why might he be of interest to people today?

You might supplement the information in the *Sourcebook* by explaining that Washington was born a slave in the South in 1856. After emancipation he moved with his family to Malden, Virginia. The family was too poor to send Booker to school regularly, so he taught himself to read and write. After graduating from college (which he paid for by working as a janitor), Washington taught school and eventually founded the Tuskegee Institute. There, he strove to educate students who were as poor and disadvantaged as he once was. His autobiography, *Up from Slavery* (1901), has become a classic.

Additional titles at the same reading level

Other Reading

Cultivate your students' interest in the genre of biography. If necessary, review the characteristics of this type of writing and then ask them to read and report on one of these books:

VINCENT VAN GOGH by Sean Connelly

FREDERICK DOUGLASS FIGHTS FOR FREEDOM by Margaret Davidson

SACAGAWEA by Jan Gleiter and Kathleen Thompson

(Lexile 440)   (Lexile 440)   (Lexile 410)

65

PAGE 3 **Skills and Strategies Overview**

Each lesson plan in the *Sourcebook* begins with a chart giving an overview of the skills covered in the lesson. The purpose is to give teachers an at-a-glance picture of the lesson.

Note in the chart the vocabulary words that are highlighted. These words from the selection are presented in the **Vocabulary** blackline master to help familiarize students with key words in the selection.

Other Resources

Each lesson in the *Sourcebook* contains a wealth of additional resources to support you and your students. In all, six blackline masters provide additional scaffolding for you at critical parts of the lesson: Vocabulary, Prereading, Comprehension, Word Work, Prewriting, and Assessment.

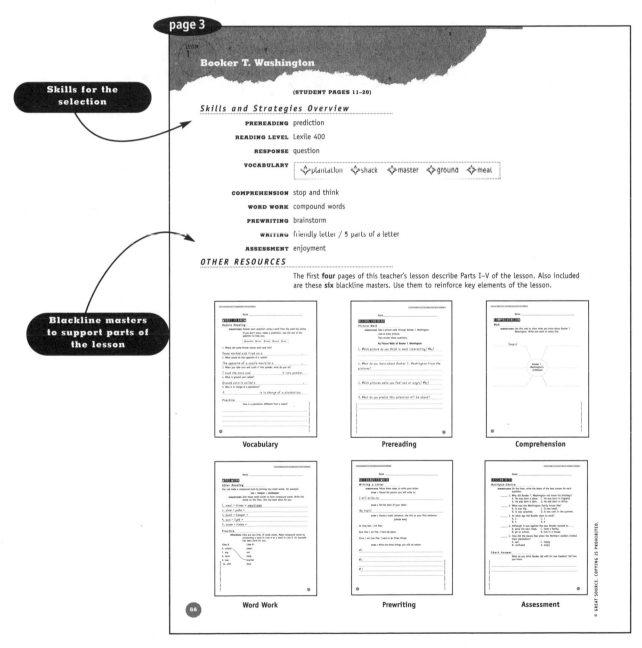

Skills for the selection

Blackline masters to support parts of the lesson

PAGE 4 **Before You Read**

- The *Teacher's Guide* walks through each lesson in the *Sourcebook*, following the five-step lesson plan and explaining how to teach each part.

- Where appropriate, additional blackline masters are cross-referenced.

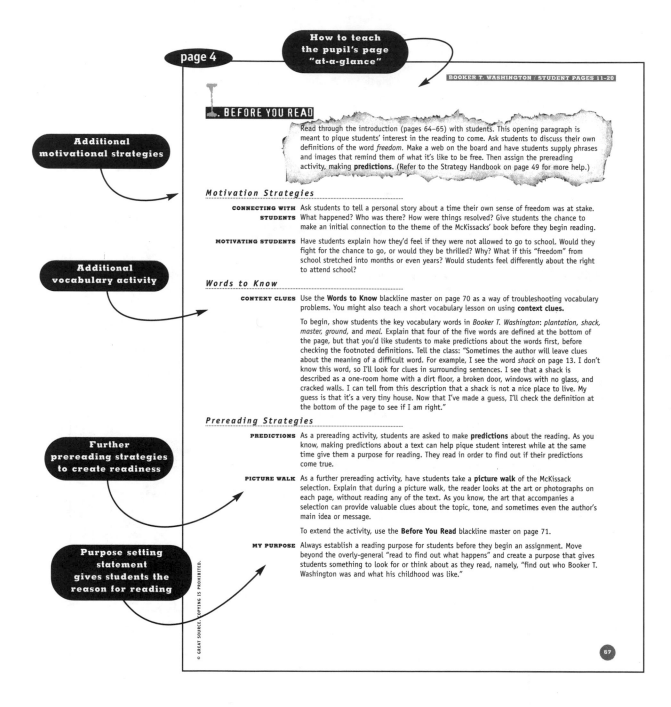

page 4

How to teach the pupil's page "at-a-glance"

BOOKER T. WASHINGTON / STUDENT PAGES 11-20

BEFORE YOU READ

Read through the introduction (pages 64–65) with students. This opening paragraph is meant to pique students' interest in the reading to come. Ask students to discuss their own definitions of the word *freedom*. Make a web on the board and have students supply phrases and images that remind them of what it's like to be free. Then assign the prereading activity, making **predictions**. (Refer to the Strategy Handbook on page 49 for more help.)

Additional motivational strategies

Motivation Strategies

CONNECTING WITH STUDENTS — Ask students to tell a personal story about a time their own sense of freedom was at stake. What happened? Who was there? How were things resolved? Give students the chance to make an initial connection to the theme of the McKissacks' book before they begin reading.

MOTIVATING STUDENTS — Have students explain how they'd feel if they were not allowed to go to school. Would they fight for the chance to go, or would they be thrilled? Why? What if this "freedom" from school stretched into months or even years? Would students feel differently about the right to attend school?

Additional vocabulary activity

Words to Know

CONTEXT CLUES — Use the **Words to Know** blackline master on page 70 as a way of troubleshooting vocabulary problems. You might also teach a short vocabulary lesson on using **context clues.**

To begin, show students the key vocabulary words in *Booker T. Washington*: *plantation, shack, master, ground,* and *meal.* Explain that four of the five words are defined at the bottom of the page, but that you'd like students to make predictions about the words first, before checking the footnoted definitions. Tell the class: "Sometimes the author will leave clues about the meaning of a difficult word. For example, I see the word *shack* on page 13. I don't know this word, so I'll look for clues in surrounding sentences. I see that a shack is described as a one-room home with a dirt floor, a broken door, windows with no glass, and cracked walls. I can tell from this description that a shack is not a nice place to live. My guess is that it's a very tiny house. Now that I've made a guess, I'll check the definition at the bottom of the page to see if I am right."

Further prereading strategies to create readiness

Prereading Strategies

PREDICTIONS — As a prereading activity, students are asked to make **predictions** about the reading. As you know, making predictions about a text can help pique student interest while at the same time give them a purpose for reading. They read in order to find out if their predictions come true.

PICTURE WALK — As a further prereading activity, have students take a **picture walk** of the McKissack selection. Explain that during a picture walk, the reader looks at the art or photographs on each page, without reading any of the text. As you know, the art that accompanies a selection can provide valuable clues about the topic, tone, and sometimes even the author's main idea or message.

To extend the activity, use the **Before You Read** blackline master on page 71.

Purpose setting statement gives students the reason for reading

MY PURPOSE — Always establish a reading purpose for students before they begin an assignment. Move beyond the overly-general "read to find out what happens" and create a purpose that gives students something to look for or think about as they read, namely, "find out who Booker T. Washington was and what his childhood was like."

67

PAGE 5 Read

- In **Part II Read**, students are directed to read the selection and are given an active reading strategy.

- Each **Part II Read** instructs students to read the selection once with an active reading strategy, and then read it again with a comprehension strategy, this time writing their thoughts or comments in the **Response Notes**.

- **Reread** asks students to go back to the selection a third time to be sure they have answered all of the questions in the comprehension activity.

- **Word Work** explains the decoding skill taught in the lesson and why the skill is important for developing readers. A cross-reference to blackline master with additional work in this same word skill also appears here.

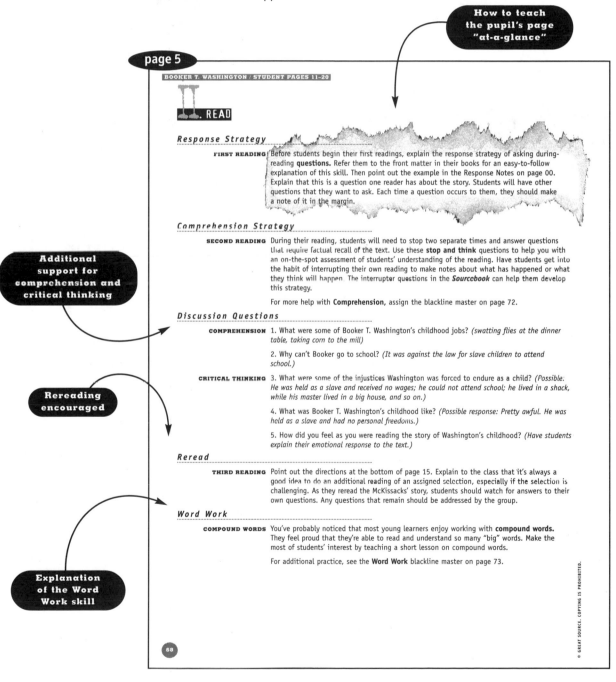

How to teach the pupil's page "at-a-glance"

page 5

BOOKER T. WASHINGTON / STUDENT PAGES 11–20

II. READ

Response Strategy

FIRST READING Before students begin their first readings, explain the response strategy of asking during-reading **questions.** Refer them to the front matter in their books for an easy-to-follow explanation of this skill. Then point out the example in the Response Notes on page 00. Explain that this is a question one reader has about the story. Students will have other questions that they want to ask. Each time a question occurs to them, they should make a note of it in the margin.

Comprehension Strategy

SECOND READING During their reading, students will need to stop two separate times and answer questions that require factual recall of the text. Use these **stop and think** questions to help you with an on-the-spot assessment of students' understanding of the reading. Have students get into the habit of interrupting their own reading to make notes about what has happened or what they think will happen. The interrupter questions in the *Sourcebook* can help them develop this strategy.

For more help with **Comprehension**, assign the blackline master on page 72.

Additional support for comprehension and critical thinking

Discussion Questions

COMPREHENSION 1. What were some of Booker T. Washington's childhood jobs? *(swatting flies at the dinner table, taking corn to the mill)*

2. Why can't Booker go to school? *(It was against the law for slave children to attend school.)*

CRITICAL THINKING 3. What were some of the injustices Washington was forced to endure as a child? *(Possible: He was held as a slave and received no wages; he could not attend school; he lived in a shack, while his master lived in a big house, and so on.)*

4. What was Booker T. Washington's childhood like? *(Possible response: Pretty awful. He was held as a slave and had no personal freedoms.)*

Rereading encouraged

5. How did you feel as you were reading the story of Washington's childhood? *(Have students explain their emotional response to the text.)*

Reread

THIRD READING Point out the directions at the bottom of page 15. Explain to the class that it's always a good idea to do an additional reading of an assigned selection, especially if the selection is challenging. As they reread the McKissacks' story, students should watch for answers to their own questions. Any questions that remain should be addressed by the group.

Word Work

COMPOUND WORDS You've probably noticed that most young learners enjoy working with **compound words.** They feel proud that they're able to read and understand so many "big" words. Make the most of students' interest by teaching a short lesson on compound words.

Explanation of the Word Work skill

For additional practice, see the **Word Work** blackline master on page 73.

68

© GREAT SOURCE. COPYING IS PROHIBITED.

PAGE 6 Get Ready to Write, Write, and Look Back

- The page begins with a prewriting activity and references another blackline master that offers additional support.

- Next, the students write. Explicit instructions for the writing assignment are included in the pupil's text. But here, students are also introduced to the **Writers' Checklist**, which is the Grammar, Usage, and Mechanics mini-lesson.

- The Writing Rubric gives teachers a way to evaluate students' writing.

- The lesson ends by encouraging students to look back and reflect on what they have read. It also introduces the **Readers' Checklist**. A final cross-reference to the Assessment blackline master, appears here as well.

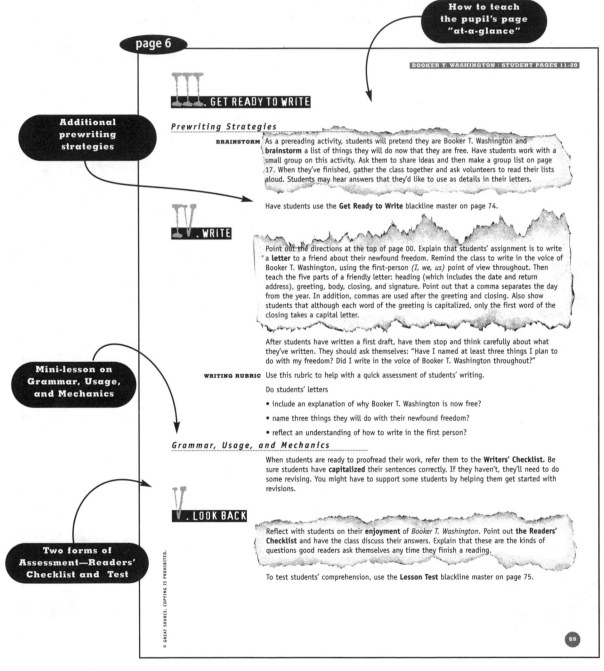

How to teach the pupil's page "at-a-glance"

page 6

BOOKER T. WASHINGTON / STUDENT PAGES 11-20

III. GET READY TO WRITE

Additional prewriting strategies

Prewriting Strategies

BRAINSTORM As a prereading activity, students will pretend they are Booker T. Washington and **brainstorm** a list of things they will do now that they are free. Have students work with a small group on this activity. Ask them to share ideas and then make a group list on page 17. When they've finished, gather the class together and ask volunteers to read their lists aloud. Students may hear answers that they'd like to use as details in their letters.

Have students use the **Get Ready to Write** blackline master on page 74.

IV. WRITE

Point out the directions at the top of page 00. Explain that students' assignment is to write a **letter** to a friend about their newfound freedom. Remind the class to write in the voice of Booker T. Washington, using the first-person (*I, we, us*) point of view throughout. Then teach the five parts of a friendly letter: heading (which includes the date and return address), greeting, body, closing, and signature. Point out that a comma separates the day from the year. In addition, commas are used after the greeting and closing. Also show students that although each word of the greeting is capitalized, only the first word of the closing takes a capital letter.

After students have written a first draft, have them stop and think carefully about what they've written. They should ask themselves: "Have I named at least three things I plan to do with my freedom? Did I write in the voice of Booker T. Washington throughout?"

WRITING RUBRIC Use this rubric to help with a quick assessment of students' writing.

Do students' letters

- include an explanation of why Booker T. Washington is now free?

- name three things they will do with their newfound freedom?

- reflect an understanding of how to write in the first person?

Mini-lesson on Grammar, Usage, and Mechanics

Grammar, Usage, and Mechanics

When students are ready to proofread their work, refer them to the **Writers' Checklist.** Be sure students have **capitalized** their sentences correctly. If they haven't, they'll need to do some revising. You might have to support some students by helping them get started with revisions.

V. LOOK BACK

Reflect with students on their **enjoyment** of *Booker T. Washington*. Point out **the Readers' Checklist** and have the class discuss their answers. Explain that these are the kinds of questions good readers ask themselves any time they finish a reading.

Two forms of Assessment—Readers' Checklist and Test

To test students' comprehension, use the **Lesson Test** blackline master on page 75.

69

As noted, each lesson plan in the *Sourcebook Teacher's Guide* has six blackline masters for additional levels of support for key skill areas.

PAGE 7 Words to Know

- Each **Words to Know** blackline master helps students learn the meanings of five words from the selection. The purpose of this blackline master is to expose students to the meanings of key words in the selection, giving them readiness before they read.

---

page 7

Meanings of five words from the selection are taught

BOOKER T. WASHINGTON / STUDENT PAGES 11–20

Name _____

WORDS TO KNOW

Before Reading

DIRECTIONS Answer each question using a word from the word box below. If you don't know, make a prediction. Use the rest of the question to help you.

◇plantation ◇shack ◇master ◇ground ◇meal

1. Where did some former slaves work and live?

Some worked and lived on a _____ .

2. What would be the opposite of a castle?

The opposite of a castle would be a _____ .

3. When you take corn and crush it into powder, what do you do?

I took the corn and _____ it into powder.

4. What is ground corn called?

Ground corn is called a _____ .

5. Who is in charge of a plantation?

A _____ is in charge of a plantation.

Practice

How is a *plantation* different from a *shack*?

_____

_____

_____

_____

70

PAGE 8 **Before You Read**

- An additional prereading activity is included to ensure that students have sufficient background for reading the selection. Generally, the purpose of the activity is to activate students' prior knowledge about a subject and help them predict what the selection is about.

page 8

Additional prereading activity builds background and activates students' prior knowledge

Name _____

BEFORE YOU READ
Picture Walk

DIRECTIONS Take a picture walk through *Booker T. Washington*.
Look at every picture.
Then answer these questions.

My Picture Walk of *Booker T. Washington*

1. Which picture do you think is most interesting? Why?

_____

_____

2. What do you learn about Booker T. Washington from the pictures?

_____

_____

3. Which pictures make you feel sad or angry? Why?

_____

_____

4. What do you predict this selection will be about?

_____

_____

71

PAGE 9 Comprehension

- Each **Comprehension** blackline master affords teachers still another way to build students' understanding of the selection, using a different strategy from the one found in the *Sourcebook*.

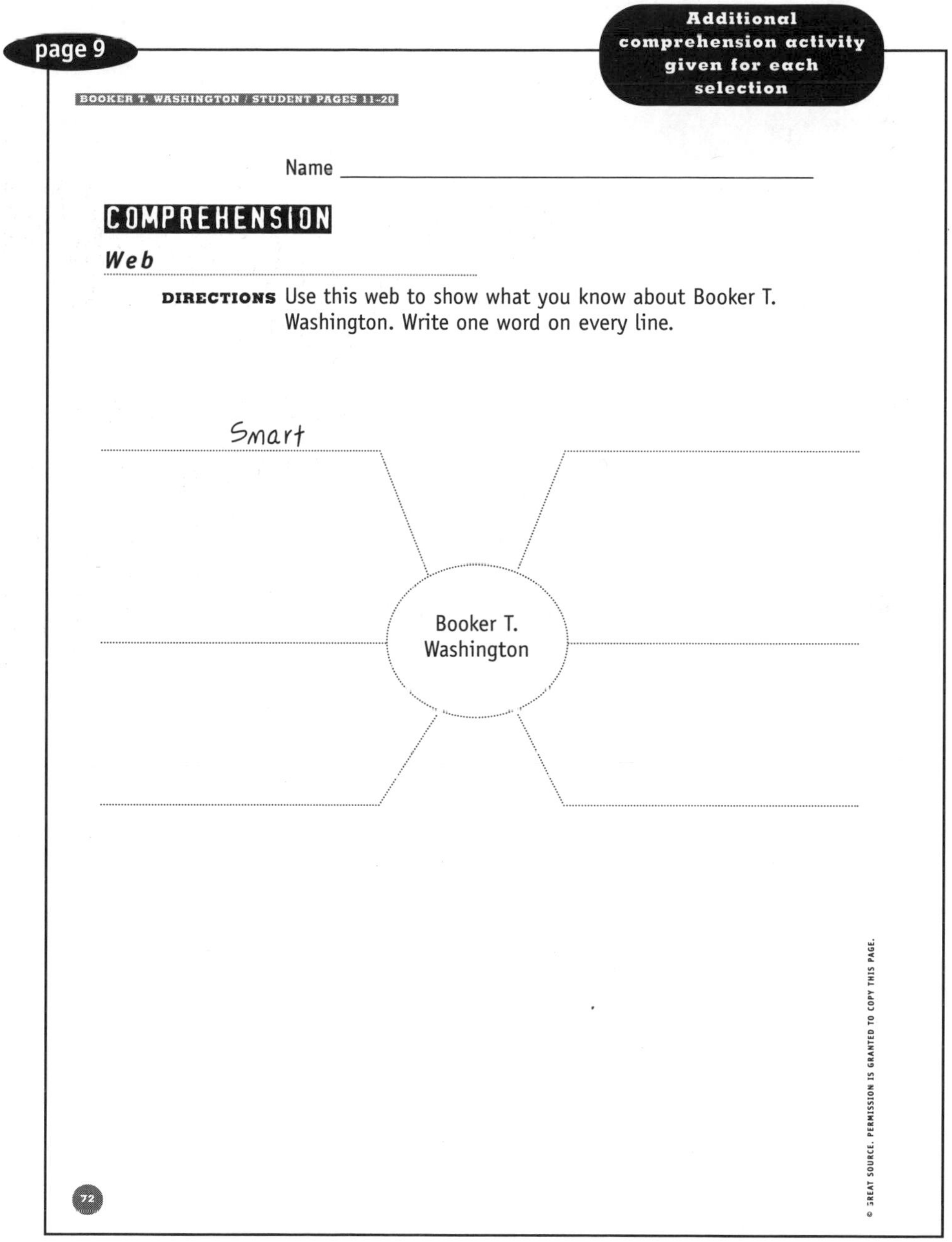

page 9

BOOKER T. WASHINGTON / STUDENT PAGES 11-20

Name _____

COMPREHENSION

Web

DIRECTIONS Use this web to show what you know about Booker T. Washington. Write one word on every line.

Smart

Booker T. Washington

72

PAGE 10 Word Work

- Each **Word Work** activity offers additional practice with the skills emphasized in the pupil's book. Often, students will need repeated practice on a skill before they internalize it.

page 10

Extra practice on
Word Work skill

Name _____

WORD WORK

After Reading

You can make a compound word by joining two small words. For example:

zoo + keeper = zookeeper

DIRECTIONS Join these small words to form compound words. Write the words on the lines. One has been done for you.

1. meal + times = _mealtimes_ _____
2. slow + poke = _____
3. book + keeper = _____
4. sun + light = _____
5. some + times = _____

Practice

DIRECTIONS Here are two lines of small words. Make compound words by connecting a word in Line A to a word in Line B. An example has been done for you.

Line A   **Line B**

6. school   paper
7. any   out
8. sand   body
9. tear   teacher
10. with   drop

73

PAGE 11 Prewriting

- Often, at least some students will need even more scaffolding than appears in the pupil's lesson as they prepare for the writing assignment.

- The "extra step" in preparing to write is the focus of the prewriting blackline master.

---

page 11

BOOKER T. WASHINGTON / STUDENT PAGES 11–20

Name _____

GET READY TO WRITE
Writing a Letter

DIRECTIONS Follow these steps to write your letter.

STEP 1 Choose the person you will write to.

I will write to: _____

STEP 2 Tell the topic of your letter.

My topic: _____

STEP 3 Choose a topic sentence. Use this as your first sentence.

(circle one)

At long last, I am free!

Now that I am free, I have big plans.

Since I am now free, I want to do three things.

STEP 4 Write the three things you will do below:

#1 _____

#2 _____

#3 _____

Another prewriting activity to get students ready to write

74

PAGE 12 Lesson Test

- The Lesson Test blackline master offers a brief multiple-choice test on the selection and a short-essay question for a more formal assessment.

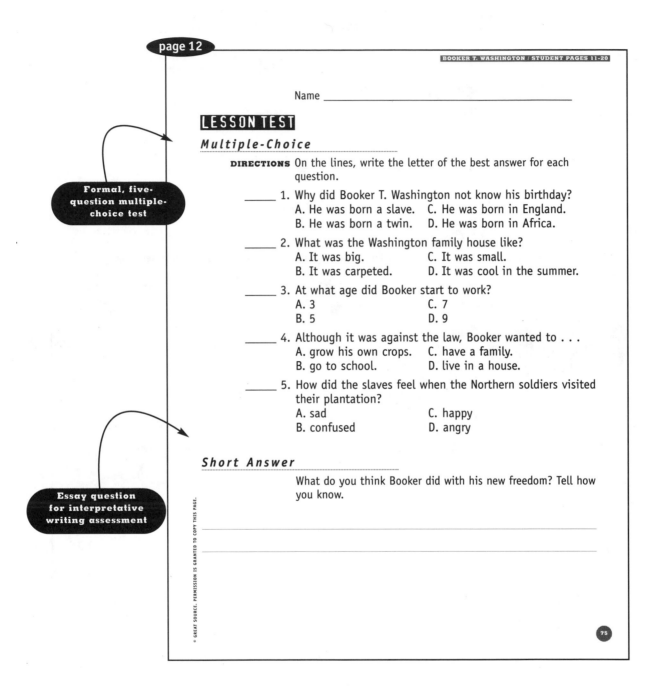

page 12

Name _____

LESSON TEST

Multiple-Choice

DIRECTIONS On the lines, write the letter of the best answer for each question.

_____ 1. Why did Booker T. Washington not know his birthday?
A. He was born a slave.   C. He was born in England.
B. He was born a twin.   D. He was born in Africa.

_____ 2. What was the Washington family house like?
A. It was big.   C. It was small.
B. It was carpeted.   D. It was cool in the summer.

_____ 3. At what age did Booker start to work?
A. 3   C. 7
B. 5   D. 9

_____ 4. Although it was against the law, Booker wanted to . . .
A. grow his own crops.   C. have a family.
B. go to school.   D. live in a house.

_____ 5. How did the slaves feel when the Northern soldiers visited their plantation?
A. sad   C. happy
B. confused   D. angry

Short Answer

What do you think Booker did with his new freedom? Tell how you know.

_____

_____

Formal, five-question multiple-choice test

Essay question for interpretative writing assessment

75

Guiding Students' Reading

BY LAURA ROBB

Whenever I coach teachers, I meet with them to learn about their teaching styles and practices, their educational philosophy, and all the time I'm jotting down questions they have for me. At a school in my community, I recently met with teachers from grades three, four, and five. Their teaching experience ranged from two to ten years, and their teaching styles included a reading/writing workshop that integrated the language arts and a more structured classroom that separated topics such as reading, writing, spelling, grammar, and punctuation skills. However, among twelve teachers, three questions surfaced again and again:

1. What can I do to support *all my readers* including those who struggle?

2. How do I find short materials for my struggling and reluctant readers?

3. Can I apply the guided reading principles primary teachers are using to older students?

Reflective teachers constantly pose questions, for questions are the foundation of inquiry. And inquiry can lead to responsive teaching—teaching that meets the needs of each child in your classroom as well as spurs teachers to explore answers to their questions.

In this article, I will address the three questions because they are crucial to supporting teachers who understand the importance of taking each struggling or reluctant reader where he or she is and gently nudging him or her forward by offering chunks of independent reading time, scaffolding instruction, and organizing and leading flexible strategic reading groups.

Independent Reading

Too often, struggling readers spend more of their time completing skill sheets than reading books they can enjoy. The skill-sheet instructional strategy comes from the traditional belief that isolated practice of such skills as finding the main idea, sequencing, learning word meanings, and syllabication would help students acquire the skills to read books, the newspaper, and magazines.

Contrary to tradition, research shows that one of teachers' most important tasks regarding comprehension instruction is to set aside ample time for actual text reading. Students who struggle need to read as much as or more than proficient readers—providing the texts are at their independent reading level. Such daily silent reading combined with strategy demonstrations and student practice can improve reading more than a diet of skill sheets.

Finding adequate materials for struggling readers who read one or more years below grade level is a challenge. Teachers recognize that there is a limited amount of easy-to-read material available for middle grade students—reading materials that are on topics that hold their interest from start to finish.

The **Sourcebooks**, however, are outstanding resources for teachers in need of independent reading materials. Selections are leveled from easy reading at the start of each student book to a final lesson that's near or on grade level. Since selections are excerpts from the finest literature, teachers have sixteen books per grade level that children can read independently throughout the school year. Moreover, teachers can offer other readable books by the authors students enjoy most. For those who require teacher support while reading, you can scaffold instruction by sitting side-by-side a student and guide the reading with questions, prompts, and modeling.

The Importance of Scaffolding

Scaffolding is the specific support offered to pairs, small groups, individuals, and the entire class that teachers provide before, during, and after reading. Teachers scaffold students' reading until each student demonstrates an understanding of a strategy. Gradually, the teacher withdraws support, moving students to independence.

In a typical middle grade classroom, where teachers work with a mix of reluctant/struggling, grade level, and proficient readers, scaffolding reading might start with the entire class, then move to those students who require additional help in order to understand and internalize a strategy.

Recent research shows that applying reading strategies to texts—strategies such as predicting, questioning, and making personal connections—improves students' comprehension before, during, and after reading. In addition, it's important to help students set purposes for reading before plunging them into a text, for this strategy focuses students on what's important in the selection.

Good teaching provides scaffolding for proficient and struggling readers and starts before reading, helping students activate their prior knowledge and experience so they can use what they know to connect to the authors' words and construct new understandings. During reading, scaffolding strategies build on setting purposes for reading as students actively interact with a text by using the reading purposes to underline words and phrases and write notes in the margin. After reading, scaffolding improves recall and deepens comprehension as students practice such strategies as rereading and skimming to answer a question, to find details about a character or an event, to locate information, or to prepare for writing. Reflecting on their reading by revisiting the piece, talking to a partner, and writing about what they've read all boost comprehension and recall of key details and ideas.

Why Sourcebooks Are a Must-have Text

We have carefully structured each *Sourcebook* lesson so that it builds on the sound, current research on scaffolding instruction and the reading strategy curriculum. We've integrated the strategic parts of each lesson to heighten the impact on struggling readers of practicing and coming to understand related strategies. Here's the support your students will receive with each lesson:

Get Ready to Read: throughout the *Sourcebook*, students practice four to six research-tested activities that prepare them for reading.

Your Purpose for Reading: each lesson sets a purpose for reading that builds on the preparation activity and focuses students' reading goals.

Read and Interact with the Text: during the first reading, students become **active readers**, underlining and circling parts of the text, then writing their thoughts and questions in the Notes.

Comprehension Builders: while reading, students are invited to stop and think about the story's structure and meaning, as well as answer questions and think about relationships such as cause and effect.

Reread: asks students to go back to the text and complete parts they haven't already completed, in order to build fluency.

Word Work: these activities help struggling readers improve their decoding strategies and learn how they can build on what they already know about words to figure out how to say new, unfamiliar words.

Getting Ready to Write: divided into two parts, students first reread their notes and the entire text because rereading improves recall and comprehension. The second part helps students prepare for their writing by creating a detailed plan of ideas.

Writing Activity: always related to the reading selection, students use their plans to write letters, poems, and expository, descriptive, and narrative paragraphs.

Look Back: this reflective part of the lesson invites students to think about what they learned, why they enjoyed the piece, the meaning of the selection, or why the piece was easy or challenging to read.

Many of your students will be able to work through each lesson independently or with the support of a reading partner. However, there will be times when you will use the entire lesson or parts of a lesson with a pair or small group of students. Moreover, you'll find the *Sourcebook* lessons ideal for group instruction because short, readable selections allow you to focus on strategies and work through part of a lesson in one to two periods.

Strategic Reading Groups

"I can't read this stuff. I'll never learn how to read." These comments, made by readers who struggle, reveal how fragile these youngsters are. Unfortunately, their self-esteem is low due to all their negative experiences with reading. At school, they watch classmates complete work easily and achieve success—these observations only reinforce struggling learners' negative thoughts about their ability to progress. At home, they avoid reading because they can't cope with grade-level texts. Often, teachers and parents read materials to them. However, this only improves students' listening. To improve reading, students must read books they CAN read and enjoy.

The best way to support your struggling readers is to organize groups that are flexible, because they respond to the ever-changing needs of students.

Responsive Grouping

Learners improve at different rates. That's why responsive grouping, where you work with students who have common needs, is the key to moving all readers forward. Once a student understands how to apply a strategy such as predicting, posing questions, or previewing, it's time to move that child to a group that's working on another strategy.

Responsive, flexible grouping is similar to the guided reading model primary teachers use. The difference in the middle grades is that students don't change groups as frequently as emergent and beginning readers. The emphasis of instruction is on developing critical thinking strategies, interpreting the meaning of texts, and learning to find the main points an author is making. In addition, those students who need to bolster their ability to pronounce long, new words and figure out their meanings using context clues receive ongoing teacher support. The question, then, that faces all of us teachers is, "How do I monitor the progress of each child so I can respond to his/her reading needs by changing group membership?"

First, teachers must systematically observe their students by doing the following:

- Jot down notes as students work independently, with a partner, or in a small group.

- Study samples of students' written work.

- Observe students during teacher-led small-group strategic reading lessons.

- Hold short one-on-one conferences and listen to students answer questions about their reading process, progress, and needs.

- Use this data to adjust group membership.

The chart below compares Responsive and Traditional Grouping. It will help you understand the benefits of responsive grouping.

Responsive Grouping	Traditional Grouping
Students grouped by assessment of a specific strategy.	Students grouped by general assessments such as standardized testing.
Responds to students' needs and changes as these needs change.	Static and unchanging for long periods of time.
Strategies practiced before, during, and after reading with a variety of genres.	Selections limited to basal. Worksheets for specific skills.
Books chosen for the group at their instructional level.	Students move through a grade-level basal whether or not they read above or below grade level.
Reading is in silent, meaningful chunks.	Round-robin oral reading.
Students actively interact with the text, discuss and reflect on it, and develop critical thinking.	Students read to find out the correct answer.
Varied vocabulary with an emphasis on solving word problems while reading.	Controlled vocabulary.
Students practice and apply strategies that enable them to connect to and think deeply about their reading.	Students complete worksheets that have little to do with the story in the basal anthology.
Students learn to apply word-solving strategies to real books.	Students practice skills with worksheets. The transfer to using word-solving strategies in real books is rarely made.
Evaluation based on careful observation of students' reading in a variety of situations.	Evaluation based on skill sheets and basal reading texts.

The Sourcebooks and Responsive Grouping

The **Sourcebooks** are ideal for small-group work that focuses on a specific reading or writing strategy. Selections are readable, and all the strategies are connected and/or related in each lesson. All the lessons have been structured according to the standards listed under "Responsive Grouping." Moreover, you don't have to use valuable time to search for short materials to frame a meaningful lesson that can nudge struggling readers forward.

If one child or a group of children is/are experiencing difficulty with a specific strategy such as previewing, taking notes, decoding, or preparing to write, the **Sourcebooks** are the perfect resource for the teacher to support and guide those students. Teachers can focus on one part of a lesson with the group or work through an entire lesson over several days. The main consideration is to offer instructional scaffolding to readers who struggle, for as you work together, you will improve their reading ability and develop their confidence and self-esteem.

Ten Suggestions for Supporting Struggling Readers

The tips that follow are from a list that I keep in my lesson plan book, so I can revisit it and make sure I am attending to the needs of every student who requires my support.

1. Be positive. Focus your energies on what students can do. Accept students where they are and use the *Sourcebook* lessons to move them forward.

2. Set reasonable and doable goals with your students. Continue to revise the goals as students improve.

3. Give students reading materials they can read independently, such as the selections in the *Sourcebook.* When students DO the reading, they will improve.

4. Get students actively involved with their learning by using strategies that ask students to interact instead of to passively listen.

5. Help students learn a strategy or information a different way if the method you've introduced isn't working.

6. Sit side-by-side and explain a point or strategy to a students who needs extra scaffolding. Closing the gap between your explanation and the student can result in improved comprehension.

7. Invite students to retell information to a partner or in small groups. Talk helps learners remember and clarify their ideas.

8. Make sure students understand directions.

9. Help struggling readers see their progress. Invite students to reflect on their progress and tell you about it. Or, tell students the progress you see.

10. Give students extra time to complete work and tests. ·

Closing Thoughts

Using the *Sourcebooks* with your reluctant and struggling readers can transform passive, unengaged readers into active and motivated learners. As your students complete the *Sourcebook* lessons and benefit from other parts of your reading curriculum, they will have had many opportunities to build their self-confidence and self-esteem, and develop a repertoire of helpful strategies by participating in reading, writing, and thinking experiences that are positive and continue to move them forward.

Fountas, Irene and Gay Su Pinnell. 1996. *Guided Reading: Good First Teaching for All Children*. Portsmouth, NH: Heinemann.

Gillet, Jean Wallace and Charles Temple. 1990. *Understanding Reading Problems: Assessment and Instruction,* third edition. New York: HarperCollins.

Robb, Laura. 2000. *Teaching Reaching in Middle School*. New York: Scholastic.

BY RUTH NATHAN

During the past thirty years, many studies centering on the reading process have identified what good readers do (Pressley and Woloshyn, 1995). We know they use efficient strategies to comprehend, and that they know when and where to use them. We know, too, that good readers monitor their comprehension, and that they are appropriately reflective. That is, strong readers know when they need to read more, read again, or ask for help. Proficient readers also possess strong vocabularies and usually have vast backgrounds of experience, either real or vicarious.

In order to grow into becoming a proficient reader, studies from the fields of both psychology and education have also shown that successful instruction will most likely occur when certain needs are met (Adams, 1990). For example, it is important for readers to be reading at their instructional level when they're learning comprehension strategies and not be frustrated by text that is too difficult. Difficult text usually has more complex syntactic structures and less-frequent words. It is equally important that teachers teach a few (one or two) strategies at a time, in context, and that these strategies be repeated frequently.

Because of what we know about proficient readers *and* quality instruction, the chapters in this **Sourcebook** have embraced three keys to promote student success:

KEY ONE: Only a few comprehension strategies are taught at a time, and these comprehension strategies are taught *in* context, practiced, and repeated (Robb, 2000; Harvey and Goudvis, 2000).

KEY TWO: The literature in the **Sourcebook** is of high interest and appropriate readability. This means that the stories selected will interest readers at this age; that the syntactic complexity is low at first, becoming ever-more difficult; and that word recognition is eased by choosing books with more frequent words and fewer rare words. Only gradually do stories contain a greater number of rare words.

KEY THREE: In each chapter, rare words are identified and explained. In addition, there are word recognition exercises in each chapter meant to help less-proficient readers gain in their word-recognition power. Students are shown how to use analogy to read new words as well as how to use words parts, such as syllables and affixes, to speed word recognition.

In addition to the three keys, the authors of the **Sourcebook** have utilized many strategies *before*, *during*, and *after* reading to engage readers and to promote transfer of learning.

Each chapter begins with readers accessing their prior knowledge and suggests a reason for reading. Research has shown prior knowledge and purpose to be important factors in comprehension (Adams, 1990). During reading, students are encouraged to talk with classmates, thus articulating their beliefs while at the same time hearing other interpretations of the text (Keene and Zimmermann, 1997; Booth and Barton, 2000). In addition, during reading students are using the text pages to reflect on their understanding through invitations to both write and draw (Clagget, 1999; Harvey and Goudvis, 2000). This practice goes back to the Middle Ages, but has received much support in all contemporary models of competent thinking (Pressley and Woloshyn, 1995). After reading, students are using all the language arts—reading, writing, listening, and speaking, as well as drawing— to write related entries, be it a summary, an invitation, a journal entry with a point of view, or a creative story ending or poem.

All in all, the **Sourcebooks** are exactly what struggling readers need to improve their comprehension and reading enjoyment. The three keys to success combined with before-, during-, and after-reading opportunities will provide students with many meaningful and joyful experiences. Our hope is that these experiences might lead students to a life filled with unforgettable encounters with texts of all types—books, newspapers, magazines, and all texts electronic.

Four Must-Have Teacher Resources

Classrooms That Work: They Can All Read and Write, 2nd edition, by Patricia M. Cunningham and Richard L. Allington. New York: Longman, 1999.

This book covers a range of topics you will find useful: teaching reading and writing in the primary and intermediate grades, organizing your classroom, and helping struggling readers cope with difficult science and history texts. You'll visit classrooms that use Cunningham's "Four-Blocks" approach to reading and better understand how the model works in the primary grades.

Easy Mini-Lessons for Building Vocabulary by Laura Robb. New York: Scholastic, 1999.

Choose from a large menu of doable strategies that build students' vocabulary before, during, and after reading. You'll also help prepare your students for standardized tests with the "Test-Taking Tips" sprinkled throughout the book. This book offers a practical and manageable approach to teaching vocabulary.

Words Their Way: Word Study for Phonics, Vocabulary, and Spelling Instruction, 2nd edition, by Donald R. Bear, Marcia Invernizzi, Francine Johnston, and Shane Templeton. Columbus, Ohio: Merrill, 2000.

This book strengthens teachers, knowledge of word study and spelling by clearly explaining developmental spelling and each of the stages children pass through. In addition, the book is packed with easy-to-implement word-study games and lessons that can improve children's ability to read and understand multi-syllable words.

Teaching Reading in Middle School: A Strategic Approach to Teaching Reading That Improves Comprehension and Thinking, by Laura Robb, New York: Scholastic, 2000.

Readers will gain deep insight in teaching reading strategies before, during, and after reading, organizing students into teacher-led strategic reading groups, setting up a reading workshop, as well as motivating and assessing middle grade and middle school readers. A chapter on struggling readers offers suggestions for helping these students read books at their independent levels without losing self-esteem. The readable text combines literacy stories, theory, and practice, and offers a practical, research-based model.

Organizing and Managing Reading Groups

BY LAURA ROBB

On the first day of school twenty-five to thirty third graders cross the threshold of your classroom. Each student differs in the experiences and knowledge he or she brings to your class. Students' reading levels vary: some will read on grade level, others will read one to two years below grade level, and a few proficient readers will be one to two years above grade level. This snapshot raises three questions for language arts and reading teachers:

1. How do I address the needs of this wide range of reading abilities?

2. How do I find appropriate pieces for strategic group work—literature students can read?

3. What does the rest of the class do while I'm working with a group?

For two to four reading groups to work both independently and with their teacher, it's important to create simple, but effective reading and writing experiences that students can complete alone or with a partner. Equally as important is showing students how to use materials they'll work on while you're with another group and negotiating behavior guidelines so students don't interrupt you.

Teach Students How to Work in Pairs, Small Groups, and Independently

It can take from four to six weeks to establish routines at the start of the year. During this time, students learn how to work on specific tasks without your guidance. Thoroughly explain the how-to's of each experience. For example, for independent reading, explain how you've organized your classroom library, where to log in the title and author of the book and the amount students have read, as well as behavior expectations for silent, independent reading.

While You Work with a Group, Students Can . . .

Provide easy-to-manage reading and writing experiences for students, making independent learning time meaningful and engaging. Such experiences can also nudge students forward and improve their reading and writing strategies and skills.

SOURCEBOOKS AND DAYBOOKS The *Reading and Writing Sourcebooks* and *Daybooks of Critical Reading and Writing* are top-notch resources for independent work and teacher-led group work. Show students how the *Sourcebooks* and *Daybooks* work by completing the first unit with them. You can order a *Daybook* at grade level and one a year above grade level to challenge students to learn at their independent reading levels.

Struggling readers can work with you in *Sourcebook,* grade 3, and gain the vocabulary, skills, and strategies they need to progress. Once students understand what they must do, parts of each lesson, such as the Word Work and Write, can be completed independently.

PAIRED READING Partners read small sections of a book or passage and retell parts to one another.

LISTENING TO A BOOK Students listen to books by *Sourcebook* authors on an audiocassette in a listening center. They can respond to this experience by drawing and/or writing about the story in a journal.

COMPLETE A JOURNAL ENTRY Students can respond to their reading by identifying the main character, the problems faced, and the outcomes; by describing the personality of the main character; by drawing and writing about important settings; or by showing how a character or an event is similar to an experience they've had.

GROUP DRAMAS Small groups select a section or chapter of a book to dramatize, using voices and gestures to reveal character.

WRITING PROJECT Students can work on a piece of writing from their *Sourcebook*, *Daybook*, or writing folder.

Group Management Tips

In a forty-five-minute to one-hour reading block, you can meet with two reading groups (35–45 minutes total reading time—15 to 20 for each teacher-led group plus five extra minutes for transitions), and have time to go over the activities and show students where they'll work. Create a signal for immediate quiet, such as flicking the lights.

Here are some suggestions that lead to productive group work:

• Select three to four reading and writing experiences from the list on pages 6 and 7 that students can work on until everyone completes each activity.

• Post these experiences on a chart or the chalkboard.

• List the names of students under their first activity. Rotate to a new activity after 15 to 20 minutes.

• List the names of the two reading groups that will work with you that day.

• If some students finish early, they should read independently, using books they can read without support.

Early in the year, take the time to establish guidelines for what students do if they have a question and you're working with reading groups. Write the four guidelines that follow on construction paper and display on a bulletin board or wall.

1. Stop and think. Try to solve your problem on your own. Think of strategies you can try that might help.

2. Ask your reading partner or a member of your group for help.

3. If your buddy or a group member can't help, ask another student.

4. If neither 1, 2, or 3 works, read your free-choice reading book and wait until your teacher can help you.

Closing Thoughts

The level of success of group work depends on two things:

• Activities students can complete on their own.

• Establishing routines and behavior guidelines BEFORE inviting students to complete activities independently or with a partner.

The **Sourcebooks** and **Daybooks** are ideal resources for students because they let you offer them reading and writing activities that are appropriate to their developmental needs. Moreover, as students experience success and pleasure in reading and writing, they will improve.

Here is a quick guide to the main prereading, comprehension, and reflective strategies used in the *Sourcebooks*. Students will benefit by explicit instruction in these strategies. You can help teach these strategies by introducing them to students.

In order to help students internalize these strategies, the number and use of them was limited so that students could encounter them repeatedly throughout the book.

Overview
....

Prereading Strategies
K-W-L
Anticipation Guide
Preview
Think-Pair-and-Share
Word Web

Active Reading (Response) Strategies
Comprehension Strategies
Stop and Think
Graphic Organizer
Double-entry Journal
Retell

Word Work Strategies
Reflective Reading Strategies
Understanding
Ease
Meaning
Enjoyment

PREREADING STRATEGIES
K-W-L

What It Is

K-W-L is a pre- and post-reading strategy designed to facilitate students' interest in and activate their prior knowledge of a topic before reading nonfiction material. The letters K, W, and L stand for "What I Know," What I Want to Know," and "What I Learned."

Look at the example of a K-W-L chart from **Sourcebook,** grade 4, *How We Learned the Earth Is Round:*

```
┌─────────────────────────────────────────────────────────────┐
│                      K-W-L CHART                             │
│ What I Know                                                  │
│                                                             │
│                                                             │
│ What I Want to Know                                         │
│                                                             │
│                                                             │
│ What I Learned                                             │
│                                                             │
│                                                             │
└─────────────────────────────────────────────────────────────┘
```

How to Introduce It

Introduce K-W-L as a whole-class activity. Give students time to write one or two questions they have. Explain that they will come back to their chart after they have finished reading, to record what they have learned.

Explain to students that K-W-L first pulls together what they know and then gives them questions that they can read for.

Be sure to return to the chart and have students list what they learned in the L column.

Why It Works

Brainstorming (the K part) activates prior knowledge. What sets K-W-L apart from other prereading strategies is that K-W-L also encourages students to ask questions (the W component), thereby setting meaningful purposes for their reading. Returning to the chart (the L component) brings closure to the activity and demonstrates the purposefulness of the task.

Comments and Cautions

Don't worry about the accuracy of what students write under the K column. Students can correct any errors later during the L part of the activity.

After students write what they know, under K, ask them to get together in groups. This will help readers benefit from the knowledge of others.

Then, as students break out of their groups to begin reading, be sure to focus them on their questions, L, "What I Want to Learn."

Anticipation Guide

What It Is

An anticipation guide is a series of statements that students respond to, first individually and then as a group, before reading a selection. The intent is not to quiz students but to prompt answers and the discussion that ensues. The discussion will build background and expectation and give students a reason to read.

Here is an example from *Sourcebook,* grade 4, *Train to Somewhere:*

✔ agree X disagree

_____   A. Every child needs a good home.

_____   B. Children who don't have parents should live with new families.

_____   C. Brothers and sisters should live together.

_____   D. Adults do not like messy children.

How to Introduce It

Have students read the statements. (When making your own guides, keep the number of statements to about five items max. More than that makes it difficult to discuss in detail.)

Discuss the students' responses. The point of an anticipation guide is to discuss students' various answers and explore their opinions. Discussion builds the prior knowledge of each student by adding to it the prior knowledge of other students. The discussion of Anticipation Guide statements can also be a powerful motivator because once students have answered them, they have a stake in seeing if they are "right."

Encourage students to make predictions about what the selection will be about based on the statements.

Then read the selection.

After reading the selection, have students return to their guides and reevaluate their responses based on what they learned from the selection.

Why It Works

Anticipation Guides are useful tools for eliciting predictions before reading, both with fiction and nonfiction. By encouraging students to think critically about a series of statements, anticipation guides raise expectations and build excitement about the selection.

Comments and Cautions

This is a highly motivational prereading activity. Try to keep the class discussion on the subject; the teacher's role is that of a facilitator, encouraging students to examine and re-examine their responses. The greater the stake students have in an opinion, the more they will be motivated to read about the issue.

The focus of the guide should not be on whether students' responses are "correct", but rather on the discussion that ensues once students complete the guide individually.

You might also turn the entire anticipation guide process into a whole-group activity by having students respond with either "thumbs up" or "thumbs down."

Preview or Walk-thru

What It Is

Previewing is a prereading strategy in which students read the title and skim the selection and then reflect on a few key questions. It asks the students to "sample" the selection before they begin reading and functions very much like the preview to a movie. Occasionally it is simply referred to as a walk-thru and is a less formal variation of skimming and scanning.

How to Introduce It

Previewing can be done as an individual or group activity. You might introduce it to the group and in later lessons encourage students to work on their own.

On the first time you use this activity, take time to model previewing carefully for students.

Direct them to the title. Have a student read it aloud.

Then ask them to look at the first sentence. Have someone read it aloud.

Then give students 10–15 seconds to look over the rest of the selection. Then ask them what words, names, or ideas they remember.

Finally, direct students to the last paragraph. Ask students what stands out in the last paragraph for them.

Then have students respond to 4–5 questions about the selection. Questions might include:

* What is the selection about?

* When does it take place?

* Who is in it?

* How does the selection end?

Read the rest of the selection.

Return to the questions and discuss the accuracy of student's predictions. Were they surprised at how the selection turned out based on their initial preview? Why or why not?

Example from **Sourcebook**, grade 4, *A Drop of Blood*:

BEFORE YOU READ

Previewing lets you think about parts of a text before you read it. It starts you thinking about the topic.

1. Read the first and last paragraphs of *A Drop of Blood*.
2. Look at the art and pictures. What do they suggest the reading will be about?
3. Read the underlined words. Read the sentence that includes each underlined word.
4. In your own words, answer each question.

• What is this reading about?

_____

_____

_____

• What questions do you have about this topic?

_____

_____

Why It Works

Previews work because they provide a frame of reference in which to understand new material. Previews build context, particularly when reading about unfamiliar topics. Discussing the questions and predicting before reading helps students set purposes for reading and creates interest in the subject matter.

Comments and Cautions

Previews work best with difficult, content-intensive reading selections. Especially with nonfiction and texts with difficult vocabulary, it helps students to understand a context for a selection—what's the subject? where's the story located? who's involved?

Think-Pair-and-Share

What It Is

Think-Pair-and-Share is a prereading strategy that encourages group discussion and prediction about what students will read. Students work in pairs or groups of three or four to discuss sentences selected from the text.

How to Introduce It

Break students into groups of three–four. Present three–five sentences from the selection. Ask group members to read the sentences and discuss what they mean and in what order they might appear in the text.

Encourage groups to make predictions and generate questions about the reading.

Then read the selection.

Have groups discuss the selection and the accuracy of their think-pair-and-share sentences. How many were able to correctly predict the order in which the sentences appeared? How many could predict what the selection was about?

Here is an example from **Sourcebook,** grade 4, *Follow That Trash!:*

.... You throw out about 4 pounds of garbage a day.

.... It's easy to get rid of everyone's trash.

.... Some trash is burned.

.... Most trash is buried in the ground.

Why It Works

Think-Pair-and-Share can be a powerful tool for getting students motivated to read. Small group work such as this gives students the chance to discover that they don't always have to come up with all the answers themselves. Sometimes two or three heads <u>are</u> better than one. Working in groups also provides reluctant readers with the understanding that all readers bring different ideas to the reading task. The activity also begins the critical process of "constructing meaning" of the text.

You can make the activity more tactile by cutting the sentences up into strips and passing them out to each group. Ask the groups to put the sentences in the order they think they occurred in the story.

Comments and Cautions

Have students help in building the think-pair-and-share activity. Have each group member write one sentence from the text on a file card. Then ask groups to exchange file cards—one group pieces together the sentences of another group.

Word Web

What It Is

A word web is a prereading activity in which students brainstorm about and make connections to a key concept from the reading material. Word webs work especially well with selections about a specific idea, such as weather.

Here is an example from **Sourcebook**, grade 4, *A River Dream:*

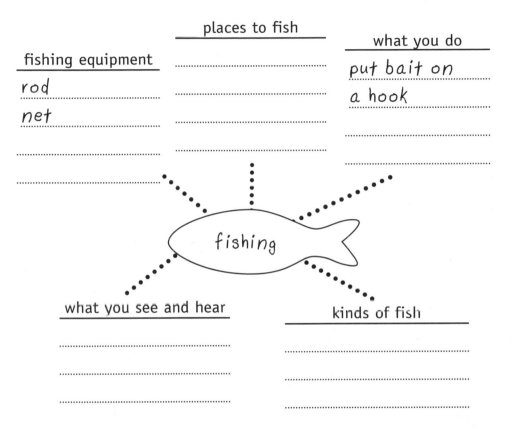

How to Introduce It

Explain what a word web is. Tell students that you will put a word in the center of the web and you want them to think of as many other words and ideas as they can that connect to that word.

Walk students through the activity as a group. Take a general idea, such as "transportation." Ask students to give examples of transportation. Then ask them how they feel about different kinds of transportation (cars, planes, trains, spaceships, etc.).

After modeling how to complete a web, ask students to complete the one in the **Sourcebook**. Then have them share their webs with two or three other students before reading the selection.

Why It Works

Word Webs are excellent tools for developing students' conceptual knowledge. They tap into students' prior knowledge and help students make connections between what they know and what they will learn.

Comments and Cautions

If students get "stuck," encourage them to write down words, phrases, examples, or images they associate with the concept. For this strategy, it is helpful for students to work together in groups. Allow sufficient time for students to experience success as they create ideas about the subject before they start the selection.

ACTIVE READING STRATEGIES

The Active Reading (Response) Strategies are introduced at the beginning of the student *Sourcebook* (pages 6–9). They are the heart of the interactive reading students are asked to do throughout the book. In **Part II** of each lesson, students are asked to read the selection actively, marking or highlighting the text or writing comments and reactions to it. In the first reading, they read and mark. In the second reading, they are asked to write or draw their thoughts in the Response Notes beside each selection.

To maintain focus, the directions ask readers to do only one thing at a time. Struggling readers do not naturally interact with a text, so the strategies are limited to four and an example is provided in each lesson.

Examples are also provided in each lesson as a way to model the strategy. The intent is to make marking up the text a natural way for students to read.

Response Strategies

1. Make clear
2. Connect
3. Question
4. Draw

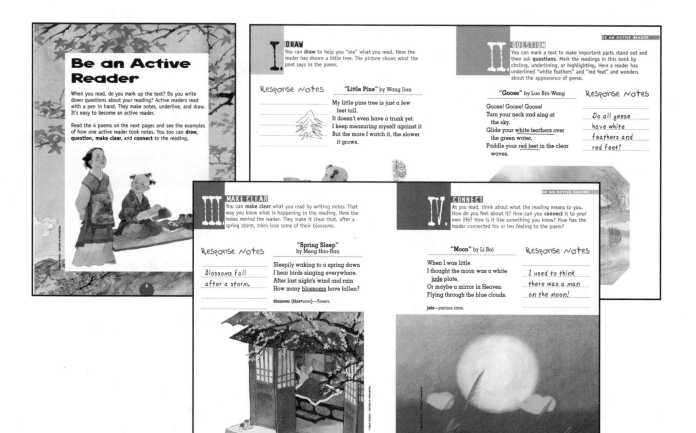

The purpose of these Response Strategies in each lesson is:

1. To help students learn how to mark up a text
2. To help students focus on specific aspects of a text and find the information they need
3. To build lifelong habits by repeating good reading practices

COMPREHENSION STRATEGIES
Stop and Think

What It Is

The Stop and Think strategy is a form of directed reading. It is designed to guide students' reading of a selection. Directed reading in its purest form consists of a series of steps, including readiness, directed silent reading, comprehension check and discuss, oral re-reading, and follow-up activities. In the *Sourcebook*, students gain readiness in **Part I**, read silently in **Part II**, and then encounter questions that check their comprehension throughout the selection.

During the Reread step at the end of **Part II**, teachers are encouraged to have students go back through the selection, reading the selection another time, and making sure they have responded to the Stop and Think questions. Repeated reading of a selection tends to increase reading fluency, which in itself improves reading comprehension.

How to Introduce It

For the first selection with Stop and Think questions, point out for students the questions placed in the middle of the selection. Have students read the selection as directed in **Part II**.

Guide them through active reading of the text on the first reading and through responding to the text on a second reading. Then, after all of the students have made it through the selection, ask students to reread. On this third reading, ask students to concentrate on the questions in the text. Tell students to answer each question when they come upon it.

Mention to students that the questions are the kind of questions they should be asking themselves as they read.

Here is an example from *Sourcebook*, grade 4, *How We Learned the Earth Is Round:*

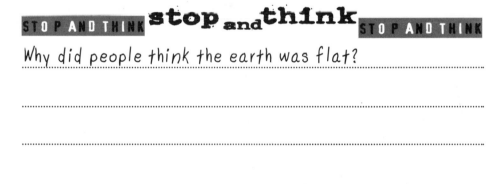

STOP AND THINK stop and think STOP AND THINK

Why did people think the earth was flat?

STOP AND THINK STOP AND THINK STOP AND THINK

Why It Works

Directed reading helps students ask the questions good readers ask of themselves. The structured format of the Stop and Think activities ensures that students will be asking the right kinds of questions.

Comments and Cautions

Directed reading may need to be modified to fit the needs of individual students. Some students may benefit by answering questions in groups or by working in pairs.

Directed reading is intended to help students take meaning from the text. But, interspersing the questions within the text may also mean an interruption of reading for some students. Especially for these students, be sure that students read all the way through the selection once before trying to tackle the Stop and Think questions. By increasing reading fluency, you will be increasing students' reading comprehension.

Graphic Organizer

What It Is

A graphic organizer is a visual representation of the information in a reading selection. Graphic organizers can be as simple as a web or as involved as a story chart. In either case, the purpose is to <u>show</u> information and organize it for the reader.

How to Introduce It

Start off by showing some graphic organizers. For example, show a 3-column "Beginning, Middle, and End Chart" and a "Story Frame." Tell students that they can use different kinds of graphic organizers to help them keep track of what they read.

After students understand what graphic organizers are, tell them their purpose: to organize information and make it easier to remember.

Here is an example from ***Sourcebook,*** grade 4, *Otherwise Known as Sheila the Great:*

What is Sheila's problem? How is it solved?

1.	2.

Why It Works

By making thinking visible, a graphic organizer helps students remember it. It also helps students make connections between ideas, especially in flow charts or cause-effect charts.

Comments and Cautions

You may want to introduce simple graphic organizers in your discussions of selections. A common and quite easy organizer is a Beginning, Middle, and End Chart for stories.

By starting with simple organizers, students will be acquainted with graphic organizers when they encounter the Story Frame later in ***Sourcebook***, grade 5.

Double-entry Journal

What It Is

A Double-entry Journal is an adaptation of the more familiar response journal. Typically, the left column includes quotes from a selection, while the right column offers students the opportunity to respond to the quotation or idea. It is a very good way to build students' ability to comprehend and interpret a text, and to make inferences.

How to Introduce It

Introduce double-entry journals by doing one as a class. Create a 2-column chart and put a quote from the selection in the left-hand column. Then ask students for their reactions to the quote and write them in the right-hand column. Explain to students that they have just completed a double-entry journal and that it is a strategy to help them understand specific quotes or sentences from a text.

In time, students can choose their own quotes to comment on. In the *Sourcebook*, the quotes are always chosen for students. The benefits of selecting the quotations for students are that the focus is then more on interpreting passages of the text and that the task is simplified, making it easier for students to succeed.

Here is an example from *Sourcebook,* grade 4, *Follow That Trash!:*

DOUBLE-ENTRY JOURNAL

Quote	What You Think This Means
"But landfills fill up. They are ugly and dangerous, too."	

Why It Works

Double-entry Journals encourage students to become more engaged in what they are reading. With a double-entry journal, students naturally make connections between the literature and their own lives. Double-entry journals expand on students' understanding of the material because they require students to make inferences about or some kind of interpretation of the text. As a beginning step in learning to analyze literature, students will find writing about a text easier as they focus on the quotations they select.

Comments and Cautions

Many students may not know what to write about the quotes. Encourage students to write how they feel about the quote or tell what they think a quotation means.

Find the students who need help in knowing what to write and work through several more examples with them.

Retell

What It Is

Retelling is both a comprehension strategy and assessment tool, in which students tell about a selection in their own words. Retelling often works best with chronological stories and as a means of checking that students followed the general "story" in a selection.

How to Introduce It

Introduce retelling as a whole-class activity. For example, you might read a fairy tale out loud or tell the story of the "Billy Goats Gruff" in which three Billy goats try to cross a bridge guarded by a troll. First, the small goat meets the troll and persuades him to wait for his bigger brother. Then, the next Billy goat meets the troll and persuades the troll to wait for his mother. Then, the mother comes and kicks the troll off the bridge. Ask a volunteer to retell the story. Then ask another volunteer to do so. Explain that retellings will differ somewhat but have the same essential features.

Here is an example from *Sourcebook,* grade 4, *Through Grandpa's Eyes:*

STOP AND RETELL stop and retell STOP AND RETELL

What does Grandpa teach John to do?

Why It Works

Explain to students the benefit of retelling as a strategy is that they understand a story better when it is translated into their own words. Mention also that retelling helps them remember the story.

Retelling also helps students make a more personal connection to the text, which makes it more meaningful, and promotes a deeper understanding of the material.

Comments and Cautions

You might tape-record the retellings and let students listen to and assess their own work.

Tell students that the goal of a retelling is not to include every detail, but only to tell what is important about the story.

As much as possible, try to make students understand that one retelling is not necessarily better than another simply because it includes more. A retelling should be accurate and reflect the story, but longer retellings are not necessarily better than shorter ones.

Word Work: Strategies for Reading and New Words

BY RUTH NATHAN, PH.D.

There's an old saying, "If you drop gold and books, pick up the books first, then the gold" (Von Hoff Johnson, 1999). Most of us who work with less-skilled readers would wish this scenario for our struggling students. But the truth is, many less-skilled readers don't enjoy reading at all. While there are many documented reasons for their feelings toward text, the most ubiquitous problem is slow, even laborious, word recognition processes. When reading words takes a great deal of attention and time, comprehension is often lost (Adams, 1990). Who would want to read if it brought no satisfaction?

The Word Work section of each lesson in the **Sourcebooks** is intended to give struggling readers strategies to read new or longer words. Once a reader reads a word a few times, rather than skipping it, word recognition time for that word decreases and soon becomes automatic. The more automatic word recognition is, the more attention is available for the important work of comprehension, reflection, and interpretation. If we want our less-skilled readers to "go for the books," not just the "gold," we have to teach them strategies to unlock the pronunciation of unknown words.

Five Useful Strategies

Recognizing complex sound/symbol combinations

Recognizing compound words

Reading new words by analogy

Syllabification

Recognizing affixes: prefixes and suffixes

Recognizing Complex Sound/Symbol Combinations

When children first learn to read, they are taught one-to-one sound/symbol correspondences. For example, **b** says /b/ as in *ball*; **t** says /t/ as in *top*. But soon this one-to-one phenomenon is lost to the truth of the matter. Our language is a mixture of many languages, mostly Anglo-Saxon, Greek, and Latin. From Anglo-Saxon we get the *many* spellings of **long a,** as in *mate, nail, play*, and *great*. From Latin we get the "schwa" (the first sound in *about*), a sound spelled with virtually every vowel: *ahead, attitude, committee, selection*, and *selection* (Henry, 1990). And from Greek we get the sound /f/ as in *phonograph*, not /f/ as in *fly*; or /k/ as in *chronology*, not /k/ as in *kite*. English is complex! This being the case, the **Sourcebooks** offer lessons in these complex letter/sound relationships using "word sorts," an active technique that highlights alternative spellings of the same sound (Bear, et al., 1999).

Recognizing Compound Words

Many long English words are simply the combination of two smaller words; these are called compound words. Compounding is one of the major ways by which English words are created. *Over* combines with *pass* to become *overpass*. *Book* combines with *store* to become *bookstore*. Students benefit tremendously by knowing that one strategy for recognizing a longer word is to look for smaller words of which it might be made.

Reading New Words by Analogy

When we say readers can read a new word by using "analogy," it means that they can use a word they know to read one that looks similar from the first vowel onward. For example, if I can read *right* I can probably read *might* by removing the **r** and substituting an **m**. Both words are part of the same word family—that is to say, from the vowel onward they are identical in both spelling and sound. Reading words by analogy is a useful technique when reading sight words, words that are in "families" that don't conform to more frequent sound/symbol relationships, such as *could, would, should*.

Syllabification

Longer words usually contain many syllables. A syllable is a word or word part with one vocalic sound. For example, *front* has one syllable while *front/ier* has two. If students have a strategy for breaking longer words into syllables, then the words become easier to read. The *Sourcebooks* contain several lessons on syllabification. Fortunately, the syllable patterns are generally the same in Latin-based words as in those of Anglo-Saxon origin. The VCCV (*muf/fin*), VCV (*mu/sic* or *sev/en*), and VCCCV (*mon/ster* or *pump/kin*) patterns are most common (Henry, 1990). It's interesting to note, again to students' advantage, that prefixes and suffixes often consist of syllables based on these patterns (for example, *in/ter-* and *in/tro-* [VCCV], *-i/ty* [VCV]).

Recognizing Affixes: Prefixes and Suffixes

In addition to knowing the meaning of frequent prefixes (*un-, re-, dis-, in-*) and the meaning *and* uses of suffixes *(-ful, -ly, -ion)*, less-skilled readers need instruction on how the spelling of a root word might change with the addition of a suffix that begins with a vowel. For example, when the suffix *-ed* or *-ing* is added to a root word, the spelling of the word it's added to often changes. This confuses less-skilled readers. A **y** might change to an **i** as in marr*i*ed; a final consonant might double, as in run*n*ing, or a **final e** might be dropped, as in rumbling. Because these subtle root word changes confuse less-skilled readers, the changes must be taught explicitly. In addition, prefixes sometimes change their spelling, depending on the word they precede. For example, the prefix *in-* is spelled four ways: <u>in</u>valid, <u>im</u>portant, <u>ir</u>relevant, and <u>il</u>legal. Spelling changes in prefixes and root words challenge less-skilled readers and need to be taught explicitly. This is why all *Sourcebook* lessons include a word work part in them.

Taken together, the Word Work lessons in the *Sourcebook* reduce the chance that less-skilled readers will just skip words they think they can't read. "Go for the books" might become a reality for all children if they have strategies for recognizing new or long words. Remember, recognition of words comes first, then automaticity. Just as drivers can talk while they drive because they've automatized the driving process, readers will comprehend, reflect on and think critically about what they read if word recognition comes at no cost to reading for meaning (Stanovich, 1995).

References

Adams, Marilyn. 1990. *Beginning to Read: Thinking and Learning about Print*. Cambridge, Massachusetts: The MIT Press.

Bear, D. and Marcia Invernizzi, Shane Templeton, and Francine Johnson. 1999. *Words Their Way: Word Study for Phonics, Vocabulary, and Spelling Instruction*. Columbus, Ohio: Prentice Hall.

Booth, David and Bob Barton. 2000. *Story Works: How Teachers Can Use Shared Stories in the Curriculum*. Pembroke.

Harvey, Stephanie and Anne Goudvis. 2000. *Strategies That Work: Teaching Comprehension to Enhance Understanding*. Stenhouse.

Henry, Marcia K. 1990. *Words: Integrated Decoding and Spelling Instruction Based on Word Origin and Word Structure*. Austin, Texas: Pro-Ed.

Keene, Ellin Oliver and Susan Zimmerman. 1997. *Mosaic of Thought: Teaching Comprehension in a Reader's Workshop*. Heinemann.

Pressley, Michael and Vera Woloshyn. 1995. *Cognitive Strategy Instruction That Really Improves Children's Academic Performance*. Brookline Books.

Robb, Laura. 2000. *Teaching Reading in Middle School: A Strategic Approach to Teaching Reading That Improves Comprehension and Thinking*. New York: Scholastic.

Stanovich, Keith. 1986. "Matthew effects in reading: Some consequences of individual differences in the acquisition of literacy." *Reading Research Quarterly, 21*, 360-407.

Von Hoff Johnson, Bonnie. 1999. *Wordworks: Exploring Language Play*. Golden, Colorado: Fulcrum Resources.

WORD WORK SKILLS

The notes below outline the skills included in the Word Work activities in *Sourcebook*, grade 4. The skills are listed here to help you reinforce and explicitly teach these ideas (and sometimes rules) about words. Some ideas are taught more than once and get progressively more difficult.

The purpose of the Word Work activities is to ease at-risk readers' stress over reading unknown or long words. Among the ways to help are to show readers how to "see" 1) the base word of a long word that might have a prefix, suffix, or both, and that might have undergone a spelling change; 2) smaller words in compound words; 3) syllables; or 4) analogous words. Once students begin to feel comfortable with word recognition strategies, they will be able to decode more words more easily and they will be able to focus on comprehension.

1. Compound Words

You can make a big word by joining 2 small words. The big word is called a compound word.

EXAMPLE: out + side = *outside*

house + boat = *houseboat*

some + time = *sometime*

2. Adding Suffixes to Words That End in Silent *e*

Many of the words you know end in a final silent *e*. Here are some: *taste*, *bake*, and *come*. Words that end in silent *e* are tricky if you are adding an ending that begins with a vowel, such as *-ed*, *-ing*, and *-er*. It's easy to make final silent *e* words longer when you follow this rule:

If a word ends in a silent *e*, drop the *e* before adding an ending that starts with a vowel.

3. Homophones

The best way to tackle confusing word pairs and homophones is to memorize their spellings.

EXAMPLE: *two, to, too*
their, there, they're
one, won
sea, see

4. Contractions

Take 2 words and make them into 1 new word, a contraction.

EXAMPLE: can not = *can't*

he will = *he'll*

5. Prefixes, Suffixes, and Base Words

Adding letters to the beginning and end of a base word makes the word longer. It can also change the base word's meaning.

EXAMPLE: Add the prefix *de-* and the suffix *-ed* to the base word, *part*.

The new word is *departed*.

6. Words with More Than One Meaning (Homographs)

Learn the base words that have more than one meaning. Use context clues to help you figure out the meaning of particular words.

7. Prefixes, Suffixes, and Base Words

Take a prefix off the beginning of a word, and a suffix off the end. The small word that's left is the base word.

EXAMPLE: The long word is *disappeared*. Take off the prefix *dis-* and the suffix *-ed*. The base word is *appear*.

8. Reading Words by Analogy

If you can read one word, you can read a word that's like it or almost the same.

EXAMPLE: You can read the word *back*. Now take off the *b* and put *st* in front of *ack*. The new word is *stack*.

9. Compound Words

You can make a big word by combining 2 small words. The big word is called a compound word.

EXAMPLE: every + one = *everyone*

10. Word Parts

You can build long words by combining a word part, such as *auto-,* with small words and other word parts.

EXAMPLE: auto + graph = *autograph*

11. Syllables

Words have beats—1, 2, 3 or more beats. Try clapping the word *breakfast*. You clapped 2 times because *breakfast* has 2 beats, or syllables.

Some 2-syllable words have 2 consonant letters in the middle. These letters can be the same (bu<u>rr</u>ow). These letters can be different (fi<u>ng</u>er).

12. Compound Words

You can make a big word by combining 2 small words. The big word is called a compound word.

EXAMPLE: moon + light = *moonlight*

13. Words That End in *y*

If a word ends in *y*, change the *y* to an *i* when you add a suffix.

EXAMPLE: dry + er = *drier*

14. Adding Suffixes to Words with One Syllable

When you add a suffix that starts with a vowel to words with one syllable, the base word changes. The last consonant is doubled.

EXAMPLE: stop + ing = *stopping*

15. Contractions

Take 2 words and make them into 1 new word, a contraction.

EXAMPLE: he is = *he's*

            could not = *couldn't*

            I am = *I'm*

16. Reading Words by Analogy

If you can read one word, then you can read a word that's almost the same.

EXAMPLE: You can read the word *hum*. Now take off the *h* and put *pl* in front of *um*.
             The new word is *plum*.

REFLECTIVE READING STRATEGIES

The Reflective Reading Strategies occur in **Part V** of each lesson. They help students take away more from what they read. All too often students are asked, "Did you get it?" Reading seems like a code they have been asked to decipher but cannot. Struggling readers especially need to understand that there is more to reading than "Did you get it?"

How can we turn around struggling readers if the only payoff for reading is "getting it"? Good readers read for a variety of reasons: to entertain themselves, to expand their understanding of a subject or develop their thinking in an area, or simply because they have to read. Yet good readers naturally take away more from what they read. For example:

- We read sports pages because they are **enjoyable**.

- We read about such topics as skiing and navigating the Internet because they have personal **meaning** to us.

- We read cartoons and magazines because they are quick and **easy** to browse.

- We read directions about setting up a stereo because we have to in order to have a particular **understanding**.

We read, in other words, for a variety of reasons. As teachers, we need to help struggling readers see this—and not just that they did not "get it" on the multiple-choice test. So, **Part V** of each lesson in the *Sourcebook* is a "reflective" assessment, a looking-back, so students can see what they gained from the lesson.

Here is an example from *Sourcebook,* grade 4, *Booker T. Washington:*

Continue your letter.

_____

_____

_____

_____

_____

_____

WRITERS' CHECKLIST

Capitalization

■ **Did all of your sentences begin with capital letters?**
EXAMPLE: *School will be wonderful.*

V. LOOK BACK

What part of Booker T. Washington's life did you enjoy reading about? Why? Write your answer below.

_____

_____

Think about your Reading

READERS' CHECKLIST

Enjoyment

■ **Did you like the reading?**
■ **Would you recommend the reading to a friend?**

20

The other important goal of **Part V** is to ask students to think about their reading. The metacognitive part of reading—what was hard, what was easy, what strategy was used—comes once students reflect back and collect their thoughts.

Students need to "think about their reading." Allow time at the end of each lesson for students to write their thoughts. These holistic assessments will offer valuable insight into what students did and did not understand and will prove to be very useful as diagnostic tools. Students will also benefit by learning to monitor their comprehension on their own.

The purpose of the Reflective Reading Assessment in each lesson is:

1. To model for students the questions good readers ask of themselves after reading

2. To expand the reasons for which students want to read

3. To build lifelong habits by repeating good reading practices

Reflective Assessment

1. **Understanding**

   Did you understand the reading?

   Can you tell a friend what the reading is about?

2. **Ease**

   Was the reading easy to read?

   Were you able to read it smoothly?

3. **Meaning**

   Did you learn something from the reading?

   Did you have a strong feeling about the reading?

4. **Enjoyment**

   Did you like the reading?

   Would you recommend the reading to a friend?

Here is an example:

Booker T. Washington

BACKGROUND

Patricia and Fredrick McKissack's *Booker T. Washington: Leader and Educator* is an informative, easy-to-read biography of the former slave who founded Tuskegee University and went on to become one of the most powerful African-American leaders of all time.

The McKissacks have written close to one hundred books for children and have won numerous awards for their work, including a Coretta Scott King Author Honor. Over the years, the McKissacks have combined their talents to make history come alive for children. They have written biographies of such famous figures as Sojourner Truth, George Washington Carver, and opera singer Marian Anderson.

BIBLIOGRAPHY Students might enjoy reading another book by one or both of the McKissacks. The following titles all have a Lexile level close to that of *Booker T. Washington* (Lexile 400).

(Lexile 400)   (Lexile 440)   (Lexile 450)

How to Introduce the Reading

Before they begin reading the selection from the McKissacks' book, students might benefit from some additional information about Booker T. Washington. Ask the class what they know about this famous man. What did he do to become famous? Why might he be of interest to people today?

Explain that Washington was born a slave in the South in 1856. After emancipation, he moved with his family to Malden, Virginia. The family was too poor to send Booker to school regularly, so he taught himself to read and write. After graduating from college (which he paid for by working as a janitor), Washington taught school and eventually founded the Tuskegee Institute. There, he strove to educate students who were as poor and disadvantaged as he once was. His autobiography, *Up from Slavery* (1901), has become a classic.

Other Reading

Cultivate your students' interest in the genre of biography by asking them to read and report on one of these books:

| (Lexile 440) | (Lexile 440) | (Lexile 410) |

Booker T. Washington

(STUDENT PAGES 11–20)

Skills and Strategies Overview

PREREADING	prediction
READING LEVEL	Lexile 400
RESPONSE	question
VOCABULARY	◆plantation ◆shack ◆master ◆ground ◆meal
COMPREHENSION	stop and think
WORD WORK	compound words
PREWRITING	brainstorm
WRITING	friendly letter / capitalization
ASSESSMENT	enjoyment

OTHER RESOURCES

The first **four** pages of this teacher's lesson describe Parts I–V of the lesson. Also included are these **six** blackline masters. Use them to reinforce key elements of the lesson.

Vocabulary

Prereading

Comprehension

Word Work

Prewriting

Assessment

BEFORE YOU READ

Read through the lesson introduction (pages 64–65) with students. These opening paragraphs are meant to spark student interest in the reading to come. Ask students to discuss their own definitions of the word *freedom*. Make a web on the board and have students supply phrases and images that remind them of what it's like to be free. Then assign the prereading activity, making **predictions**. (Refer to the Strategy Handbook on page 49 for more help.)

Motivation Strategies

CONNECTING WITH STUDENTS
Ask students to tell a personal story about a time their own sense of freedom was at stake. What happened? Who was there? How were things resolved? Give students the chance to make an initial connection to the theme of the McKissacks' book before they begin reading.

MOTIVATING STUDENTS
Have students explain how they'd feel if they were not allowed to go to school. Would they fight for the chance to go, or would they be thrilled? Why? What if this "freedom" from school stretched into months or even years? Would students feel differently about the right to attend school?

Words to Know

CONTEXT CLUES
Use the **Words to Know** blackline master on page 70 as a way of troubleshooting vocabulary problems. You might also teach a short vocabulary lesson on using **context clues.**

To begin, show students the key vocabulary words in *Booker T. Washington*: *plantation, shack, master, ground,* and *meal*. Explain that four of the five words are defined at the bottom of the page, but that you'd like students to make predictions about the words first, before checking the footnoted definitions. Tell the class: "Sometimes the author will leave clues about the meaning of a difficult word. For example, I see the word *shack* on page 13. I don't know this word, so I'll look for clues in surrounding sentences. I see that a shack is described as a one-room home with a dirt floor, a broken door, windows with no glass, and cracked walls. I can tell from this description that a shack is not a nice place to live. My guess is that it's a very tiny house. Now that I've made a guess, I'll check the definition at the bottom of the page to see if I am right."

Prereading Strategies

PREDICTIONS
As a prereading activity, students are asked to make **predictions** about the reading. As you know, making predictions about a text can help spark student interest while at the same time give them a purpose for reading. They read in order to find out if their predictions come true.

PICTURE WALK
As a further prereading activity, have students take a **picture walk** of the McKissack selection. Explain that during a picture walk, the reader looks at the art or photographs on each page, without reading any of the text. As you know, the art that accompanies a selection can provide valuable clues about the topic, tone, and sometimes even the author's main idea or message.

To extend the activity, use the **Before You Read** blackline master on page 71.

MY PURPOSE
Always establish a reading purpose for students before they begin an assignment. Move beyond the overly general "read to find out what happens" and create a purpose that gives students something to look for or think about as they read, namely, "Find out who Booker T. Washington was and what his childhood was like."

Response Strategy

FIRST READING Before students begin their first readings, explain the response strategy of asking during-reading **questions.** Refer them to the front matter in their books for an easy-to-follow explanation of this skill. Then point out the example in the Response Notes on page 13. Explain that this is a question one reader has about the story. Students will have other questions that they want to ask. Each time a question occurs to them, they should make a note of it in the margin.

Comprehension Strategy

SECOND READING During their reading, students will need to stop two separate times and answer questions that require factual recall of the text. Use these **stop and think** questions to help you with an on-the-spot assessment of students' understanding of the reading. Have students get into the habit of interrupting their own reading to make notes about what has happened or what they think will happen. The interrupter questions in the *Sourcebook* can help them develop this strategy.

For more help with **Comprehension,** assign the blackline master on page 72.

Discussion Questions

COMPREHENSION 1. What were some of Booker T. Washington's childhood jobs? *(swatting flies at the dinner table, taking corn to the mill)*

2. Why can't Booker go to school? *(It was against the law for slave children to attend school.)*

CRITICAL THINKING 3. What were some of the injustices Washington was forced to endure as a child? *(Possible: He was held as a slave and received no wages; he could not attend school; he lived in a shack, while his master lived in a big house, and so on.)*

4. What was Booker T. Washington's childhood like? *(Possible response: It was pretty awful. He was held as a slave and had no personal freedoms.)*

5. How did you feel as you were reading the story of Washington's childhood? *(Have students explain their emotional response to the text.)*

Reread

THIRD READING Point out the directions at the bottom of page 15. Explain to the class that it's always a good idea to do an additional reading of an assigned selection, especially if the selection is challenging. As they reread the McKissacks' story, students should watch for answers to their own questions. Any questions that remain should be addressed by the group.

Word Work

COMPOUND WORDS You've probably noticed that most young learners enjoy working with **compound words.** They feel proud that they're able to read and understand so many "big" words. Make the most of students' interest by teaching a short lesson on compound words.

For additional practice, see the **Word Work** blackline master on page 73.

III. GET READY TO WRITE

Prewriting Strategies

BRAINSTORM As a prereading activity, students will pretend they are Booker T. Washington and **brainstorm** a list of things they will do now that they are free. Have students work in small groups on this activity. Ask them to share ideas and then make a group list on page 17. When they've finished, gather the class together and ask volunteers to read their lists aloud. Students may hear answers that they'd like to use as details in their letters.

For additional help, have students use the **Get Ready to Write** blackline master on page 74.

IV. WRITE

Point out the directions at the top of page 19. Explain that students' assignment is to write a **letter** to a friend about their newfound freedom. Remind the class to write in the voice of Booker T. Washington, using the first-person *(I, we, us)* point of view throughout. Then teach the five parts of a friendly letter: heading (which includes the date and return address), greeting, body, closing, and signature. Point out that a comma separates the day from the year. In addition, commas are used after the greeting and closing. Also show students that although each word of the greeting is capitalized, only the first word of the closing takes a capital letter.

After students have written a first draft, have them stop and think carefully about what they've written. They should ask themselves: "Have I named at least three things I plan to do with my freedom? Did I write in the voice of Booker T. Washington throughout?"

WRITING RUBRIC Use this rubric to help with a quick assessment of students' writing.

Do students' letters

• include an explanation of why Booker T. Washington is now free?

• name three things they will do with their newfound freedom?

• reflect an understanding of how to write in the first person?

Grammar, Usage, and Mechanics

When students are ready to proofread their work, refer them to the **Writers' Checklist.** Be sure students have **capitalized** their sentences correctly. If they haven't, they'll need to do some revising. You might have to support some students by helping them get started with revisions.

V. LOOK BACK

Reflect with students on their **enjoyment** of *Booker T. Washington*. Point out the Readers' Checklist and have the class discuss their answers. Explain that these are the kinds of questions good readers ask themselves any time they finish a reading.

To test students' comprehension, use the **Lesson Test** blackline master on page 75.

Name _____

WORDS TO KNOW

Before Reading

DIRECTIONS Answer each question using a word from the word box below.

If you don't know the meaning of the words, make a prediction. Use the rest of the question to help you.

◇plantation ◇shack ◇master ◇ground ◇meal

1. Where did some former slaves work and live?

Some worked and lived on a _____ .

2. What would be the opposite of a castle?

The opposite of a castle would be a _____ .

3. When you take corn and crush it into powder, what do you do?

I took the corn and _____ *it into powder.*

4. What is ground corn called?

Ground corn is called _____ .

5. Who is in charge of a plantation?

A _____ *is in charge of a plantation.*

Practice

How is a *plantation* different from a *shack*?

_____

_____

_____

Name _____

BEFORE YOU READ

Picture Walk

DIRECTIONS Take a picture walk through *Booker T. Washington*.

Look at every picture.

Then answer these questions.

My Picture Walk of Booker T. Washington

1. Which picture do you think is most interesting? Why?

_____

_____

2. What do you learn about Booker T. Washington from the pictures?

_____

_____

3. Which pictures make you feel sad or angry? Why?

_____

_____

4. What do you predict this selection will be about?

_____

_____

Name _____

COMPREHENSION

Web

DIRECTIONS Use this web to show what you know about Booker T. Washington. Write one word on every line.

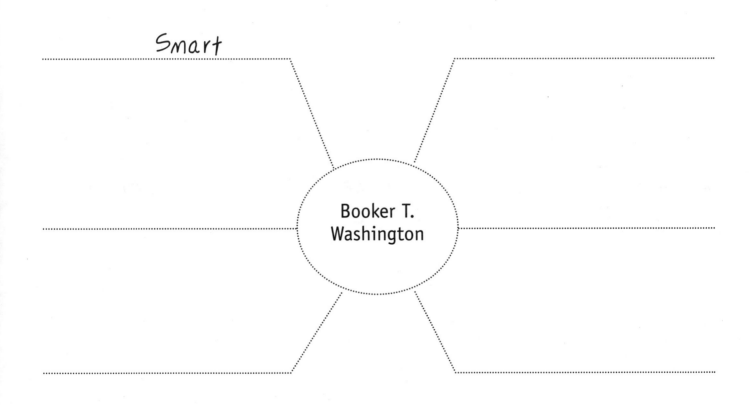

Smart

Booker T. Washington

Name _____

WORD WORK

After Reading

You can make a compound word by joining two small words. An example follows:

zoo + keeper = zookeeper

DIRECTIONS Join these small words to form compound words. Write the words on the lines. One has been done for you.

1. meal + times = _mealtimes_____

2. slow + poke = _____

3. book + keeper = _____

4. sun + light = _____

5. some + times = _____

Practice

DIRECTIONS Here are two columns of small words. Make compound words by connecting a word in Column A to a word in Column B. An example has been done for you.

Column A

6. school
7. any
8. sand
9. tear
10. with

Column B

paper
out
body
teacher
drop

Name

GET READY TO WRITE
Writing a Letter

DIRECTIONS Follow these steps to write your letter.

STEP 1 Choose the person you will write to.

I will write to:

STEP 2 Tell the topic of your letter.

My topic:

STEP 3 Choose a topic sentence. Use this as your first sentence.

(circle one)

At long last, I am free!

Now that I am free, I have big plans.

Since I am now free, I want to do three things.

STEP 4 Write the three things you will do below:

#1

#2

#3

Name _____

LESSON TEST

Multiple-Choice

DIRECTIONS On the lines, write the letter of the best answer for each question.

_____ 1. Why did Booker T. Washington not know his birthday?
A. He was born a slave.   C. He was born in England.
B. He was born a twin.   D. He was born in Africa.

_____ 2. What was the Washington family house like?
A. It was big.   C. It was small.
B. It was carpeted.   D. It was cool in the summer.

_____ 3. At what age did Booker start to work?
A. 3   C. 7
B. 5   D. 9

_____ 4. Although it was against the law, Booker wanted to . . .
A. grow his own crops.   C. have a family.
B. go to school.   D. live in a house.

_____ 5. How did the slaves feel when the Northern soldiers visited their plantation?
A. sad   C. happy
B. confused   D. angry

Short Answer

What do you think Booker did with his new freedom? Tell how you know.

_____

_____

_____

Gloria's Way

BACKGROUND

In her book *Gloria's Way*, Ann Cameron explores the ups and downs of friendship and the importance of feeling good about yourself. *Gloria's Way* is an anthology of six spirited stories, all of which feature Gloria as the protagonist and the ever-popular Julian and Huey in supporting roles. In one of the tales (part of which is reprinted in the **Sourcebook)**, Gloria is unintentionally hurt by Julian, Huey, and their new friend, Latisha. As a result, she must cope with feelings of insecurity and unhappiness.

As you probably know, Cameron's *Julian* books are enormously popular with children. Some of the *Julian* stories are loosely based on Cameron's own childhood and her friendship with a boy named Bradley and his little sister, Carolyn.

Today, Cameron and her husband live in Panajachel, Guatemala, "in a small house with a view of three volcanoes and a waterfall." Her award-winning book *The Most Beautiful Place in the World* is set in Guatemala and based on the stories a young neighbor told her.

BIBLIOGRAPHY Students might enjoy reading another book about Gloria, Julian, and Huey. Recommend these three, all of which have a Lexile level close to that of *Gloria's Way* (Lexile 410):

MORE STORIES JULIAN TELLS (Lexile 430)

JULIAN, SECRET AGENT (Lexile 460)

THE STORIES HUEY TELLS (Lexile 470)

How to Introduce the Reading

Ask a volunteer to read aloud the opening introductory paragraph on page 21. Have students discuss the first question: "What is the most important thing for a friend to do?" Brainstorm a list of responses on the board, some of which may reflect the themes in Cameron's story. Later, after students have finished reading, return to the list as a class and have students add ideas that have occurred to them as a result of the reading. Help students see that one of the reasons we read is to learn new things or find new ways of looking at familiar topics.

Other Reading

Read aloud another Ann Cameron book or other stories written at this same reading level. Choose from among the following high-interest books:

(Lexile 410)   (Lexile 410)   (Lexile 420)

Gloria's Way

(STUDENT PAGES 21-32)

Skills and Strategies Overview

PREREADING	think-pair-and-share
READING LEVEL	Lexile 410
RESPONSE	connect
VOCABULARY	◆prisoner ◆remember ◆sighed ◆jiggled ◆patient
COMPREHENSION	double-entry journal
WORD WORK	silent *e* endings
PREWRITING	word web
WRITING	journal entry / spelling
ASSESSMENT	ease

OTHER RESOURCES

The first **four** pages of this teacher's lesson describe Parts I–V of the lesson. Also included are these **six** blackline masters. Use them to reinforce key elements of the lesson.

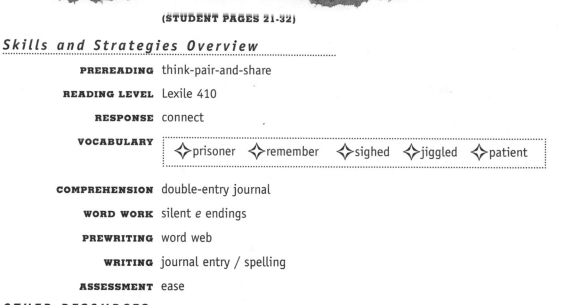

Vocabulary   **Prereading**   **Comprehension**

Word Work   **Prewriting**   **Assessment**

BEFORE YOU READ

Explain to students that they're about to read a story about friendship. Have students tell a funny friendship story from their own lives. Then ask them to turn to the prereading activity, a **think-pair-and-share**. (Refer to the Strategy Handbook, page 50, for more help.)

Motivation Strategies

MOTIVATING STUDENTS   Ask the class: "Can a person be a friend to himself or herself? Can you be your own best friend? Why or why not?" A short discussion on this topic will serve as an excellent warm-up to the theme of Cameron's story.

CONNECTING WITH STUDENTS   Ask students to tell about a time they were angry or hurt because of something a friend did. If students are uncomfortable discussing this out loud, have them write what happened in the margin of their books. Encourage students to forge a personal connection to the selection before they begin reading.

Words to Know

SYNONYMS   Use the **Words to Know** blackline master on page 82 as a way to troubleshoot vocabulary problems. After working through the page, you might decide to teach a short vocabulary lesson on **synonyms.**

To begin, show students the key vocabulary words in *Gloria's Way*: *prisoner, remember, sighed, jiggled,* and *patient.* Ask students to volunteer one or more synonyms for each word. Then explain that learning the synonym for an unfamiliar word can be a shortcut to learning the word's dictionary definition. Help students add new words (and definitions) to their vocabularies each time they read.

Prereading Strategies

THINK-PAIR-AND-SHARE   Students are asked to complete a **think-pair-and-share** activity as a warm-up to Cameron's story. In a think-pair-and-share, students work together to solve sentence "puzzles" related to the selection. In this case, they'll read a series of five statements about friendship and then say whether they agree or disagree with the statements. Of course, it's not important that students know the right answer at this point. The purpose of this activity is to help them do some initial thinking about the topic and theme of the reading.

GRAPHIC ORGANIZER   As an additional prereading activity, have students make a **graphic organizer** that explores their relationship with a friend. Ask students to record on the cluster what they like to do with their friend, how they feel about this friend, and some of the friend's special qualities. This activity will also serve as an excellent warm-up to the prewriting web students will complete in **Part III.**

To extend the activity, use the **Before You Read** blackline master on page 83.

MY PURPOSE   Read aloud the purpose statement on page 22 and be sure students understand that you'd like them to think about Gloria's troubles as they are reading. Students may want to "borrow" some of these troubles when they write their journal entries for **Part IV.**

READ

Response Strategy

FIRST READING Before students begin their first readings, explain the response strategy of **connect.** Refer to the explanation on page 9 of the student book, or explain in your own words that connecting to a story or an article means putting yourself in the place of a character or imagining yourself in a situation described. Most students will welcome the opportunity to compare what they're reading to their own lives.

Comprehension Strategy

SECOND READING During their reading of the story, students will need to stop and record their thoughts in a **double-entry journal.** As you know, using a Double-entry journal encourages active response to a text. Explain to students that their responses should be personal reactions to a sentence or an idea in the story. Their goal is to *react,* not summarize. To help them get started, work together on the first journal entry. Read the quote aloud and ask volunteers to respond.

For more help with **Comprehension,** assign the blackline master on page 84.

Discussion Questions

COMPREHENSION 1. Why is Gloria in bed? *(She is sick.)*

2. What advice does Gloria's mom give her? *(She tells her not to badger Julian about their friendship. She also tells her to be her own best friend.)*

CRITICAL THINKING 3. What kind of a person is Gloria? *(Ask students to support their inferences about her character with evidence from the selection.)*

4. Do you agree with the mother's advice—that you should be your own best friend? Explain why or why not. *(Invite students to make a personal connection to the text and the mother's advice. Have them explain what she means and apply it to their own experiences.)*

5. How does Gloria feel about herself? *(Answers will vary. Have students reread the final two paragraphs before answering this question.)*

Reread

THIRD READING The directions on page 28 ask students to reread the story and think carefully about their own ideas of friendship. As an option, return to the brainstorming list you made with students before reading the selection. How have students' ideas about friendship changed as a result of reading the story?

Word Work

SILENT E The Word Work lesson on page 29 offers students some additional practice on words with **silent *e*** endings. Review the rule for adding an ending to this type of word and then assign the exercise. Many of the words in the exercise come from *Gloria's Way.*

For additional practice, see the **Word Work** blackline master on page 85.

III. GET READY TO WRITE

Prewriting Strategies

WEB For a prewriting activity, students will create a **web** that explores their thoughts and ideas about friendship. Explain to the class that you'd like them to think of one or more answers to each of the questions on the web. Encourage them to support what they say with examples from their own lives. They can use these examples in their journal entries.

Have students use the **Get Ready to Write** blackline master on page 86.

IV. WRITE

Students should understand that their assignment is to write a **journal entry** about friendship and what it means. Have them provide examples from their own lives to support what they say. Remind them to refer as needed to the web they created on page 30.

After students have written a first draft, have them stop and think carefully about what they've written. They should ask themselves: "Have I offered details from my own life to support what I say about friendship? Do I stay focused on the topic of friendship throughout?"

WRITING RUBRIC Use this rubric to help with a quick assessment of students' writing.

Do students' journal entries

• begin with a topic sentence that explains their view of friendship?

• offer at least three personal details in support of the topic sentence?

• end with a closing sentence that tells how a good friend makes them feel?

Grammar, Usage, and Mechanics

When students are ready to proofread their work, refer them to the **Writers' Checklist** at the top of page 32. Ask them to read each word of their journal entry, checking carefully for **spelling** errors. To help, assign proofreading partners and have them lightly circle in pencil any spelling errors. The writer should then correct the word by checking a dictionary or a class word list. Here are some commonly misspelled words:

friend	received	together	trouble	bought	always	everybody	knew/know

V. LOOK BACK

Reflect with students on the **ease** or difficulty with which they read Cameron's story. Point out the **Readers' Checklist** and have the class discuss their answers to the questions. Suggest reading strategies they might use in the future to help with a selection such as *Gloria's Way*.

To test students' comprehension, use the **Lesson Test** blackline master on page 87.

Name _____

WORDS TO KNOW

Before Reading

DIRECTIONS Read this paragraph. Then match the underlined words with their definitions.

> Gloria was sick. She felt like a <u>prisoner</u> in her own house. "<u>Remember</u> how much fun I used to have?" she asked. She <u>jiggled</u> the soup bowl until her mother told her to stop.
>
> Her mom <u>sighed</u>. "Be <u>patient</u>, Gloria."

1. prisoner
2. remember
3. sighed
4. jiggled
5. patient

a. call back to mind; recall
b. calm
c. someone who is not free
d. shook
e. breathed out deeply

Practice

Write a sentence about a time you were *patient*. Your sentence should show what *patient* means.

_____

_____

_____

_____

Name _____

BEFORE YOU READ

Graphic Organizer

DIRECTIONS Think of someone who is a good friend to you.

Write about your friend on this organizer.

Use plenty of details.

What my friend looks like	**What my friend acts like**

My friend

What I like best about my friend	**How my friend feels about me**

Name _____

COMPREHENSION

Reciprocal Reading

DIRECTIONS Get together with a reading partner.
Answer these questions together.
Check your book if you need to.

1. What is Gloria upset about?

_____

_____

2. What advice about friendship would you like to give to Gloria?

_____

_____

3. What does friendship mean to Gloria?

_____

_____

4. What does friendship mean to you?

_____

_____

Name _____

WORD WORK

After Reading

DIRECTIONS Add *-ed* and *-ing* to the words below. Write the new words on the lines. One has been done for you.

1. fine + -ed = fined _____

2. live + -ing = _____

3. smile + -ed = _____

4. bake + -er = _____

5. vote + -er = _____

Practice

DIRECTIONS Take the *-ed* or *-ing* ending off these words. Write the new word on the line. One has been done for you.

6. shaming   shame _____

7. scraped _____

8. timing _____

9. writing _____

10. moping _____

Name

GET READY TO WRITE

Writing a Journal Entry

STEP 1 Write three words that describe friendship.

Friendship is . . .

_____

_____

_____

STEP 2 Write a topic sentence that uses the three words.

Friendship is_____,

_____, and _____.

STEP 3 Find examples from the story that support your topic sentence. Find one example for each word.

example #1 _____

_____

example #2 _____

_____

example #3 _____

_____

Name _____

LESSON TEST

Multiple-Choice

DIRECTIONS On the lines, write the letter of the best answer for each question.

_____ 1. Gloria and her mother are discussing . . .
  A. schoolwork.   C. plans for dinner.
  B. friendship.   D. plans to buy a pet.

_____ 2. Gloria wants to ask Julian if he . . .
  A. could get her work.   C. will walk her dog.
  B. likes her best.   D. will call her.

_____ 3. What is the setting of this story?
  A. Gloria's bedroom   C. Gloria's classroom
  B. Julian's kitchen   D. a doctor's office

_____ 4. How does Gloria feel throughout the story?
  A. sad   C. happy
  B. mad   D. scared

_____ 5. Gloria follows her mother's advice because . . .
  A. she is sick.   C. she trusts her mother.
  B. she has no friends. D. None of these answers

Short Answer

What lesson does Gloria learn from her mother about friendship?

_____

_____

_____

Train to Somewhere

BACKGROUND

Eve Bunting's award-winning picture book *Train to Somewhere* tells the heartbreaking and historically accurate story of a nineteenth-century Orphan Train that traveled West in order to find homes for children nobody wanted.

Bunting's story is narrated by a fictional character, fourteen-year-old Marianne. Marianne sits back and watches while child after child is chosen for adoption instead of her. Some of the orphans are chosen because of their looks; others are chosen because they look useful. Because Marianne is neither strong nor pretty, she is passed over at every train stop. In the end, she is taken in by a kind-hearted elderly couple who lives in a town called Somewhere.

Eve Bunting grew up in Northern Ireland. When she was young, Bunting's family taught her to respect the art of storytelling and admire a well-drawn character and an interesting plot. She is the author of over 130 books for children, including the critically acclaimed *Fly Away Home*.

BIBLIOGRAPHY Students might enjoy reading another book by Eve Bunting. Check the Lexile website (www.Lexile.com) for titles that have a Lexile level close to that of *Train to Somewhere* (Lexile 440), or choose from among the following:

A TURKEY FOR THANKSGIVING	DUCKY	FLY AWAY HOME
(Lexile 410)	(Lexile 440)	(Lexile 450)

How to Introduce the Reading

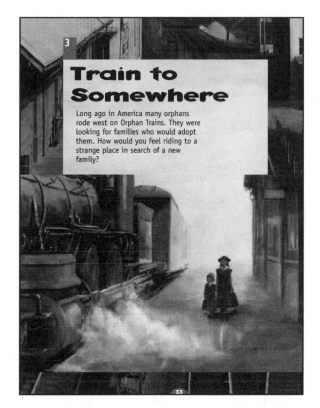

Explain to students that *Train to Somewhere* is a work of historical fiction, but Orphan Trains really did exist. In the 1850s, thousands of children roamed the streets of New York in search of money, food, and shelter. In 1853, a young minister named Charles Loring Brace became concerned about the plight of these children.

That same year, Brace founded the Children's Aid Society, which arranged trips West for orphans who lived in New York. Between 1854 and 1929, more than 100,000 children were sent, via Orphan Trains, to new homes in rural America. The Orphan Train program, controversial as it was, would turn out to be a forerunner of modern foster care.

For additional reading on this topic, see *Aggie's Home* by Joan Lowery Nixon, *Orphan Train Rider, or One Boy's True Stor*y by Andrea Warren.

Other Reading

Read aloud other high-interest books that are written at the same reading level as *Train to Somewhere.* These three all receive high ratings from children:

(Lexile 430)   (Lexile 430)   (Lexile 440)

Train to Somewhere

Skills and Strategies Overview

PREREADING anticipation guide

READING LEVEL Lexile 440

RESPONSE make clear

VOCABULARY ◇ conductor ◇ platform ◇ coach ◇ bundles ◇ aboard

COMPREHENSION stop and think

WORD WORK homophones

PREWRITING topic sentence and details

WRITING expository paragraph / homophones

ASSESSMENT meaning

OTHER RESOURCES

The first **four** pages of this teacher's lesson describe Parts I–V of the lesson. Also included are these **six** blackline masters. Use them to reinforce key elements of the lesson.

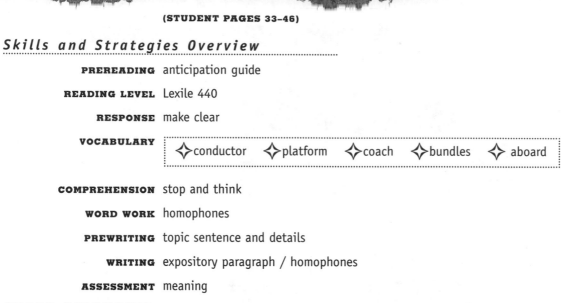

Vocabulary

Prereading

Comprehension

Word Work

Prewriting

Assessment

1. BEFORE YOU READ

Read through the introduction (page 33) with students. Offer background information about Orphan Trains as needed. Then assign the prereading activity, an **anticipation guide**. (Refer to the Strategy Handbook, page 48, for more help.)

Motivation Strategies

MOTIVATING STUDENTS Borrow a copy of *Train to Somewhere* from the library and do a whole-class picture walk of the book. Himler's moving watercolor illustrations are sure to capture your class's interest. After students finish reading the excerpt reprinted in the *Sourcebook*, they may enjoy hearing more of Marianne's story.

CONNECTING WITH STUDENTS Ask students to answer the question on the opening page of the lesson: "How would you feel riding to a strange place in search of a new family?" Have volunteers fully explain their responses. Help students make a before-reading connection to the main character of Bunting's story.

Words to Know

CONTEXT CLUES Use the **Words to Know** blackline master on page 94 as a way to troubleshoot vocabulary problems. After working through the page, you might decide to teach a short vocabulary lesson on using **context clues.**

To begin, show students the key vocabulary words in *Train to Somewhere*: *conductor, platform, coach, bundles,* and *aboard.* Explain that these (and other) words are defined at the bottom of the page, but that you'd like students to make predictions about the meaning of unfamiliar words before they check the footnoted definitions. Model this by saying: "I don't know the meaning of the word *bundles.* I see, though, that it appears in the same sentence as the word *trunks* and that bundles are something the children need to load on the train. I know that bundles are not suitcases. Could they be 'packages'? I'll check the footnote to see if my prediction is correct."

Prereading Strategies

ANTICIPATION GUIDE **Anticipation guides** are easy to create and interesting for students. They work especially well with lower-level readers because they give students a head start on topic and theme work. Have the class work independently on the guide, marking a √ for answers they agree with and an X for answers they disagree with. Then pair students and ask them to compare answers. Have students explain their answers to each other. Ask them to call on personal experiences as support for their answers.

THINK-PAIR-AND-SHARE As an additional prereading activity, have students work together on a **think-pair-and-share** that explores their knowledge of Orphan Trains. Have them begin by marking "agree" or "disagree" in response to four statements about Orphan Trains. Then ask them to share answers with a partner. They'll finish by making a prediction about Bunting's story.

Use the **Before You Read** blackline master on page 95 with the think-pair-and-share activity.

MY PURPOSE Most of your students will be motivated to read Bunting's story, since the topic of orphans and orphanages is usually of interest to this age group. Point out the reading purpose on page 34 and ask students to watch carefully for important details.

Response Strategy

FIRST READING When students are ready to do their first readings, explain the response strategy of **make things clear.** Tell the class that good readers think carefully about the words they are reading and *what they mean.* The response strategy of making clear shows students how important it is to keep track of clarification comments that they make unconsciously as they're reading. Later, when they begin the prewriting activity, have students return to their Response Notes and use what they've written.

Comprehension Strategy

SECOND READING At two separate points during their reading of Bunting's story, students will need to pause and answer **stop and think** questions that are meant to help them reflect on the facts of the reading. The stop and think questions in the *Sourcebook* serve several purposes. First, they help slow the speed with which students read. A slower reader is quite often a more careful reader. Second, they allow students to self-assess their own comprehension of the selection. If the student can't answer the question, he or she knows to reread in the area of the question. This is a boon for low-level readers who have a hard time skimming an entire text in search of one detail.

For more help with **Comprehension,** assign the blackline master on page 96.

Discussion Questions

COMPREHENSION 1. What were the Orphan Trains? *(They were trains that carried children with no parents to new homes in the West, most often Illinois and Iowa.)*

CRITICAL THINKING 2. What is the setting for this story? *(a train station in the year 1878)*

3. What's sad about this story? *(Have students explain their emotional reactions to the plight of these orphans.)*

4. What inferences (reasonable guesses) can you make about Marianne? *(Possible: She is bright, obedient, and helpful. She has a plain appearance and not a lot of self-confidence.)*

5. What do you think it was like to ride on an Orphan Train? *(Ask students to imagine themselves in the place of one of the characters and say how they'd feel.)*

Reread

THIRD READING Your students will benefit from an additional reading of Bunting's story. Try doing a round-robin reading, switching readers at the bottom of each page. Have students follow along in their books and listen for details about the Orphan Trains.

Word Work

HOMOPHONES **Homophones** are words that sound the same but are spelled differently. Offer practice with these homophones: *ate/eight; blue/blew; pair/pare/pear; our/hour;* and *road/rode/rowed.*

For additional practice, see the **Word Work** blackline master on page 97.

III. GET READY TO WRITE

Prewriting Strategies

TOPIC SENTENCE AND DETAILS As an initial prewriting activity, students will write a topic sentence that explains what it was like to ride on an Orphan Train. Point out the formula in the middle of page 43 and explain that this is the formula students should use each time they write a **topic sentence**.

On the next page, students will need to find **details** that support their topic sentence. Many of these details can come from the notes students made as they were reading the selection. Remind the class that good writers support their topic sentences with at least three details.

Have students use the **Get Ready to Write** blackline master on page 98.

IV. WRITE

Read aloud the directions on page 45 to be sure students understand that their assignment is to write an **expository paragraph** about Orphan Trains. Help students get into the habit of using standard paragraph structure: topic sentence, followed by two to three supporting details, followed by a closing sentence that restates the topic sentence.

After students have written a first draft, have them exchange papers with an editing partner. Ask: "Has the writer offered at least three details from the story in support of the topic sentence?"

WRITING RUBRIC Use this rubric to help with a quick assessment of students' writing.

Do the students' paragraphs

• open with a topic sentence that states the topic and a feeling about it?

• contain three or more accurate details about Orphan Trains?

• end with an appropriate closing sentence?

Grammar, Usage, and Mechanics

When students are ready to edit their work, refer them to the **Writers' Checklist.** Read aloud the question about the **homophones** *to/two/too* and ask students to check to be sure they've used these words correctly in their writing. Encourage students to ask their reading partners for help as needed.

V. LOOK BACK

Reflect with students on the **meaning** of *Train to Somewhere*. Point out the **Readers' Checklist** on page 46. Help students discuss what the story meant to them personally.

To test students' comprehension, use the **Lesson Test** blackline master on page 99.

Name _____

WORDS TO KNOW

Before Reading

DIRECTIONS Look at the picture.

Use words from the box to complete each sentence.

◇conductor ◇platform ◇coach ◇bundles ◇aboard

1. The _____ is in charge of the train.

2. There are _____ and packages ready to be brought onto the train.

3. Once everyone is _____, the train will pull out.

4. People may enter both doors of the _____.

5. The train is waiting by the _____.

Practice

Write a sentence about a train ride you or someone you know took. Use one vocabulary word in the sentence.

_____

_____

_____

_____

Name _____

BEFORE YOU READ

Think-Pair-and-Share

DIRECTIONS Read the statements below about Orphan Trains.

If you agree, check the AGREE box. If you disagree, check the DISAGREE box.

Share your ideas with a reading partner.

agree	disagree	Think-Pair-and-Share
⬭	⬭	Orphan Trains really existed.
⬭	⬭	Children loved riding on Orphan Trains.
⬭	⬭	Orphan Trains are still used today.
⬭	⬭	Orphan Trains were only for bad kids.

What do you think *Train to Somewhere* will be about?

_____

_____

_____

Name _____

COMPREHENSION

Double-entry Journal

DIRECTIONS Read the quotations from the story in the left column.
Write how the quotes make you feel in the right column.

Double-entry Journal

Quote from the story	How it makes me feel
"I hear there are still a lot of people in the New West wanting children to adopt."	
"Most of the people will only want one child. Don't spoil it for each other."	
"I know Nora will be one of the first ones taken."	
"I'm coming, Mama. Wait for me."	

Name _____

WORD WORK

After Reading

DIRECTIONS Read the homophones in the box.

Write the correct homophone in the blank in each sentence below.

| two, too, to | see, sea | one, won |

1. We are going to _____ the ocean.

2. My cousin is coming _____ .

3. We _____ our tickets in a contest.

4. I love watching the dolphins play in the _____ .

5. Last year I saw _____ of them swimming near shore and splashing each other.

Practice

DIRECTIONS Match the homophone in Column A with its correct definition in Column B.

Column A	Column B
they're	a word that shows ownership
there	a contraction for *they are*
their	a word that points out direction

Name _____

GET READY TO WRITE

Writing Sensory Words

Sensory words are words that appeal to the five senses: **sight, sound, taste, touch,** and **smell.** Writers use sensory words to help you see, hear, taste, touch, and smell what they describe.

For example, Eve Bunting uses the sensory words *clickety-clack, clickety-clee* to help you "hear" the Orphan Train.

DIRECTIONS Write sensory words that describe the Orphan Train. Write 3 words for each sense.

Use some of Bunting's words if you like.

Sensory Words That Describe the Orphan Train

sight words	sound words	taste words	touch words	smell words
1.	1.	1. thick milk out of a can	1.	1.
2.	2.	2.	2.	2.
3.	3.	3.	3.	3.

Name _____

LESSON TEST

Multiple-Choice

DIRECTIONS On the lines, write the letter of the best answer for each question.

_____ 1. Marianne and Nora are . . .
   A. sisters.   C. cousins.
   B. orphans.   D. nurses.

_____ 2. Miss Randolph's job is to . . .
   A. drive the train.   C. watch over the children.
   B. find a husband.   D. None of these answers

_____ 3. This story takes place . . .
   A. in the South.   C. at an orphanage.
   B. on a train.   D. in Chicago.

_____ 4. The girls change out of their new clothes so they . . .
   A. can go to sleep.   C. can buy other clothes.
   B. can play.   D. don't get them messy.

_____ 5. An important idea in *Train to Somewhere* is:
   A. Apples grow on trees.   C. All children need a home.
   B. Fleas are everywhere.   D. Orphans cause trouble.

Short Answer

How does Marianne feel as she rides the Orphan Train? Give support for your answer.

_____

_____

_____

First Flight

BACKGROUND

George Shea's *First Flight* is a fictionalized account of a real-life boy named Tom Tate. In the early 1900s, Tate, who lived in Kitty Hawk, North Carolina, befriended Orville and Wilbur Wright and watched as they fulfilled their dream to "fly through the air like birds."

In Shea's story, Tom observes Will and Orv's first flight, joins as a crew member on the second, and then stays to watch Orv's first machine-powered flight in 1903. Throughout the book, Shea carefully maintains his story line while at the same time provides his readers with a fascinating glimpse of the trial-and-error methodology involved in invention.

George Shea, who lives in Los Angeles, is the author of another popular book for children, *Amazing Rescues*. Known for his methodical research, Shea spent many hours interviewing Tom Tate's son for his book *First Flight*.

BIBLIOGRAPHY Students might enjoy reading another book by Tom Shea or a different work of historical fiction. Invite them to choose from among the following:

AMAZING RESCUES by George Shea

SMALL WOLF by Nathaniel Benchely

FINDING PROVIDENCE: THE STORY OF ROGER WILLIAMS by Avi

(Lexile 400)   (Lexile 430)   (Lexile 450)

How to Introduce the Reading

Read the introduction to the lesson on page 47. Ask students what they know about Wilbur and Orville Wright. As background, explain that the Wrights were American brothers, inventors, and aviation pioneers who achieved the first powered, sustained, and controlled airplane flight (1903) and built and flew the first airplane (1905). For reference, encourage students to consult these two nonfiction books, both of which are meant for readers at this age level: *Will and Orv* by Walter A. Schultz and *The Wright Brothers* by Margaret Hudson.

As an alternate introductory activity, ask students to tell about their experiences on airplanes. Have any of them taken a trip on a small plane or in a helicopter? Have any of them dreamed of becoming a pilot? Then ask the class to discuss the questions in the introductory paragraph. What would they do and where would they go if they could fly?

Use your discussion to create a sense of expectation about the reading.

Other Reading

Read aloud other works of historical fiction. These three books are written at the same reading level as *First Flight* (Lexile 460):

(Lexile 460)

(Lexile 460)

(Lexile 450)

First Flight

Skills and Strategies Overview

PREREADING	word web
READING LEVEL	Lexile 460
RESPONSE	draw
VOCABULARY	✧beach ✧tent ✧machine ✧windiest ✧imagining
COMPREHENSION	double-entry journal
WORD WORK	contractions
PREWRITING	5 Ws
WRITING	news story / contractions
ASSESSMENT	understanding

OTHER RESOURCES

The first **four** pages of this teacher's lesson describe Parts I–V of the lesson. Also included are these **six** blackline masters. Use them to reinforce key elements of the lesson.

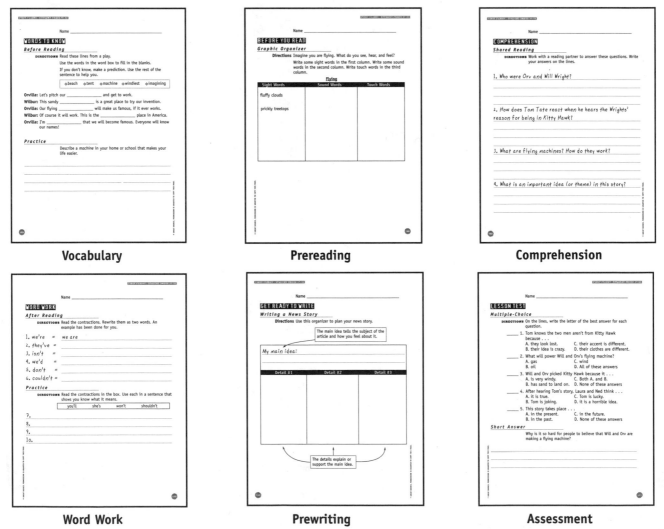

Vocabulary

Prereading

Comprehension

Word Work

Prewriting

Assessment

1. BEFORE YOU READ

Explain to students that *First Flight* is an excerpt from a historical fiction novel by George Shea. Remind the class that historical fiction combines fictional characters and real historical events. When you feel students are ready to begin, assign the prereading activity, a **word web**. (Refer to the Strategy Handbook, page 51, for more help.)

Motivation Strategies

MOTIVATING STUDENTS   Show a film or video about Orville and Wilbur Wright's life and work. (Check your library's video section or your local video store.) Use the movie as a factual warm-up to the topic of this selection.

CONNECTING WITH STUDENTS   Ask students to think about a person in history that they'd like to meet. Have them name the person, say why they'd like to meet him or her, and then explain what they'd ask and what they'd say. This discussion will help prepare students for the juxtaposition of fictional characters (e.g., Tom Tate) and real people (Orville and Wilbur Wright) in Shea's story.

Words to Know

CONTEXT CLUES   Use the **Words to Know** blackline master on page 106 as a way to troubleshoot vocabulary problems. After working through the page, you might decide to teach a short vocabulary lesson on using **context clues**.

Draw students' attention to the lesson's key vocabulary words: *beach, tent, machine, windiest,* and *imagining*. The footnotes define only one of these words for students, so you'll want to encourage them to define in context. Help students build their vocabularies by modeling using these words in several different sentences.

Prereading Strategies

WORD WEB   As a prereading activity, students are asked to make a **word web** for the words *flying machine*. A web like the one on page 48 will help activate students' prior knowledge about the topic while at the same time allow them to make some initial connections between the literature and their own lives. Students can share their webs with a reading partner or the whole class. Leave some of the most interesting webs on the board for the duration of the lesson. Students should refer to them as they read, and while they are preparing for the writing assignment in **Part IV**.

BRAINSTORM   As a further prereading activity, ask students to **brainstorm** a list of sensory words that they associate with the word *flying*. This quick activity will give students the chance to experiment with language. Remind the class that sensory language can add vibrancy to a description. Sensory words give readers the "you are there" feeling that is such an important part of good writing. Create a chart that asks for "sight," "sound," and "touch" words that describe flying.

Or, if you prefer, use the graphic organizer printed on the **Before You Read** blackline master on page 107.

MY PURPOSE   Read the purpose statement on page 48 aloud and be sure students understand that you'd like them to look for factual details about flying and flying machines as they are reading this fictional account. Explain that they'll use these details later to help them complete a writing assignment.

II. READ

Response Strategy

FIRST READING Before students begin their first readings, explain the response strategy, **draw.** Refer to the explanation on page 6 of the student book, or explain in your own words that drawing is like making pictures in your mind as you read. Most students will welcome the opportunity to doodle as they read.

Comprehension Strategy

SECOND READING As they are reading Shea's story, students should think carefully about the connections they can make to the people and action described. To help, have students stop and reflect on what they're reading using the **double-entry journals** that are scattered throughout the text. Point out the first journal entry on page 50. Explain that students need to read the quote in the left-hand column and then respond to it in the right-hand column. Emphasize that their responses should be in the form of their thoughts and feelings.

For more help with **Comprehension,** assign the blackline master on page 108.

Discussion Questions

COMPREHENSION 1. What reason do Orv and Will give for being in Kitty Hawk? *(They explain they've come to build a flying machine.)*

2. What will they use to make their machine fly? *(the wind)*

CRITICAL THINKING 3. Why do you think the children don't believe what Tom Tate tells them about Will and Orv? *(Possible: They can't fathom a machine that flies through the air. No one has ever seen such a thing.)*

4. Do you think it's common for people to disbelieve inventors when they talk about their inventions for the first time? Explain. *(Ask students to discuss specific examples—e.g., How do they think people responded when they first heard about television, the automobile, or the radio?)*

Reread

THIRD READING The directions on page 52 ask students to reread the story and pay close attention to the drawings they made on their first readings. The purpose of this activity is to show students that doing an additional reading can enhance their understanding and enjoyment of a work. Encourage students to make additional sketches as they go. What do they see that they missed on their first readings?

Word Work

CONTRACTIONS The Word Work lesson on page 53 affords you an excellent opportunity to review **contractions.** Have students practice forming the more common contractions, and explain that contractions are used in informal writing (letters and stories). In formal writing (e.g., reports), contractions should be avoided.

For additional practice, see the **Word Work** blackline master on page 109.

III. GET READY TO WRITE

Prewriting Strategies

5 Ws If students are not familiar with the **5 Ws,** carefully explain the importance of understanding the who, what, where, when, why (and sometimes how) of a topic. Be sure they know that a 5 Ws organizer can help them locate the main idea and supporting details in a piece of writing. Have students get into the habit of completing a quick 5 Ws organizer each time they read, especially when reading historical fiction or nonfiction. If your students are unfamiliar with this strategy, try completing the organizer on page 54. Duplicate the chart on the board or on an overhead. Ask volunteers to suggest details for each section. Then have students work individually on their closing sentences.

Have students use the **Get Ready to Write** blackline master on page 110.

IV. WRITE

Read aloud the directions on page 55. Students' assignment is to write a **news story** about two men trying out a flying machine in Kitty Hawk. Explain that all good news stories tell who, what, where, when, and why. Remind the class to refer to their organizers as they write.

After students have written a first draft, have them exchange papers with an editing partner. Editors should read the news story and ask: "Does the news story give three or more interesting details about the first flight?" If the answer is no, the editor can suggest additional details.

WRITING RUBRIC Use this rubric to help with a quick assessment of students' writing.

Do students' news stories

- open with a topic sentence that names the topic and what's important or interesting about it?

- contain three or more details about the flying machine and/or who will fly it?

- end with a closing sentence that ties things together?

Grammar, Usage, and Mechanics

When students are ready to proofread their work, refer them to the **Writers' Checklist.** Read aloud the question on the checklist and review the rules for forming **contractions.** For practice, ask students to form contractions for *they are, we are, he will, does not,* and *cannot.*

V. LOOK BACK

Use the **Readers' Checklist** to reflect with students on their **understanding** of *First Flight.* Were there parts of the story that were confusing? If so, what could students have done to make things clear? (They could have reread, asked a question, or visualized what is described.)

To test students' comprehension, use the **Lesson Test** blackline master on page 111.

Name _____

WORDS TO KNOW

Before Reading

DIRECTIONS Read these lines from a play.

Use the words in the word box to fill in the blanks.

If you don't know, make a prediction. Use the rest of the sentence to help you.

> ✧beach   ✧tent   ✧machine   ✧windiest   ✧imagining

Orville: Let's pitch our _____ and get to work.

Wilbur: This sandy _____ is a great place to try our invention.

Orville: Our flying _____ will make us famous, if it ever works.

Wilbur: Of course it will work. This is the _____ place in America.

Orville: I'm _____ that we will become famous. Everyone will know our names!

Practice

Describe a *machine* in your home or school that makes your life easier.

_____

_____

_____

_____

Name _____

BEFORE YOU READ

Graphic Organizer

DIRECTIONS Imagine you are flying. What do you see, hear, and feel?

Write some sight words in the first column. Write some sound words in the second column. Write touch words in the third column.

Flying

Sight Words	Sound Words	Touch Words
fluffy clouds prickly treetops		

Name _____

COMPREHENSION

Shared Reading

DIRECTIONS Work with a reading partner to answer these questions. Write your answers on the lines.

1. Who were Orv and Will Wright?

_____

_____

2. How does Tom Tate react when he hears the Wrights' reason for being in Kitty Hawk?

_____

_____

3. What are flying machines? How do they work?

_____

_____

4. What is an important idea (or theme) in this story?

_____

_____

Name _____

WORD WORK

After Reading

DIRECTIONS Read the contractions. Rewrite them as two words. An example has been done for you.

1. we're   =   we are
2. they've =   _____
3. isn't   =   _____
4. we'd   =   _____
5. don't   =   _____
6. couldn't =   _____

Practice

DIRECTIONS Read the contractions in the box. Use each in a sentence that shows you know what it means.

you'll	she's	won't	shouldn't

7. _____

8. _____

9. _____

10. _____

Name _____

GET READY TO WRITE

Writing a News Story

DIRECTIONS Use this organizer to plan your news story.

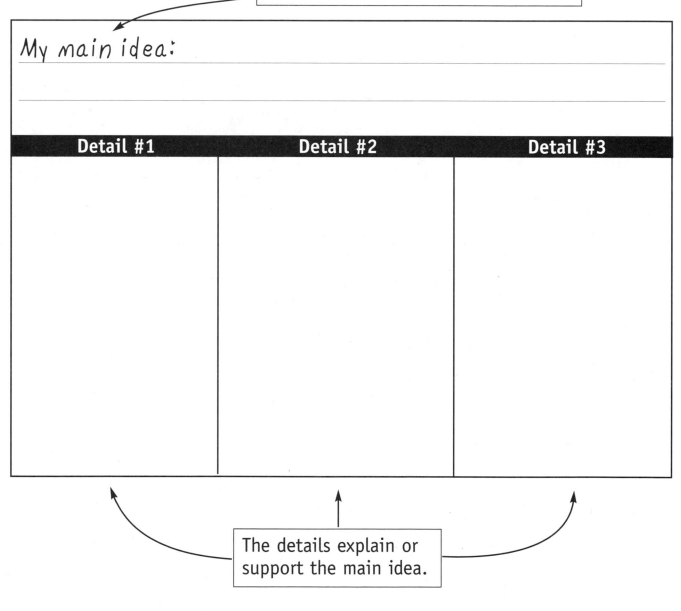

The main idea tells the subject of the article and how you feel about it.

My main idea:

| Detail #1 | Detail #2 | Detail #3 |

The details explain or support the main idea.

Name _____

LESSON TEST

Multiple-Choice

DIRECTIONS On the lines, write the letter of the best answer for each question.

_____ 1. Tom knows the two men aren't from Kitty Hawk because . . .
A. they look lost.   C. their accent is different.
B. their idea is crazy.   D. their clothes are different.

_____ 2. What will power Will and Orv's flying machine?
A. gas   C. wind
B. oil   D. All of these answers

_____ 3. Will and Orv picked Kitty Hawk because it . . .
A. is very windy.   C. Both A. and B.
B. has sand to land on.   D. None of these answers

_____ 4. After hearing Tom's story, Laura and Ned think . . .
A. it is true.   C. Tom is lucky.
B. Tom is joking.   D. it is a horrible idea.

_____ 5. This story takes place . . .
A. in the present.   C. in the future.
B. in the past.   D. None of these answers

Short Answer

Why is it so hard for people to believe that Will and Orv are making a flying machine?

_____

_____

_____

A Drop of Blood

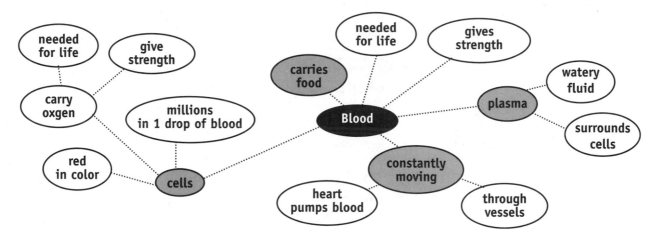

BACKGROUND

A Drop of Blood offers a simple introduction to the form, composition, and functions of blood. Thanks to Paul Showers' simple writing style, even difficult scientific concepts will be easy for your students to understand.

To reinforce the learning in *A Drop of Blood,* supplement the illustrations in the **Sourcebook** with a cluster diagram that explores the characteristics of human blood:

needed for life — give strength — carry oxgen — millions in 1 drop of blood — red in color — cells — needed for life — gives strength — carries food — Blood — plasma — watery fluid — surrounds cells — constantly moving — heart pumps blood — through vessels

BIBLIOGRAPHY Students might enjoy another nonfiction book by critically acclaimed author Paul Showers. These three books all have a Lexile level close to that of *A Drop of Blood* (Lexile 480):

(Lexile 480)   (Lexile 480)   (Lexile 520)

How to Introduce the Reading

Ask a volunteer to read aloud the introduction to *A Drop of Blood*. Have students tell what they know about blood: its composition, characteristics, and functions. Create a cluster diagram such as the one on page 112 of this book. Work with students to fill in any blank parts of the diagram after the class has finished the reading.

If possible, use the ***Sourcebook*** selection to make a link to your science or health curriculum. Explain that *A Drop of Blood* will help students learn more about the human body. As they read, they should keep in mind what they've learned in school about human anatomy.

Other Reading

Read aloud nonfiction titles that you feel might interest students and help create a link between your reading and science curriculums. Among the titles at the same reading level (Lexile 480) are these:

WHY I SNEEZE, SHIVER, HICCUP, AND YAWN by Melvin Berger

SLEEP AND REST by Alice B. McGinty

HUNGRY ANIMALS: MY FIRST LOOK AT A FOOD CHAIN by Pamela Hickman

(Lexile 480)   (Lexile 480)   (Lexile 480)

A Drop of Blood

Skills and Strategies Overview

PREREADING	preview
READING LEVEL	Lexile 480
RESPONSE	draw
VOCABULARY	✦cells ✦fluid ✦stomach ✦microscope ✦intestines
COMPREHENSION	stop and think
WORD WORK	suffixes and base words
PREWRITING	topic sentence and details
WRITING	descriptive paragraph / commas in a series
ASSESSMENT	ease

OTHER RESOURCES

The first **four** pages of this teacher's lesson describe Parts I–V of the lesson. Also included are these **six** blackline masters. Use them to reinforce key elements of the lesson.

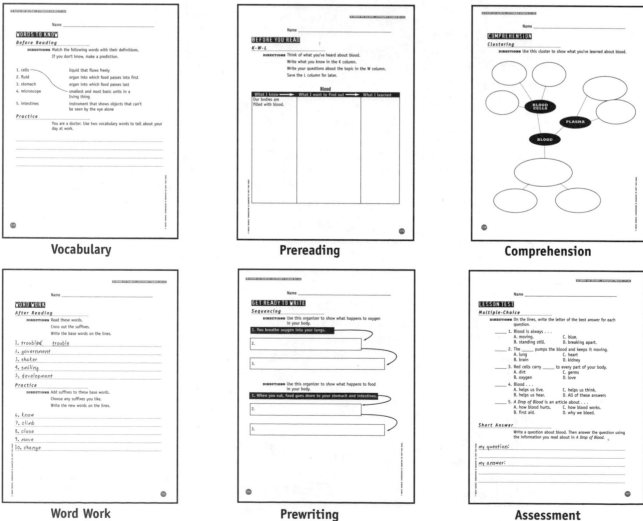

Vocabulary

Prereading

Comprehension

Word Work

Prewriting

Assessment

I. BEFORE YOU READ

Read aloud the directions at the top of page 58. Explain that students are about to read a nonfiction article about blood. Ask students to think of facts about blood they'd like to have confirmed by the reading. Write a list of the facts on the board. Help students see that one reason for reading is to find out information or answers to important questions. Then have the class complete the prereading activity, a **preview**. (Refer to the Strategy Handbook, page 49, for more help.)

Motivation Strategy

MOTIVATING STUDENTS Before class begins, check your library for an interesting film or video on blood cells or the heart. Show the film to the class as a warm-up to the reading. This activity will help students who are mainly visual learners, or students who sometimes have a difficult time gleaning information from a reading. If the film is particularly good, it may also serve to pique interest in the reading.

Words to Know

CONTEXT CLUES Use the **Words to Know** on page 118 as a way to troubleshoot vocabulary problems. After working through the page, you might decide to teach a short vocabulary lesson on using **context clues.**

As students read, point out such key vocabulary words as *cells, fluid, stomach, microscope,* and *intestines.* Ask volunteers to pronounce the words and offer definitions without checking the footnoted definitions. Then ask for sample sentences that use the words. Help students become accustomed to hearing the words in many different contexts.

Prereading Strategies

PREVIEW Before they do their careful readings, students should complete a **preview** of *A Drop of Blood.* A preview is a helpful prereading strategy because it gives readers a glimpse of what's to come. Thumbing through the pages they are about to read allows students to do some initial learning about the subject and can help them anticipate any comprehension problems they might have. To that end, you might have students note any glossed words that are unfamiliar. Also have them glance at the questions that interrupt the text. Their quick previews of these items will show them what's expected when it comes time to read. Students should finish their previews by writing three questions they have about blood.

K-W-L As an additional prereading activity, have students complete a **K-W-L** for the selection. Ask them to note what they know or have heard about blood (form, composition, and function) in the K column. Their questions belong in the W column. After they've finished reading, have students fill out the L column in anticipation of the writing assignment.

To extend the activity, use the **Before You Read** blackline master on page 119.

MY PURPOSE Read aloud the purpose statement on page 58. Explain that students will need to watch for information about two subjects: what's in a drop of blood and why we need blood. Write the students' purpose on the board and remind them to reread it once or twice along the way. The notes they make in the margins should help them meet their purpose.

II. READ

Response Strategy

FIRST READING As they read *A Drop of Blood,* students should try to imagine the information Showers describes. Each time they "see" something new, they should **draw** in the Response Notes. Visualizing while reading helps the reader stay actively involved in the text. It's a way of keeping him or her focused and on track.

Comprehension Strategy

SECOND READING As they read, students will need to strive to uncover as many facts as they can about blood. The **stop and think** questions that interrupt the text encourage them to reflect on the facts they've learned and then draw conclusions about what those facts mean. If you think this reading will be particularly challenging for students, have the class read through the piece once without stopping. On their second readings, they can pause and answer the questions.

For more help with **Comprehension,** assign the blackline master on page 120.

Discussion Questions

COMPREHENSION 1. Where in the body are red cells found? *(in the blood)*

2. What muscle pumps the blood? *(the heart)*

CRITICAL THINKING 3. What are two important functions of blood? *(Blood carries oxygen and food, both of which are necessary to sustain life.)*

4. What is the purpose of blood vessels? *(They allow the blood to pass through to all different parts of your body. They are like little tubes that link one part of the body to another.)*

5. What do you think happens if a blood vessel becomes blocked? *(Blood can no longer move freely through the vessel. This means that the part of the body on the receiving end of the vessel does not get the necessary nutrients.)*

Reread

THIRD READING The directions on page 61 ask students to reread *A Drop of Blood* for a second or third time. On this reading, they should pay particular attention to their original purpose: finding out what's in a drop of blood and why we need blood. When students have finished this reading, have them spend a few moments completing the L column on the **Before You Read** blackline master on page 119.

Word Work

SUFFIXES AND BASE WORDS Use the Word Work lesson on page 62 to review **suffixes** and **base words**. Help students get into the habit of checking for suffixes when they come across a word they don't know. In some cases, the suffix can offer a clue about the word's meaning, or at the very least show how the word should be used in a sentence. Begin with the common suffixes *-ed, -ing, -ment,* and *-er.* Add to the suffix list when students have mastered these four.

For additional practice, see the **Word Work** blackline master on page 121.

III. GET READY TO WRITE

Prewriting Strategies

TOPIC SENTENCE AND DETAILS Be sure to offer plenty of time for students to complete the prewriting pages. Students will begin by brainstorming what they know about blood. Then they'll write a **topic sentence** and three **details** for a paragraph that describes how red blood cells can help you. To assist students in writing their topic sentences, show this formula:

subject + what I want to say about the subject = a good topic sentence.

Red blood cells + carry oxygen and food to different parts of the body = Red blood cells are important because they carry oxygen and food to different parts of the body.

Have students use the **Get Ready to Write** blackline master on page 122.

IV. WRITE

Students' assignment is to write a **descriptive paragraph** that tells how red blood cells can help humans. They'll need to open with the topic sentence they wrote on page 64. In the body of the paragraph, they'll incorporate ideas from their organizer and brainstorming notes. Students' concluding sentences should be a restatement of their topic sentences.

After students have written a first draft, have them stop and think carefully about what they've written. They should ask themselves: "Have I offered at least three details in support of my topic sentence?" If the answer is no, have them go back to the reading and find another detail or two.

WRITING RUBRIC Use this rubric to help with a quick assessment of students' writing.

Do students' paragraphs

• show they understand the purpose of red blood cells?

• open with a topic sentence?

• contain at least three details in support of the topic sentence?

Grammar, Usage, and Mechanics

When students are ready to proofread, refer them to the **Writers' Checklist** and reiterate the rules for using **commas** in a series. Offer additional practice or support as needed.

V. LOOK BACK

Reflect with students on their responses to *A Drop of Blood*. Were they able to read the selection with **ease?** Point out the **Readers' Checklist** and have the class discuss their answers.

To test students' comprehension, use the **Lesson Test** blackline master on page 123.

Name _____

WORDS TO KNOW

Before Reading

DIRECTIONS Match the following words with their definitions. If you don't know, make a prediction.

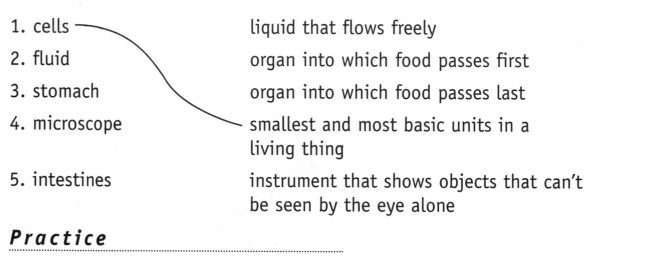

1. cells

2. fluid

3. stomach

4. microscope

5. intestines

liquid that flows freely

organ into which food passes first

organ into which food passes last

smallest and most basic units in a living thing

instrument that shows objects that can't be seen by the eye alone

Practice

You are a doctor. Use two vocabulary words to tell about your day at work.

_____

_____

_____

Name _____

BEFORE YOU READ

K-W-L

DIRECTIONS Think of what you've heard about blood.

Write what you know in the K column.

Write your questions about blood in the W column.

Save the L column for later.

Blood

What I know ⟶	What I want to find out ⟶	What I learned
Our bodies are filled with blood.		

Name _____

COMPREHENSION

Clustering

DIRECTIONS Use this cluster to show what you've learned about blood.

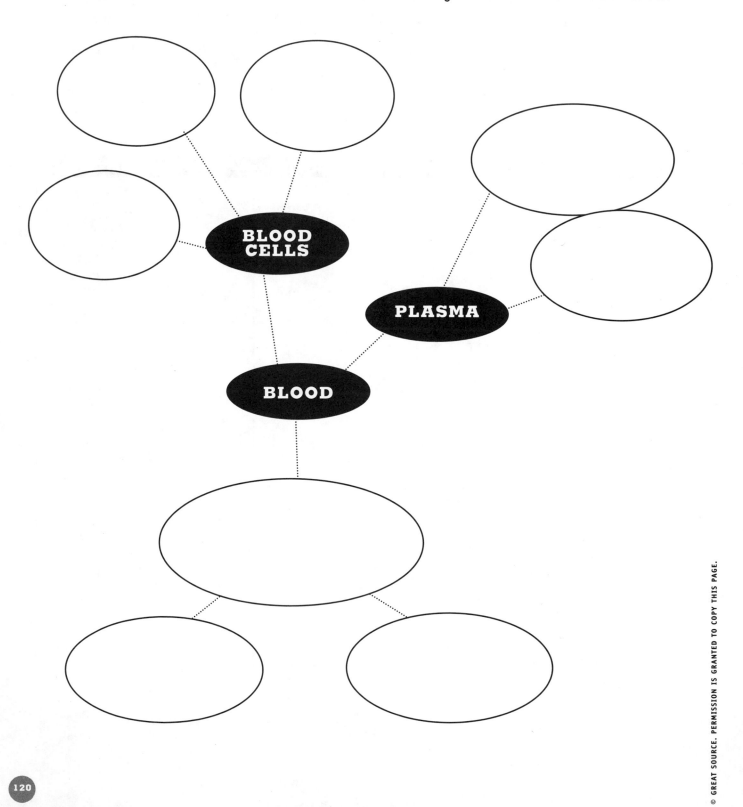

Name _____

WORD WORK

After Reading

DIRECTIONS Read these words.

Cross out the suffixes.

Write the base words on the lines.

1. trouble~~d~~   trouble
2. government   _____
3. shaker   _____
4. smiling   _____
5. development   _____

Practice

DIRECTIONS Add suffixes to these base words.

Choose any suffixes you like.

Write the new words on the lines.

6. know   _____
7. climb   _____
8. close   _____
9. move   _____
10. change   _____

Name _____

GET READY TO WRITE

Sequencing

DIRECTIONS Use this organizer to show what happens to oxygen in your body.

1. You breathe oxygen into your lungs.

2.

3.

DIRECTIONS Use this organizer to show what happens to food in your body.

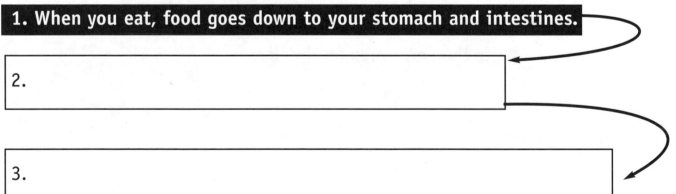

1. When you eat, food goes down to your stomach and intestines.

2.

3.

Name _____

LESSON TEST

Multiple-Choice

DIRECTIONS On the lines, write the letter of the best answer for each question.

_____ 1. Blood is always . . .
A. moving.   C. blue.
B. standing still.   D. breaking apart.

_____ 2. The _____ pumps the blood and keeps it moving.
A. lung   C. heart
B. brain   D. kidney

_____ 3. Red cells carry _____ to every part of your body.
A. dirt   C. germs
B. oxygen   D. love

_____ 4. Blood . . .
A. helps us live.   C. helps us think.
B. helps us hear.   D. All of these answers

_____ 5. *A Drop of Blood* is an article about . . .
A. how blood hurts.   C. how blood works.
B. first aid.   D. why we bleed.

Short Answer

Write a question about blood. Then answer the question using the information you read about in *A Drop of Blood*.

my question: _____

_____

my answer: _____

_____

_____

A River Dream

BACKGROUND

Allen Say's award-winning book *A River Dream* tells the story of a little boy named Mark who takes a fantasy trip up the river in order to fly-fish with his adoring uncle. Because Mark is sick in bed, he can't actually take the fishing trip. Instead, he lies in bed and allows his thoughts to roam free, proving once again that imagining a thing can be almost as good as actually doing it.

The talented Allen Say was born in Yokohama, Japan, in 1937. At the age of six, he began working toward fulfilling his dream of becoming a cartoonist. When he was twelve, he apprenticed himself to his favorite cartoonist, Noro Shinpei. Say calls the four years he studied under Shinpei the happiest in his life. (His book *The Ink-Keeper's Apprentice* describes the inspiring teacher-pupil relationship between himself and Shinpei.)

For the several decades after leaving Shinpei, Say drew and painted only on a part-time basis. In 1987, he was awarded a Caldecott Honor Medal for his book *The Boy of Three Year Nap*.

For more information about Allen Say and his works, visit the website
http://www.eduplace.com/rdg/author/say/

Offer students the opportunity to e-mail questions and comments to Say from this website.

BIBLIOGRAPHY Students might enjoy thumbing through another book by Allen Say to get a sense of his writing and artistic style. Encourage them to choose from among the following:

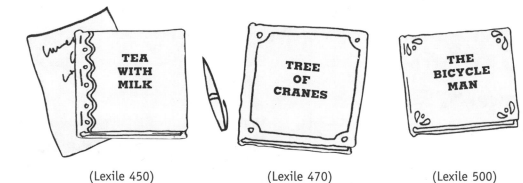

(Lexile 450)   (Lexile 470)   (Lexile 500)

How to Introduce the Reading

Read aloud the introduction to the lesson on page 67. Ask students to discuss a time they did something that they'd never thought they'd be able to do. How did they feel? How did others react? A short discussion on this topic will help students make a personal connection to an important theme in Say's story.

Other Reading

Read aloud other fiction and nonfiction books that relate to the subject or theme of *A River Dream*. These three books all have a Lexile level close to that of Say's book (Lexile 490):

(Lexile 490)   (Lexile 500)   (Lexile 510)

A River Dream

Skills and Strategies Overview

PREREADING	word web
READING LEVEL	Lexile 490
RESPONSE	connect
VOCABULARY	✧cast ✧gaping ✧leapt ✧mighty ✧magnificent
COMPREHENSION	stop and think
WORD WORK	homographs
PREWRITING	storyboard
WRITING	narrative paragraph / spelling
ASSESSMENT	enjoyment

OTHER RESOURCES

The first **four** pages of this teacher's lesson describe Parts I–V of the lesson. Also included are these **six** blackline masters. Use them to reinforce key elements of the lesson.

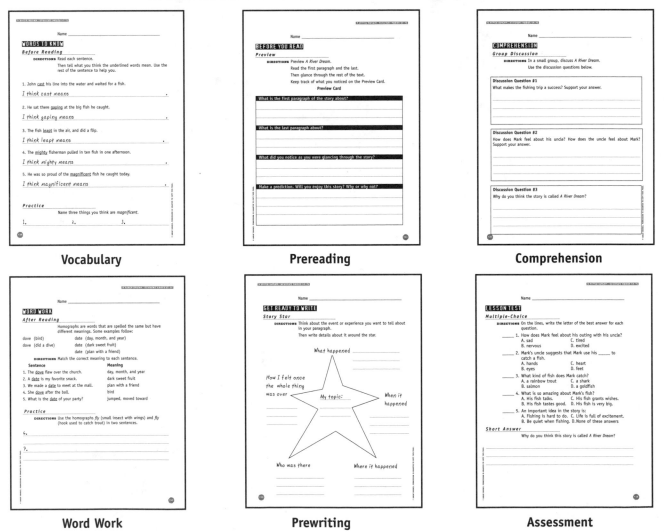

Vocabulary **Prereading** **Comprehension**

Word Work **Prewriting** **Assessment**

BEFORE YOU READ

Ask volunteers to tell about a time they went fishing. Have them explain the equipment that is needed, what's involved, locations of good fishing spots nearby, and so on. Allow students to generate their own excitement about the reading to come. When you feel they are ready to begin work on the unit, assign the prereading activity, a **word web**. (Refer to the Strategy Handbook, page 51, for more help.)

Motivation Strategy

MOTIVATING STUDENTS   Borrow a copy of *A River Dream* from the library and do a whole-class picture walk of the story. Ask students to respond to Say's vivid illustrations. How does the art make them feel? What does it remind them of? Is this a book they'd normally choose at the library? Why or why not?

Words to Know

CONTEXT CLUES   Use the **Words to Know** blackline master on page 130 as a way to troubleshoot vocabulary problems. After working through the page, you might decide to teach a short vocabulary lesson on using **context clues.**

To begin, show students the key vocabulary words in *A River Dream*: *cast, gaping, leapt, mighty,* and *magnificent*. Explain to students that these (and other) words are defined at the bottom of the page, but that you'd like them to try to make a prediction about the meaning of the words first, before checking the footnoted definitions. Tell the class: "Sometimes the author will leave clues in nearby sentences about the meaning of a difficult word. For example, I see the word *magnificent* on page 72. I don't know what this word means, so I'll look for context clues. In the sentences before the 'magnificent' sentence, I see that Mark has called the fish 'beautiful.' Could 'beautiful' be a synonym for 'magnificent'? I'll check the definition at the bottom of the page to see if I'm right."

Prereading Strategies

WORD WEB   For a prereading activity, students are asked to make a **web** for the word *fishing*. Encourage the class to think of sensory words (words that appeal to the five senses) that could help a reader *visualize* what fishing is like. Ask: "What does fishing look like and feel like? What does it smell like or sound like?" Help students get into the habit of choosing vivid verbs and adjectives. This will improve their writing.

PREVIEW   As an additional prereading activity, have students **preview** *A River Dream*. Ask them to read the first and last paragraphs and then glance through the rest of the text. Encourage them to pay attention to interrupter questions, vocabulary words, and any other text elements that catch their attention.

When they've finished, have them complete the preview card on the **Before You Read** blackline master on page 131.

MY PURPOSE   The reading purpose on page 68 asks students to think about the river dream that Allen Say describes. Have students watch for elements that give the narrative a dreamlike quality. Do they notice any words, phrases, or pictures that lead them to believe that Mark is dreaming instead of actually experiencing the fishing trip? When students have finished reading, return to the reading purpose and have the class discuss what they've found.

II. READ

Response Strategy

FIRST READING Before students begin their first readings, explain the response strategy of **connecting** to the literature. Tell students that as they read, they should think about how they would feel if they were in the main character's place. Considering their own thoughts, feelings, and reactions will help them better understand the thoughts, feelings, and reactions of the character in question.

Comprehension Strategy

SECOND READING As they're reading Say's story, students will need to pause twice and answer **stop and think** questions that require inferential response. Remind students that not everyone will interpret a text in the same way. Encourage the class to share their answers to the two interrupter questions. Have them support their ideas with facts and details from the text.

For more help with **Comprehension,** assign the blackline master on page 132.

Discussion Questions

COMPREHENSION 1. Is Mark's "fishing trip" a successful one? Explain. *(Yes, because he catches a magnificent trout.)*

2. How does Mark's uncle feel about the fish Mark catches? *(He shares Mark's excitement.)*

CRITICAL THINKING 3. Why is Mark "flushed with excitement" in this story? *(Possible: It is from the exhilaration of fly fishing.)*

4. What examples of figurative language can you find in Say's story? *(Point out the simile in the last sentence of the first page of the story. What other similes can students find?)*

5. What does the title *A River Dream* mean to you? *(Remind students of their reading purpose and ask them to comment on the dreamlike quality of the narrative.)*

Reread

THIRD READING The directions on page 72 ask students to reread the story with an eye to the meaning of the "river dream." Have students work in pairs to complete the rereading. Then ask them to discuss the dream and what it might mean. Students should feel free to make additional notes in the margins of their books.

Word Work

HOMOGRAPHS The Word Work lesson on page 73 offers students some practice on **homographs,** which often cause trouble for low-level readers or students who speak English as a second language. Once they've mastered the homographs on the page, ask them to consider these:

bark (tree covering / sound a dog makes / sailing ship); *baste* (pour liquid on while roasting / sew); *stable* (building for horses / unchanging); and *post* (support / job or position / system for mail delivery).

For additional practice, see the **Word Work** blackline master on page 133.

III. GET READY TO WRITE

Prewriting Strategies

STORYBOARD For a prewriting activity, students will create a **storyboard** that shows a time they did something they really wanted to do. Remind the class that the best stories often open right before the most exciting part. (This will help students avoid the problem of meandering story openings.) Explain that you'd like students to draw a quick sketch in each box, and then write a sentence describing the sketch underneath. Have students exchange storyboards before they write their paragraphs. Partners should offer advice on reordering the boxes, ideas of how to make the narrative more exciting, and so on.

Have students use the **Get Ready to Write** blackline master on page 134.

IV. WRITE

Students should write a **narrative paragraph** about a time they did something they really wanted to do. Have them begin with a topic sentence that identifies the event and explains how it made them feel. Also remind them that a good narrative has a beginning, a middle, and an end.

After students have written a first draft, have them stop and think carefully about what they've written. They should ask themselves: "Have I offered three or more details that tell about the event? Have I used sensory language to make my writing vivid and interesting?"

WRITING RUBRIC Use this rubric to help with a quick assessment of students' writing.

Do students' paragraphs

- open with a topic sentence that states the event to be described and how it made them feel?

- tell what happens in chronological order?

- offer at least three details to support the topic sentence?

Grammar, Usage, and Mechanics

When students are ready to proofread their work, refer them to the **Writers' Checklist** and have them double-check the **spelling** of their words. Remind them to look carefully at homophones and homographs. Students should work with an editing partner if they find proofreading their own writing difficult.

V. LOOK BACK

Reflect with students on their **enjoyment** of *A River Dream*. Point out the **Readers' Checklist** and have the class discuss their answers to the questions. If they didn't like the story, have them explain why. What do they think would have improved the writing?

To test students' comprehension, use the **Lesson Test** blackline master on page 135.

Name _____

WORDS TO KNOW

Before Reading

DIRECTIONS Read each sentence.

Then tell what you think the underlined words mean. Use the rest of the sentence to help you.

1. John <u>cast</u> his line into the water and waited for a fish.

I think <u>cast</u> means _____ .

2. He sat there <u>gaping</u> at the big fish he caught.

I think <u>gaping</u> means _____ .

3. The fish <u>leapt</u> in the air and did a flip.

I think <u>leapt</u> means _____ .

4. The <u>mighty</u> fisherman pulled in ten fish in one afternoon.

I think <u>mighty</u> means _____ .

5. He was so proud of the <u>magnificent</u> fish he caught today.

I think <u>magnificent</u> means _____ .

Practice

Name three things you think are *magnificent*.

1. _____ 2. _____ 3. _____

Name _____

BEFORE YOU READ

Preview

DIRECTIONS Preview *A River Dream*.

Read the first paragraph and the last.

Then glance through the rest of the text.

Keep track of what you noticed on the Preview Card.

Preview Card

What is the first paragraph of the story about?

What is the last paragraph about?

What did you notice as you were glancing through the story?

Make a prediction. Will you enjoy this story? Why or why not?

Name _____

COMPREHENSION

Group Discussion

DIRECTIONS In a small group, discuss *A River Dream*.
Use the discussion questions below.

Discussion Question #1

What makes the fishing trip a success? Support your answer.

_____

_____

_____

Discussion Question #2

How does Mark feel about his uncle? How does the uncle feel about Mark? Support your answer.

_____

_____

_____

Discussion Question #3

Why do you think the story is called *A River Dream*?

_____

_____

_____

Name _____

WORD WORK

After Reading

Homographs are words that are spelled the same but have different meanings. Some examples follow:

dove (bird)   date (day, month, and year)

dove (did a dive)   date (dark sweet fruit)

                               date (plan with a friend)

DIRECTIONS Match the correct meaning to each sentence.

Sentence

1. The <u>dove</u> flew over the church.

2. A <u>date</u> is my favorite snack.

3. We made a <u>date</u> to meet at the mall.

4. She <u>dove</u> after the ball.

5. What is the <u>date</u> of your party?

Meaning

day, month, and year

dark sweet fruit

plan with a friend

bird

jumped, moved toward

Practice

DIRECTIONS Use the homographs *fly* (small insect with wings) and *fly* (hook used to catch trout) in two sentences.

6. _____

7. _____

Name _____

GET READY TO WRITE

Story Star

DIRECTIONS Think about the event or experience you want to tell about in your paragraph.

Then write details about it around the star.

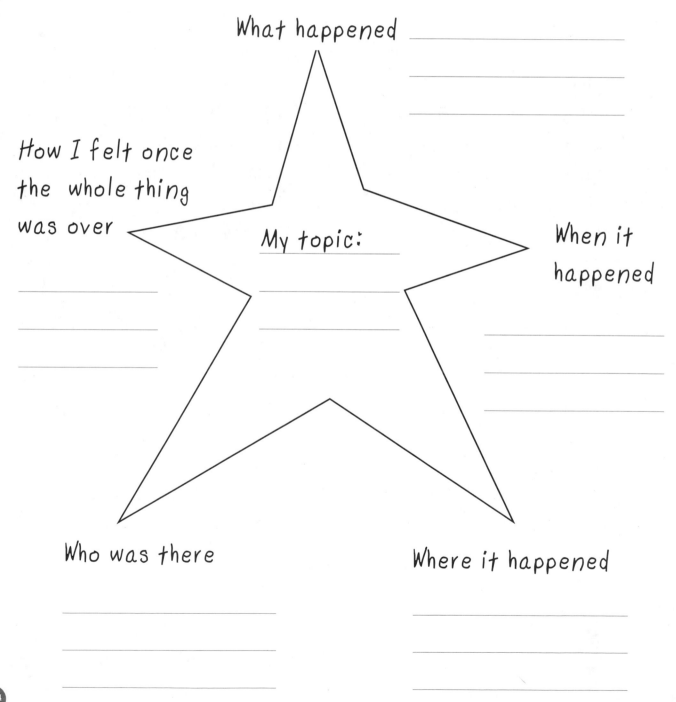

What happened _____
_____
_____

How I felt once
the whole thing
was over
_____
_____
_____

My topic: _____

When it
happened
_____
_____

Who was there
_____
_____
_____

Where it happened
_____
_____

Name _____

LESSON TEST

Multiple-Choice

DIRECTIONS On the lines, write the letter of the best answer for each question.

_____ 1. How does Mark feel about his outing with his uncle?
   A. sad   C. tired
   B. nervous   D. excited

_____ 2. Mark's uncle suggests that Mark use his _____ to catch a fish.
   A. hands   C. heart
   B. eyes   D. feet

_____ 3. What kind of fish does Mark catch?
   A. a rainbow trout   C. a shark
   B. a salmon   D. a goldfish

_____ 4. What is so amazing about Mark's fish?
   A. His fish talks.   C. His fish grants wishes.
   B. His fish tastes good. D. His fish is very big.

_____ 5. An important idea in the story is:
   A. Fishing is hard to do. C. Life is full of excitement.
   B. Be quiet when fishing. D. None of these answers

Short Answer

Why do you think this story is called *A River Dream*?

_____

_____

_____

How We Learned the Earth Is Round

BACKGROUND

In *How We Learned the Earth Is Round,* award-winning children's author Patricia Lauber shows readers that good learning often begins with a question. In the case of the ancient Greeks, the question was a simple one: *Why do boats seem to sink and rise as they disappear and appear over the horizon?*

For centuries, ancient Greek men and women stood on land and watched boats sail to what they assumed was the end of the earth. What puzzled them was why the bottom of the boat—on its trip out—would disappear first, while the top of the boat would be the first thing to appear on the trip back. After countless observations of this same phenomenon, the Greeks began to ask themselves: *Could the earth have a curved surface?* That would explain why ships seem to sink and rise.

Many of your students will be familiar with Patricia Lauber's work and her simple, straightforward writing style. Lauber has written over 80 books for children. Although the majority of her books are nonfiction, she has written several award-winning novels as well. When Lauber discusses her writing with children, she explains that her ideas come from everywhere—from things she reads and from things she hears, sees, tastes, and touches. Her goal as a writer is to share these interesting things with young readers.

Lauber has won many prestigious awards for her books, including a Lifetime Achievement Commendation for Children's Science books from Carnegie-Mellon University.

BIBLIOGRAPHY Suggest students read another nonfiction book by Patricia Lauber. She has several titles that should tie in nicely with your social studies curriculum. Have students read one of these three or check for alternates in the stacks at your school library:

YOU'RE ABOARD SPACESHIP EARTH

(Lexile 460)

BE A FRIEND TO TREES

(Lexile 500)

WHAT YOU NEVER KNEW ABOUT FINGERS, FORKS, AND CHOPSTICKS

(Lexile 580)

How to Introduce the Reading

Ask students to consider the question: "Why did people of long ago think that the earth was flat?" Help them see that it's impossible to see the curvature of the earth while standing on the ground. Since these people had no air or space travel, they believed the earth was flat because it *looked* flat.

Other Reading

Read aloud other Patricia Lauber books or other nonfiction selections that are written at this same reading level (Lexile 490). Among the titles at the same reading level are these:

(Lexile 490)   (Lexile 500)   (Lexile 490)

How We Learned the Earth Is Round

Skills and Strategies Overview

PREREADING K-W-L

READING LEVEL Lexile 490

RESPONSE make clear

VOCABULARY ◇prairie ◇harbor ◇hull ◇disappears ◇surface

COMPREHENSION stop and think

WORD WORK prefixes, suffixes, and base words

PREWRITING main idea and supporting details

WRITING expository paragraph / end punctuation

ASSESSMENT understanding

OTHER RESOURCES

The first **four** pages of this teacher's lesson describe Parts I–V of the lesson. Also included are these **six** blackline masters. Use them to reinforce key elements of the lesson.

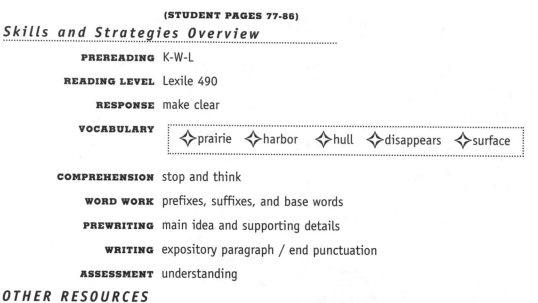

Vocabulary

Prereading

Comprehension

Word Work

Prewriting

Assessment

I. BEFORE YOU READ

Read through the introduction on page 77 with students. Ask students to predict the answer these "great thinkers" came up with. Allow your discussion and students' predictions to generate interest in the reading to come. Then assign the prereading activity, a **K-W-L**. (Refer to the Strategy Handbook, page 47, for more help.)

Motivation Strategy

MOTIVATING STUDENTS To help motivate students and familiarize them with the subject, find one or two books from your library about the ancient Greeks. (For example, *Eyewitness Books: Ancient Greece* offers an excellent visual introduction to the subject.) Encourage students to discuss what they see in the illustrations and compare it to what they know from other sources, such as books, TV shows, movies, and so on.

Words to Know

CONTEXT CLUES Use the **Words to Know** blackline master on page 142 as a way to troubleshoot vocabulary problems. After working through the page, you might decide to teach a short vocabulary lesson on using **context clues**.

Draw attention to the key vocabulary words for this lesson: *prairie, harbor, hull, disappears,* and *surface.* Ask students to volunteer definitions of the words. Also have them use the words in sentences of their own. A series of quick vocabulary exercises will help students become more comfortable with any words that are new to them.

Prereading Strategies

K-W-L As a prereading activity, students are asked to complete a **K-W-L**. As you know, a K-W-L can be helpful to those students who have difficulty beginning a new reading or writing project. In addition to assisting with organization, a K-W-L gives students the chance to activate prior knowledge about a topic. After recording what they already know, they can think carefully about "gaps" in their knowledge. This way, *they* (as opposed to *you)* decide what they need to learn about the discovery that the earth is round.

QUICKWRITE As an alternate prereading strategy, ask students to do a **quickwrite** that relates to the topic of the lesson. If you like, assign a topic from the list below and ask students to write for one minute about this topic without stopping. Later, they may want to use some of their ideas in their expository paragraphs. Possible topics for a quickwrite include these:

• The ancient Greeks

• How *I* know the earth is round

• Why I'd like to sail around the world

The **Before You Read** blackline master on page 143 offers support for this activity.

MY PURPOSE Students' purpose for reading Lauber's article will be to find out how the ancient Greeks discovered that the earth is round. Ask them to watch for particular clues about how the Greeks made this discovery. Also have them think about what the impact of this discovery might have been.

II. READ

Response Strategy

FIRST READING Before students begin their first readings, review the purpose of the response strategy, **make things clear.** Point out the example on page 79 and explain that this is the kind of note that a reader can return to later, when it comes time to clarify an idea or recall a detail. Help students get into the habit of making notes like this while they're reading articles and stories for their various school subjects.

Comprehension Strategy

SECOND READING As they are reading Lauber's piece, students will need to stop occasionally and answer **stop and think** questions designed to test their factual recall of the text. For some of the questions (e.g., "What made the Greeks wonder about the shape of the earth?"), students will need to make connections between different parts of the text. Encourage them to be brief in their responses. It's important that students don't leave the reading itself for an extended period of time. Encourage them to answer each stop and think question in a minute or less. If they get stuck, have them return to the question later, on their third reading.

For more help with **Comprehension,** assign the blackline master on page 144.

Discussion Questions

COMPREHENSION 1. Why does the earth look flat to us? *(We are small and the earth is big. We can only see a small amount of the earth at a given time, which means we can't see its curvature.)*

CRITICAL THINKING 2. How do you imagine people reacted when they first heard the earth was round? *(Possible: with shock, disbelief, and anger that they had been wrong, and so on.)*

3. How did the ancient Greeks learn that the earth is round? *(They watched the way ships appeared and disappeared over the horizon and formed the hypothesis that the earth must be curved.)*

4. Explain the idea that all good learning begins with a question. *(Ask students to consider how asking questions helps people learn. Remind them of the questions the Greeks asked that led them to the discovery that the earth is round.)*

Reread

THIRD READING Have students reread (or skim) Lauber's piece in order to find answers to the questions they wrote in the W section of their K-W-L charts. Remind them to consult the notes they made in the margins of the reading. Some of their comments may relate to the questions on the K-W-L.

Word Work

PREFIXES, SUFFIXES, AND BASE WORDS The Word Work lesson on page 83 offers students practice on **prefixes, suffixes,** and **base words.** Help students master common prefixes *(dis-, re-,* and *un-)* and suffixes *(-ing* and *-ed).* Over the course of the year, reinforce the importance of looking for the base word first when thinking about the meaning of a longer word.

For additional practice, see the **Word Work** blackline master on page 145.

III. GET READY TO WRITE

Prewriting Strategies

MAIN IDEA AND SUPPORTING DETAILS Before they begin the diagram on page 84, you might review with students some tips on how to find the main idea in a nonfiction reading.

Step 1 Check the title. The most important idea is sometimes there.

Step 2 Look at the first and last sentences of every paragraph.

Step 3 Watch for key words in italics or boldface or words that are repeated. These words often point the way to the main idea.

Once students have read the main idea in the center of the diagram, they can begin gathering details. Remind the class that each detail they list should relate to the main idea.

Have students use the **Get Ready to Write** blackline master on page 146.

IV. WRITE

The directions at the top of page 85 ask students to write an **expository paragraph.** If necessary, review the characteristics of this type of writing. An expository paragraph explains something or gives information. It includes all the facts a reader needs to understand the subject. These facts are presented in the form of details that support the main idea.

WRITING RUBRIC Use this rubric to help with a quick assessment of students' writing.

Do students' expository paragraphs

• open with a main idea sentence that identifies the topic to be discussed?

• contain three or more details from Lauber's article that support the topic sentence?

• end with a closing sentence that is a restatement of the paragraph's main idea?

Grammar, Usage, and Mechanics

When students are ready to proofread, refer them to the **Writers' Checklist**. Review the rules for end punctuation. Offer additional support as needed.

V. LOOK BACK

Reflect with students on their **understanding** of *How We Learned the Earth Is Round*. Point out the **Readers' Checklist** and have the class discuss their answers to the questions. Were there parts of the article that confused the students? If so, what could they have done to clear up their confusion? (*Possible: They might have reread, asked a question, or visualized what is described.*)

To test students' comprehension, use the **Lesson Test** blackline master on page 147.

Name  _____

WORDS TO KNOW

Before Reading

DIRECTIONS Read this paragraph.

Then choose a word from the word box to fill in each blank.

If you're not sure, make a prediction and correct your work later.

> ✦prairie   ✦harbor   ✦hull   ✦disappears   ✦surface

Kyle works all day to repair the hole in the _____ of his boat. He is leaving the _____ tomorrow. As he works, he notices the sun is shining on the _____ of the water. Later the sun _____ behind a cloud. The calm water reminds him of a flat Kansas _____ .

Practice

Write a question to Kyle about his day. Use one vocabulary word in your question.

_____

_____

_____

_____

Name _____

BEFORE YOU READ

Quickwrite

DIRECTIONS Choose a topic from the list below.

Then write for 1 minute about your topic.

Write everything you can think of.

My topic: (circle one)

The ancient Greeks

How *I* know the earth is round

Why I'd like to sail around the world

My Quickwrite

_____

_____

_____

_____

_____

_____

_____

Name _____

COMPREHENSION

Research

DIRECTIONS Work with a partner to find answers to these questions.
Look for information at the library or on the Internet.
Write what you find on this research card.

Research Card

Who were the ancient Greeks?

_____

When did they live?

_____

What are the names of two great thinkers who lived in
ancient Greece?

_____

What did these two people study?

_____

This is where I found my information:

_____

Name _____

WORD WORK

After Reading

DIRECTIONS Put an X through the suffix of each word. Then write the base word. One has been done for you.

Word with suffix	Base word
1. appear~~ed~~	appear
2. trusting	
3. guessed	
4. moving	

Practice

DIRECTIONS Add a suffix or prefix from the box to each of these base words. Write the new word on the line. One has been done for you.

prefixes: *re-, un-*   suffixes: *-ed, -ing*

5. stop ___stopped___

6. tie _____

7. shut _____

8. do _____

9. play _____

10. tell _____

Name _____

GET READY TO WRITE

Graphic Organizer

DIRECTIONS Use this organizer to show how the Greeks learned that the earth is round.

Check your book if you need to.

Then use the organizer to help you write your expository paragraph.

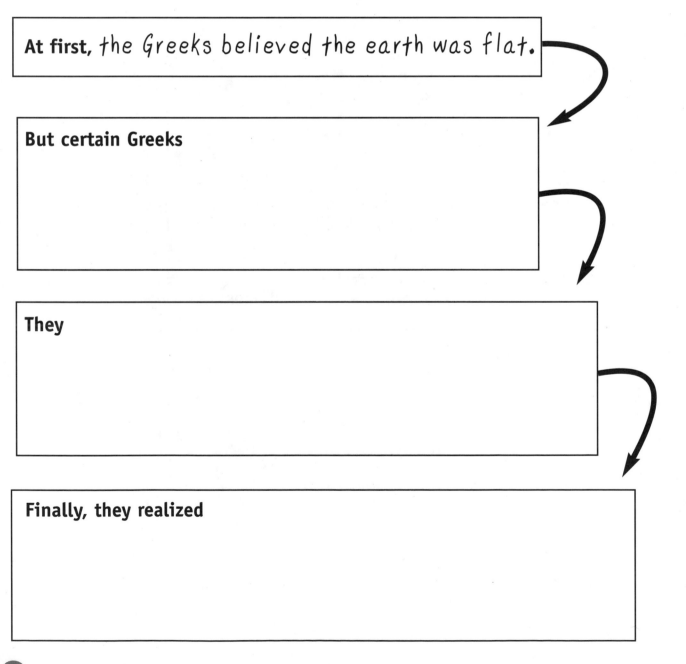

At first, *the Greeks believed the earth was flat.*

But certain Greeks

They

Finally, they realized

Name _____

LESSON TEST

Multiple-Choice

DIRECTIONS On the lines, write the letter of the best answer for each question.

_____ 1. People long ago thought the earth was . . .
A. round.   C. tiny.
B. flat.   D. endless.

_____ 2. The earth's real shape was discovered . . .
A. 25 years ago.   C. 2,500 years ago.
B. 250 years ago.   D. 2 million years ago.

_____ 3. The Greeks realized the earth was round when . . .
A. they discovered   C. they saw it from a
   gravity.   plane.
B. they traveled by foot. D. they saw a ship sail away.

_____ 4. The Greeks also realized the earth . . .
A. is flat in some areas.   C. curves in all directions.
B. has three moons.   D. is shaped like a football.

_____ 5. An important idea in *How We Learned the Earth Is Round* is . . .
A. always ask questions.   C. round is better than flat.
B. be careful sailing.   D. none of these answers

Short Answer

How did the Greeks figure out the earth is round?

_____

_____

_____

_____

I Am Rosa Parks

BACKGROUND

I Am Rosa Parks is Parks's autobiography, which she wrote for an audience of eight- to ten-year-olds. To create the book, Parks simplified her award-winning work, *Rosa Parks: My Story,* and made it accessible to younger readers.

In this version of her autobiography, Parks uses simple, direct language to tell the story of why she refused to give up her bus seat to a white man. Later in the book, Parks explains her role in the ground-breaking struggle that became the Civil Rights Movement. Parks's gentle tone and matter-of-fact descriptions serve to emphasize her quietly courageous message of peace: "I hope that children today will . . . learn to respect one another no matter what color they are."

Rosa Louise McCauley Parks was born in 1913 in Tuskegee, Alabama. After graduating from Alabama State College, she made her living as a seamstress. In 1943, Parks became a member of the Montgomery chapter of the National Association for the Advancement of Colored People (NAACP). On December 1, 1955, she was arrested for refusing to relinquish her seat on a public bus to a white man, a violation of the city's racial segregation ordinances. Her refusal touched off the 1955 Montgomery, Alabama, bus boycott, which in turn helped to ignite the Civil Rights Movement.

Her award-winning autobiography was published in 1992. Seven years later, she was awarded the Congressional Gold Medal of Honor, the highest honor a civilian can receive in the United States.

BIBLIOGRAPHY Students might enjoy reading another story about a famous American. Suggest they choose one of these books, all three of which have the same Lexile level as *I Am Rosa Parks* (Lexile 520):

How to Introduce the Reading

Your students already may be familiar with Rosa Parks and the stand she made for civil rights. Have volunteers tell what they know about her work and her momentous decision to remain seated on a Montgomery bus.

As an alternate introduction, read aloud the questions on page 87 and ask the class to respond. What recourse do they have when they think a rule in school is not fair? What recourse do they have when they think a rule at home is not fair? Ask students to explain which they think is more effective: kicking and yelling in protest, or quietly making your position known. Use your discussion as a way of introducing Dr. Martin Luther King's belief that quiet voices can sometimes be the loudest of all.

Other Reading

Read aloud other books that relate to the theme of *I Am Rosa Parks*. Choose one of these three:

(Lexile 540)   (Lexile 520)   (Lexile 520)

I Am Rosa Parks

(STUDENT PAGES 87-96)

Skills and Strategies Overview

PREREADING	preview
READING LEVEL	Lexile 520
RESPONSE	question
VOCABULARY	◇restaurants ◇arrested ◇obeyed ◇apart ◇section
COMPREHENSION	cause-effect chart
WORD WORK	consonants and consonant clusters
PREWRITING	character web
WRITING	letter / commas in compound sentences
ASSESSMENT	meaning

OTHER RESOURCES

The first **four** pages of this teacher's lesson describe Parts I–V of the lesson. Also included are these **six** blackline masters. Use them to reinforce key elements of the lesson.

Vocabulary

Prereading

Comprehension

Word Work

Prewriting

Assessment

1. BEFORE YOU READ

Read through the directions at the top of page 88 and discuss the purpose of a **preview** with students. Ask the class: "How many times have you thumbed through a book first, just to look at the pictures, find out how long it is, or find out how hard it is?" Explain that when they thumb through a book, what they're really doing is previewing the text, which can help them become better readers. After your discussion, set students to work on the activity of previewing *I Am Rosa Parks*. (Refer to the Strategy Handbook, page 49, for more help.)

Motivation Strategies

MOTIVATING STUDENTS Show students a picture book about the Civil Rights Movement. Point out important leaders and discuss the impact the Movement had on the United States. Have students share stories they've heard from family members or friends. Use your discussion to help students activate prior knowledge about this important historical period.

CONNECTING WITH STUDENTS Ask students to tell about a time they stood up for what they believed in. Who was there, when did it happen, and what issue was at stake? Guide students toward a discussion of their civil rights. Have any of them ever felt that their rights were taken away from them?

Words to Know

CONTEXT CLUES Use the **Words to Know** blackline master on page 154 as a way to troubleshoot vocabulary problems. After working through the page, you might decide to teach a short vocabulary lesson on using **context clues**.

Some of your students may find the vocabulary of this selection challenging. Help them by pointing out difficult words and modeling how to search for the words' meanings. To begin, show students the key vocabulary words for the selection: *restaurants, arrested, obeyed, apart,* and *section*. Remind the class that using context clues to uncover the meaning of an unfamiliar word is faster than stopping each time to check the dictionary. Model using context clues by pointing out clues for the word *arrested* (page 89) and the word *obeyed* (page 90).

Prereading Strategies

PREVIEW During a **preview**, the reader looks carefully at the first and last paragraphs of the selection and then glances through the rest of the text, paying particular attention to headlines, questions, vocabulary words, art, and captions. A preview can familiarize the reader with the topic of the selection and will often provide valuable clues about the author's main idea. Have students make notes on the preview cards (page 88) after they've finished.

SKIM As an additional prereading activity, have students **skim** the selection. During a skim, readers glance through the selection quickly, looking for words and phrases that reveal information about the topic. Skimming gives readers an idea of what they can expect during their close readings and can alert them to words or ideas that might cause difficulty during their careful readings. This strategy may be particularly helpful to those who feel intimidated by nonfiction.

To extend the activity, use the **Before You Read** blackline master on page 155.

MY PURPOSE Point out the reading purpose at the bottom of page 88. Ask a volunteer to read it aloud. Clear up any confusion about the purpose before making the reading assignment.

READ

Response Strategy

FIRST READING Discuss the response strategy of **questioning.** Point out the Response Notes question on page 89 and explain that this is an example of a question that might occur to students as they are reading. Other readers might have completely different questions. Request that students write at least one question per page of text. Help them get into the habit of automatically noting questions as they read.

Comprehension Strategy

SECOND READING Before students begin their first readings, point out the first **cause-effect** chart, which appears on page 90. Be sure students understand what *cause and effect* means. If necessary, model the relationship between the two by showing the effect of a "cause" you demonstrate, such as closing the door (effect: hallway noise is muted).

For more help with **Comprehension,** assign the blackline master on page 156.

Discussion Questions

COMPREHENSION 1. Why did the bus driver ask Rosa Parks to give up her seat? *(because a white man was standing)*

2. What is the setting for Rosa Parks's story? *(the South in the 1950s)*

CRITICAL THINKING 3. What kind of a person is Rosa Parks? *(Possible: She is brave and determined, and knows what's right.)*

4. What did she do that made her famous? *(She refused to give up her seat to a white man on a Montgomery bus. She became famous for this act of defiance.)*

5. Whom do you know that reminds you of Rosa Parks? *(Ask students to make a connection to their own lives. Have them explain the ways in which the person they name is similar to Parks. What personality traits does this person share with Parks?)*

Reread

THIRD READING As you know, reading a selection for a second (or third) time can greatly increase comprehension. Tell students that when they reread, they should watch carefully for information about Parks. What kind of a person is she? Encourage students to make additional notes in the margins of the text.

Word Work

CONSONANTS AND CONSONANT CLUSTERS Use the Word Work lesson on page 93 to reinforce students' understanding of **consonants** and **consonant clusters.** Review problematic clusters such as *ck, br, sh,* and *th.* Offer the opportunity to practice forming more words than are required on the page.

If you feel students need additional practice, assign the **Word Work** blackline master on page 157.

III. GET READY TO WRITE

Prewriting Strategies

CHARACTER WEB As a prewriting activity, students will create a **web** that explores Rosa Parks's personality. Point out the directions at the top of page 94. Explain that students will need to read the quality named in each section of the web *(brave, peaceful, stubborn, fair)* and then find evidence from the text that supports that quality. You may want to finish the activity by having students write a topic sentence for their letters.

Have students use the **Get Ready to Write** blackline master on page 158.

IV. WRITE

Read aloud the directions on page 95. Students should understand that they're to write a **letter** that tells who Rosa Parks is and what she is like. Have them refer to their webs as they write. Remind them to begin with a topic sentence. In the body of the letter, they'll offer support for the topic sentence. Encourage students to use direct quotations from the text when appropriate.

After students have written a first draft, have them stop and think carefully about what they've created. They should ask themselves: "Have I offered at least three pieces of support for my topic sentence? Do I paint a detailed picture of Rosa Parks and what made her famous?"

WRITING RUBRIC Use this rubric to help with a quick assessment of students' writing.

Do students' letters

• include a personality description of Rosa Parks?

• contain details from the text that support that description?

• follow the proper form for a friendly letter? (See page 18.)

Grammar, Usage, and Mechanics

When students are ready to edit their work, refer them to the **Writers' Checklist.** Read aloud the question on the checklist and then teach a brief lesson on using a **comma** to separate the two parts of a compound sentence. Be sure to point out that a comma and a connecting word (conjunction) must be used together in order for a compound sentence to be grammatically correct. For extra practice, have students edit these two sentences:

Rosa Parks was brave⌃and she had strong convictions. She said she would not give up her seat⌃so the bus driver had her arrested.

V. LOOK BACK

Point out the **Readers' Checklist** and reflect with students on the **meaning** of the selection. What did Parks's autobiography mean to them personally? Why?

To test students' comprehension, use the **Lesson Test** blackline master on page 159.

Name _____

WORDS TO KNOW

Before Reading

DIRECTIONS Read each sentence.

Tell what you think the underlined words mean.

If you don't know, use context clues.

1. I refuse to eat in <u>restaurants</u> that don't serve everyone.

I think <u>restaurants</u> means _____ .

2. You will be <u>arrested</u> if you don't follow the law.

I think <u>arrested</u> means _____ .

3. The white man said I should have <u>obeyed</u> the bus driver.

I think <u>obeyed</u> means _____ .

4. The boys were asked to stay <u>apart</u> from each other on the playground.

I think <u>apart</u> means _____ .

5. Rosa Parks was supposed to sit in the back <u>section</u> of the bus.

I think <u>section</u> means _____ .

Practice

Think of the rules in your school. Which have you *obeyed* this week? Describe one of them.

_____

Name _____

BEFORE YOU READ

Skim

DIRECTIONS Skim *I Am Rosa Parks*.

Let your eyes run down the page.

Watch for words and sentences that pop out at you.

Then make some skimming notes.

Skimming Notes: *I Am Rosa Parks*

(circle one)

1. *I Am Rosa Parks* is fiction / nonfiction because

_____

_____

_____

2. What words and phrases did you notice?

_____

_____

_____

_____

3. What is *I Am Rosa Parks* about?

_____

_____

_____

_____

Name _____

COMPREHENSION

Double-entry Journal

DIRECTIONS Read the quotations from the article in the left column. Say how they make you feel in the right column. What do you think about as you read these sentences?

Quotation	How it makes me feel
"Many years ago black people in the South could not go to the same schools as white people."	
"The driver said, 'Let me have those seats.'"	
"I asked him, 'Why do you push us black people around?'"	

Name _____

WORD WORK

After Reading

DIRECTIONS Cross out the beginning consonants and consonant clusters in these words. Replace them with a new consonant or consonant cluster. One has been done for you.

1. ~~cr~~ack   _tack_____
2. spot   _____
3. stay   _____
4. blame   _____

Practice

DIRECTIONS Make a list of words that use the consonant clusters in the box. Write as many words as you can think of.

tr	bl	cr	sp

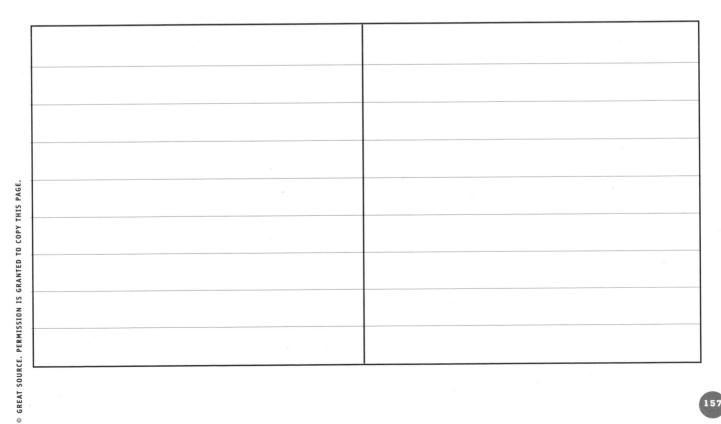

Name _____

GET READY TO WRITE

Writing a Letter

DIRECTIONS Follow these steps to write your letter.

STEP 1 Choose the person you will write to.

I will write to _____ .

STEP 2 Decide what you will say about Rosa Parks. Write a topic sentence.

Rosa Parks is _____ ,

_____ , and

_____ .

STEP 3 Find support from the text for your topic sentence. Use direct quotations when you can.

detail #1 _____

_____

_____

detail #2 _____

_____

_____

detail #3 _____

_____

_____

Name _____

LESSON TEST

Multiple-Choice

DIRECTIONS On the lines, write the letter of the best answer for each question.

_____ 1. Many years ago, black and white children didn't . . .
A. eat in the same places.
B. go to school together.
C. drink from the same water fountains.
D. All of these answers

_____ 2. Many years ago in the South, segregation was taken . . .
A. very seriously.
B. not seriously.
C. seriously only sometimes.
D. None of these answers

_____ 3. Who was the first to ask Rosa Parks to give up her seat?
A. a policeman
B. a bus driver
C. a judge
D. her friend

_____ 4. Rosa Parks is famous for . . .
A. being a hard worker.
B. inventing the bus.
C. standing up for herself.
D. working with children.

_____ 5. Another good title for this selection might be . . .
A. *Rosa Wouldn't Move*
B. *Rosa Likes the Bus*
C. *Rosa Gave Up Her Seat*
D. *Rosa and Her Friends*

Short Answer

What kind of a person is Rosa Parks? Use what you wrote in the lesson to help you answer this question.

_____

_____

Germs Make Me Sick!

BACKGROUND

Melvin Berger's *Germs Make Me Sick!* is an interesting and informative look at how bacteria and viruses spread infection and the ways in which the human body fights back. Berger's descriptions are accurate and to the point, yet his light-hearted writing style makes this a book that even your most reluctant readers will enjoy.

As students read the ***Sourcebook*** selection, they'll need to keep track of the characteristics of viruses and bacteria. A Venn diagram like the one below can help:

Viruses
- tinier than bacteria
- balls with spikes sticking out
- "loaves of bread"
- "tadpoles"
- metal screws with spider legs

- can make you sick
- found everywhere
- not all are harmful
- skin, nose can block them
- body can fight them

Bacteria
- little round balls
- rods
- spiral-shaped

Melvin Berger is the author of more than 200 books for children, including the award-winning science picture book, *Why I Sneeze, Shiver, Hiccup, and Yawn.*

BIBLIOGRAPHY Students might enjoy reading another science-related book by Melvin Berger, who writes for many different age levels. The three titles below reflect a range in difficulty from very easy to somewhat challenging:

WHY I SNEEZE, SHIVER, HICCUP, AND YAWN

ALL ABOUT ELECTRICITY

WHY DON'T HAIRCUTS HURT?

(Lexile 480)   (Lexile 510)   (Lexile 630)

How to Introduce the Reading

Ignite students' interest in Berger's text by asking them to tell stories about a time they had a cold or the flu. Model a story of your own (for example, about a time you had a fever and had to call a substitute teacher). Then ask students to say what all the stories have in common. Students might notice that colds and the flu are always "caught" from another person. Ask students to say how they think these types of germs are transmitted.

Finish your discussion by explaining that the selection students are about to read explains what kinds of germs cause colds and the flu.

Other Reading

Read aloud other nonfiction books that relate to the topic of Berger's book. Choose books such as these that are written at the same reading level as *Germs Make Me Sick!* (Lexile 530):

TASTING by Helen Frost

LET'S EXERCISE by Alice B. McGinty

NURSES by Dee Ready

(Lexile 520)   (Lexile 540)   (Lexile 520)

Germs Make Me Sick!

Skills and Strategies Overview

PREREADING	think-pair-and-share
READING LEVEL	Lexile 530
RESPONSE	make clear
VOCABULARY	✦ache ✦viruses ✦spiral ✦harmful
COMPREHENSION	retell
WORD WORK	compound words
PREWRITING	5 Ws
WRITING	expository paragraph / sentence fragments
ASSESSMENT	understanding

OTHER RESOURCES

The first **four** pages of this teacher's lesson describe Parts I–V of the lesson. Also included are these **six** blackline masters. Use them to reinforce key elements of the lesson.

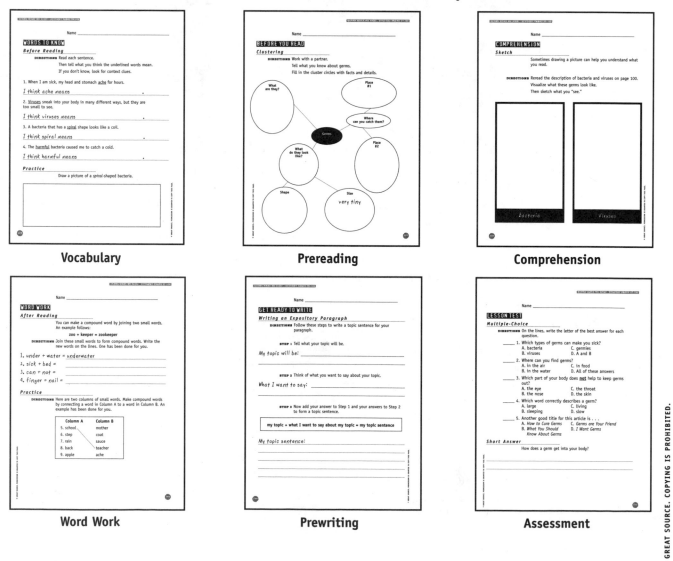

Vocabulary

Prereading

Comprehension

Word Work

Prewriting

Assessment

I. BEFORE YOU READ

Read aloud the introduction to the lesson on page 97. Ask students to answer the first question on the page: *Have you ever felt like you couldn't get out of bed?* See what kind of prior knowledge they have about the topic of contagious diseases and what causes them. Write the words *bacteria* and *virus* on the board. Then ask for ideas about what these words mean. Finish your warm-up by assigning the prereading activity, a **think-pair-and-share.** (Refer to the Strategy Handbook, page 50, for more help.)

Motivation Strategy

CONNECTING WITH STUDENTS Ask students to name "cures" they think are best for the cold and flu. What helps them feel better when they're sick? Does it help to stay in bed, or is it better to watch TV under a blanket on the couch? Help set the mood for the reading by asking students to tell about how they feel when they're sick. Also ask them to say what they can do to prevent illness. Students may say that taking vitamins, washing your hands more often during cold and flu season, and refraining from sharing drinks can help.

Words to Know

CONTEXT CLUES Use the **Words to Know** blackline master on page 166 as a way to troubleshoot vocabulary problems. After working through the page, you might decide to teach a short vocabulary lesson on **context clues.**

Help students use context clues as they read to figure out the meanings of difficult words, especially the key vocabulary for this lesson: *ache, viruses, spiral,* and *harmful.* Some of these words may be familiar to students, and some may be completely new. Demonstrate how to search for and apply context clues in order to define these and other challenging words in the selection.

Prereading Strategies

THINK-PAIR-AND-SHARE Students are asked to complete a **think-pair-and-share** activity as a warm-up to Berger's writing. In a think-pair-and-share, students work together to solve sentence "puzzles" related to the selection. In this case, they'll read a series of five statements about germs and then say whether they agree or disagree with the statements. Of course, it's not important that students know the right answer at this point. The purpose of this activity is to help them do some initial thinking about the topic of the selection.

CLUSTER As an additional prereading activity, ask students to make a **cluster** about germs that shows their prior knowledge of this topic. Clustering can help students recall information in an organized way, as if they were following a train of thought. This activity will also serve as an excellent warm-up to the 5 Ws cluster students will complete in **Part III.**

To extend the activity, use the **Before You Read** blackline master on page 167.

MY PURPOSE Always establish a reading purpose for students before they begin an assignment. Move beyond the overly general "read to find out everything you can" and create a purpose that gives students something to look for or think about as they read. Point out the reading purpose at the bottom of page 98. Have a volunteer read it aloud and another volunteer rephrase it. Be sure all students know exactly what their purpose is.

II. READ

Response Strategy

FIRST READING As they read, students will make notes that help **make clear** important facts or details, especially those that relate to their reading purpose. Invite them to use a highlighter to mark specific words and sentences that they think are interesting or puzzling. Then, in the Response Notes, students should write what they think the word or sentence means and how it relates to the topic of germs.

Comprehension Strategy

SECOND READING The **retell** boxes scattered throughout the Berger excerpt invite students to pause and say what they've learned so far. This strategy is a good one to use with challenging texts since it forces students to reflect on important information as they go, rather than wait until the end to gather facts and details. Have students use their interrupter notes to help them write their paragraphs for **Part IV**.

For more help with **Comprehension**, assign the blackline master on page 168.

Discussion Questions

COMPREHENSION 1. What two types of germs does Berger discuss? *(viruses and bacteria)*

2. How do these germs get inside the human body? *(People breathe them in or ingest them through eating and drinking. Germs are also on just about any surface a person touches.)*

CRITICAL THINKING 3. Explain the difference between harmful and nonharmful germs. *(Viruses and bacteria can be either harmful or not harmful. Harmful germs are the ones that make people sick.)*

4. What can a person do to prevent germs from entering his or her body? *(Answers will vary. Review with students the way germs get into the body and then ask for ideas about how to keep those areas germ-free: by washing, not sharing food and drink with others, and so on.)*

Reread

THIRD READING As they reread, students should watch for additional details about germs and how they make a person sick. Before they begin, have them read again the purpose statement on page 98. Their purpose for this rereading is to find even more details that relate to the purpose statement. On this reading, students might make another set of notes in a different color pen. When they finish, they can review what they wrote. This additional set of notes will prove to students how valuable a third reading can be. Not even the best readers can take *everything* in on a first or second reading.

Word Work

COMPOUND WORDS By the time they reach grade 4, students should be very familiar with **compound words** and how they are formed. Use the Word Work lesson on page 103 to reinforce their understanding of compounds.

Have the class complete the **Word Work** blackline master on page 169 if you feel they need practice forming their own compound words.

III. GET READY TO WRITE

Prewriting Strategies

5 Ws If students are not familiar with the **5 Ws**, carefully explain the importance of understanding the who, what, where, when, why (and sometimes how) of a topic. Be sure they know that this type of organizer also can reveal the main idea and supporting details of a piece of writing. Help students get into the habit of completing a quick 5 Ws organizer each time they read nonfiction. If your students are unfamiliar with this strategy, try completing the organizer on page 104 as a class. Duplicate the diagram on the board or on an overhead. Ask volunteers to suggest details for each section. Then have students work individually on their closing sentences.

Have students use the **Get Ready to Write** blackline master on page 170.

IV. WRITE

In their **expository paragraphs,** students should explain how germs make a person sick. In the opening of the paragraph, they should also discuss what germs are and where they come from. As always, students should begin their paragraphs with a topic sentence that identifies the subject of the paragraph and what they plan to say about the subject. Then they'll need to offer three or more details as support. Supporting details belong in the body of the paragraph.

After students have written a first draft, have them stop and carefully reread what they've written. Ask them: "Did you define and describe bacteria and viruses? Did you say where they come from and how they can make people sick?"

WRITING RUBRIC Use this rubric to help with a quick assessment of students' writing.

Do students' paragraphs

• open with a topic sentence that explains germs and how they affect people?

• offer three or more details about why and when germs can make a person sick?

• close with a sentence that says what they think about germs?

Grammar, Usage, and Mechanics

When students are ready to edit their work, refer them to the **Writers' Checklist**. Review the rules of avoiding **sentence fragments**. Tell students to make sure that each of their sentences has a subject and a verb and expresses a complete thought.

V. LOOK BACK

Reflect with students on their **understanding** of *Germs Make Me Sick!* Point out the **Readers' Checklist** and have the class discuss their answers to the questions. Were there parts of the article that confused them? If so, what could they have done to clear up their confusion? (*Possible: They might have reread, asked a question, or visualized what is described.*)

To test students' comprehension, use the **Lesson Test** blackline master on page 171.

Name _____

WORDS TO KNOW

Before Reading

DIRECTIONS Read each sentence.

Then tell what you think the underlined words mean.

If you don't know, look for context clues.

1. When I am sick, my head and stomach <u>ache</u> for hours.

I think <u>ache</u> means _____.

2. <u>Viruses</u> sneak into your body in many different ways, but they are too small to see.

I think <u>viruses</u> means _____.

3. A bacteria that has a <u>spiral</u> shape looks like a coil.

I think <u>spiral</u> means _____.

4. The <u>harmful</u> bacteria caused me to catch a cold.

I think <u>harmful</u> means _____.

Practice

Draw a picture of a *spiral*-shaped bacteria.

┌──┐
│   │
│   │
│   │
│   │
│   │
│   │
└──┘

Name _____

BEFORE YOU READ

Clustering

DIRECTIONS Work with a partner.

Tell what you know about germs.

Fill in the cluster circles with facts and details.

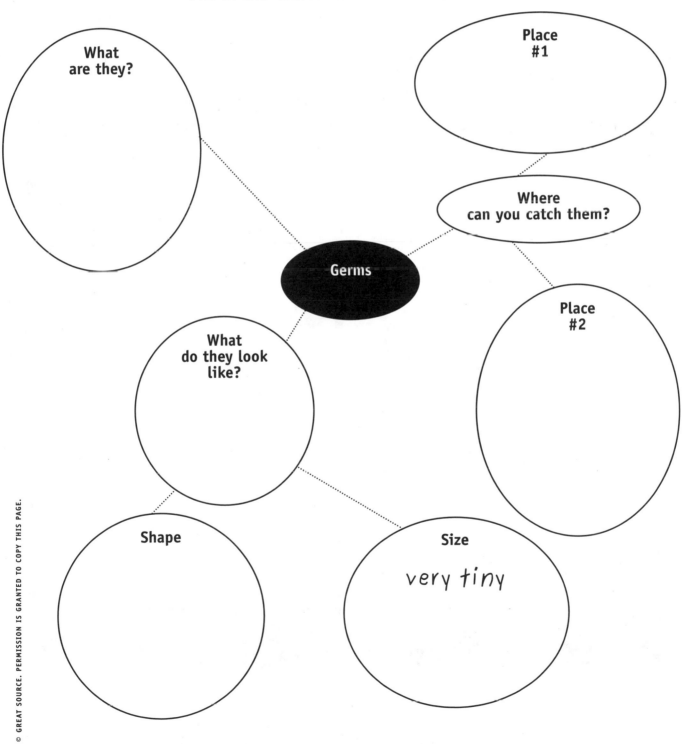

**What
are they?**

**Place
#1**

**Where
can you catch them?**

Germs

**Place
#2**

**What
do they look
like?**

Shape

Size

very tiny

167

Name _____

COMPREHENSION

Sketch

Sometimes drawing a picture can help you understand what you read.

DIRECTIONS Reread the description of bacteria and viruses on page 100.

Visualize what these germs look like.

Then sketch what you "see."

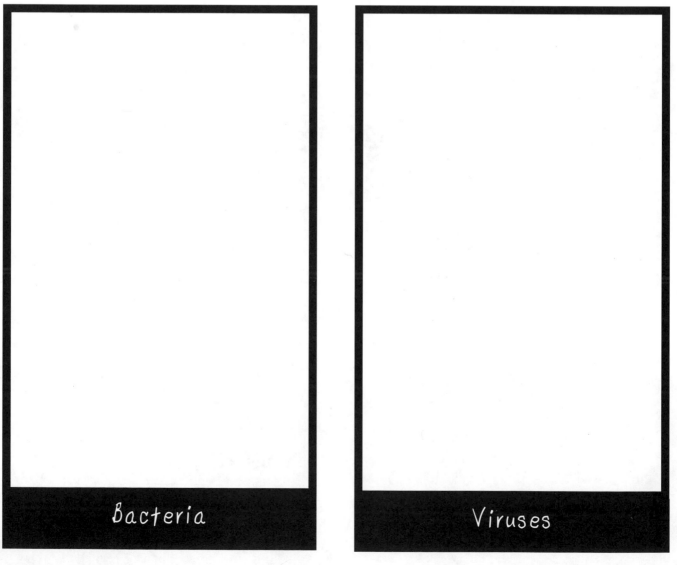

Bacteria

Viruses

Name _____

WORD WORK

After Reading

You can make a compound word by joining two small words. An example follows:

zoo + keeper = zookeeper

DIRECTIONS Join these small words to form compound words. Write the new words on the lines. One has been done for you.

1. under + water = underwater
2. sick + bed = _____
3. can + not = _____
4. finger + nail = _____

Practice

DIRECTIONS Here are two columns of small words. Make compound words by connecting a word in Column A to a word in Column B. An example has been done for you.

Column A	Column B
5. school	mother
6. step	coat
7. rain	sauce
8. back	teacher
9. apple	ache

Name _____

GET READY TO WRITE

Writing an Expository Paragraph

DIRECTIONS Follow these steps to write a topic sentence for your paragraph.

STEP 1 Tell what your topic will be.

What my topic will be: _____

_____

STEP 2 Think of what you want to say about your topic.

What I want to say: _____

_____

STEP 3 Now add your answer to Step 1 and your answers to Step 2 to form a topic sentence.

---
my topic + what I want to say about my topic = my topic sentence

---

My topic sentence: _____

_____

_____

_____

_____

Name _____

LESSON TEST

Multiple-Choice

DIRECTIONS On the lines, write the letter of the best answer for each question.

_____ 1. Which types of germs can make you sick?
A. bacteria   C. germies
B. viruses   D. both A. and B.

_____ 2. Where can you find germs?
A. in the air   C. in food
B. in the water   D. All of these answers

_____ 3. Which part of your body does **not** help to keep germs out?
A. the eye   C. the throat
B. the nose   D. the skin

_____ 4. Which word correctly describes a germ?
A. large   C. living
B. sleeping   D. slow

_____ 5. Another good title for this article might be . . .
A. *How to Cure Germs*   C. *Germs Are Your Friends*
B. *What You Should Know About Germs*   D. *I Want Germs*

Short Answer

How does a germ get into your body?

_____

_____

The Skirt

BACKGROUND

Gary Soto's novel *The Skirt* is a cheerful look at a contemporary Mexican-American family living in California. The central conflict of the story involves one of the children in the family—a girl named Miata—who mistakenly leaves her folklórico skirt on the school bus. Miata is devastated by the error and knows that her mother, who wore the skirt as a girl, will be angry about the loss. Tension builds as Miata and her friend Ana try their hardest to get the skirt back in time for the show on Sunday.

Gary Soto is a poet, a short story writer, and an essayist who focuses much of his writing on his experiences growing up in the barrio of Fresno, California. In *The Skirt,* a short novel for children, Soto explores the theme of family relationships and the importance of having a strong cultural identity.

Soto is known for his use of clear imagery and vivid prose. When he visits a school, he explains to students that the finest praise a reader can give him is to say: "I can see your stories." Soto says that he hopes to please these readers the most, which is why he works to create stories that are "alive and meaningful in the reader's mind."

BIBLIOGRAPHY Students might enjoy listening to a poem by Gary Soto. Check your library for one of his ten poetry anthologies and then read a couple of his poems aloud. If you prefer that students read on their own, you might suggest one of these novels by Soto:

(Lexile 540)   (Lexile 440)   (Lexile 420)

How to Introduce the Reading

Ask a volunteer to read the opening paragraph on page 107. Then have students tell about big and little mistakes they've made in the past. What were the mistakes, and how did they rectify them? If students are uncomfortable discussing this topic aloud, have them make notes in their books. They can use these notes later to help them complete the writing assignment.

Other Reading

Read aloud other high-interest multicultural titles. These three have a Lexile level similar to that of *The Skirt* (Lexile 540):

(Lexile 520)   (Lexile 540)   (Lexile 550)

The Skirt

(STUDENT PAGES 107-118)

Skills and Strategies Overview

PREREADING picture walk

READING LEVEL Lexile 540

RESPONSE connect

VOCABULARY ◇exhaustion ◇troupe ◇scolding ◇rear ◇ragged

COMPREHENSION stop and think

WORD WORK word parts

PREWRITING story chart

WRITING narrative paragraph / capitalization

ASSESSMENT enjoyment

OTHER RESOURCES

The first **four** pages of this teacher's lesson describe Parts I–V of the lesson. Also included are these **six** blackline masters. Use them to reinforce key elements of the lesson.

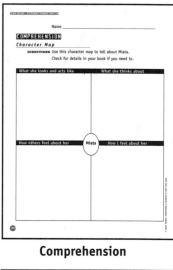

Vocabulary

Prereading

Comprehension

Word Work

Prewriting

Assessment

BEFORE YOU READ

As a warm-up to the topic of Soto's story, have students make a list of their notable family mistakes. Even if they don't share their list with anyone else, this short project will help students begin thinking about the theme of making and correcting mistakes. Remind the class that sometimes the hardest thing about making a mistake is figuring out a way to correct it. Have students provide an example of a time they made an "easy" mistake that was difficult to correct. Then assign the prereading activity, a **picture walk.** (Refer to the Strategy Handbook, page 49, for more help.)

Motivation Strategy

MOTIVATING STUDENTS   Use the Internet to introduce folklórico to those students who are not familiar with it. Begin by previewing the website www.alegria.org to be sure it is appropriate for students. Then show students the various links about folklórico at this site, as well as the information about dancers, costumes, customs, and so on.

Words to Know

SUFFIXES   The **Words to Know** blackline master on page 178 can assist you in troubleshooting vocabulary problems. After working through the page, you might decide to teach a short vocabulary lesson on using **suffixes.**

As students read, point out key vocabulary words for this lesson: *exhaustion, troupe, scolding, rear,* and *ragged.* Have students identify which of these five words has a suffix (*scolding, exhaustion,* and *ragged.)* Tell them that the suffixes *-ing* and *-ion* change a verb to a noun and mean "act of." The noun *rag* becomes the adjective *ragged* thanks to the addition of the suffix *-ed.* Ask someone to find the definition of *troupe* in a dictionary. Have the student tell how to pronounce the word and then have him or her say what it means. What sorts of "troupes" have students heard about? What is the difference between *troupe* and *troop?*

Prereading Strategies

PICTURE WALK   As a prereading activity, students are asked to do a **picture walk** of *The Skirt.* Remind the class that on a picture walk, they should look at the title of the selection, all of the art, and any captions. Then, after thinking about what they've seen, they'll need to make some careful predictions about the selection. Remind the class that most readers do a before-reading picture walk without even realizing it. (How many times have students picked up a book or magazine and thumbed through it to look at the pictures?) Good readers know that the art can very often provide valuable clues about the content of the selection.

THINK-PAIR-AND-SHARE   As an alternate prereading activity, have students complete a **think-pair-and-share** that relates to the central conflict in Soto's story. Encourage students to listen carefully to each other's ideas about how to solve the problem of the lost article. If they disagree with a possible solution, have them say why. Ask each pair to report to the class on the decision their group made. Have students in the audience comment on each group's report.

Use the **Before You Read** blackline master on page 179 as support for this activity.

MY PURPOSE   As they read Soto's story, students will need to watch for details that reveal something about Miata's character. Have them think about why the skirt is so important to her, what the exact problem is, and how they think she should solve it.

II. READ

Response Strategy

FIRST READING Before students begin their first readings, remind them of the importance of **connecting** to what they read. Have students think about what they would do if they were in Miata's place. How would they feel? What would they say to their mother if they lost something of great importance? The personal connections students make to a text can help them feel more involved in a reading. In addition, they can help the reader think carefully about story elements such as character motivation, plot, and theme.

Comprehension Strategy

SECOND READING As they read Soto's story, students will need to think carefully about issues of character and plot. The **stop and think** questions scattered throughout the text will help them make inferential responses about these literary elements. In addition, the interrupter questions may assist students in considering the theme or underlying meaning of the writing.

For more help with **Comprehension,** assign the blackline master on page 180.

Discussion Questions

COMPREHENSION 1. What is Miata's main problem? *(She left her folklórico skirt on the school bus. She needs to wear it on Sunday.)*

2. Why is the skirt special to Miata? *(Her mother wore it when she was a girl growing up in Mexico. Also, Miata is excited about dancing in the folklórico.)*

CRITICAL THINKING 3. What advice would you give Miata? *(Ask students to fully explain their ideas and why they think their advice might work.)*

4. How does Miata feel about herself after she loses the skirt? *(Possible: She is upset with herself and seems a little disgusted as well. She seems like she's ready to make a change.)*

5. What do you learn about Miata from reading this story? *(Possible: She is conscientious, but forgetful. She knows that her forgetfulness causes trouble, but feels like there's nothing she can do about it.)*

Reread

THIRD READING On their third readings, students will need to watch for clues about Miata: what she's like, why she lost the skirt, and how she might solve the problem. Ask students to make predictions as they read. Judging from what they know about her, what will Miata do to make things right?

Word Work

WORD PARTS The Word Work lesson on page 114 offers students a lesson on **word parts** such as *auto-*. If you feel the activity will be challenging for some students, complete it as a class. Then have students do another web on their own using the word part *some-*. What words can students come up with?

For additional practice, see the **Word Work** blackline master on page 181.

III. GET READY TO WRITE

Prewriting Strategies

STORY CHART Students will complete a **story chart** on page 115 that will help them consider Miata's character and the main conflict in Soto's story. When they've finished the first chart, students will complete a second chart that explores a time they made a mistake.

At the end of the prewriting session, you might have students spend a few minutes thinking about a possible topic sentence for their paragraphs. Remind them of this formula:

subject + my thoughts and feelings about the subject = a good topic sentence

Have students use the **Get Ready to Write** blackline master on page 182.

IV. WRITE

Read aloud the directions on page 117. Students will write a **narrative paragraph** about a time they made a mistake. If necessary, review the characteristics of this type of writing. A narrative paragraph tells a story about an event in the writer's life. The events in a narrative paragraph are usually told in chronological (time) order.

After students have written a draft, have them think about the story they've told. Does it make sense? Is it interesting to read? Does the story have a beginning, a middle, and an end?

WRITING RUBRIC Use this rubric to help with a quick assessment of students' writing.

Do students' narrative paragraphs

• open with a topic sentence that names the mistake and how it made them feel?

• offer three or more details that tell what they did as a result of the mistake?

• close with a sentence that tells the outcome or how they felt once the event was over?

Grammar, Usage, and Mechanics

When students are ready to proofread, have them look at the **Writers' Checklist**. Review the rules for **capitalization:** the first word of every sentence is capitalized, as are important words in the title and the pronoun *I*. Ask students to correct this sentence:

<u>my</u> mother and <u>i</u> ran after the bus.

V. LOOK BACK

Finish by asking students to comment on their **enjoyment** of Soto's story. Would they be interested in reading more about Miata? Why or why not? Use the **Readers' Checklist** as a starting point for your discussion.

To test students' comprehension, use the **Lesson Test** blackline master on page 183.

Name _____

WORDS TO KNOW

Before Reading

DIRECTIONS Read this conversation. Write what you think the underlined words mean. Look for context clues.

"Miata, how could you lose your skirt? I am always scolding you for losing things."

"Mother, I ran after the bus and tried to pound on the rear door. My lungs burned with exhaustion," Miata exclaimed.

"What does your dance troupe say now that you have no skirt?" Mother asked.

"I could make a new one," Miata replied, "but it might look ragged because I can't sew well."

---

1. I think <u>scolding</u> means _____ .

2. I think <u>rear</u> means _____ .

3. I think <u>exhaustion</u> means _____ .

4. I think <u>troupe</u> means _____ .

5. I think <u>ragged</u> means _____ .

Practice

Use *scolding* in a sentence that shows you know what it means.

_____

_____

_____

Name _____

BEFORE YOU READ

Think-Pair-and-Share

DIRECTIONS Read the problem.

Read two possible solutions to this problem.

Suggest another solution that you like better.

Discuss your ideas with your reading group.

Problem	Solution

It's Friday. You've left something on the bus that you need for Sunday. What do you do?

1. Tell a family member and let him or her fix the mistake.

2. Call the school's transportation department and explain what happened.

3. _____
_____
_____

Name _____

COMPREHENSION

Character Map

DIRECTIONS Use this character map to tell about Miata.
Check for details in your book if you need to.

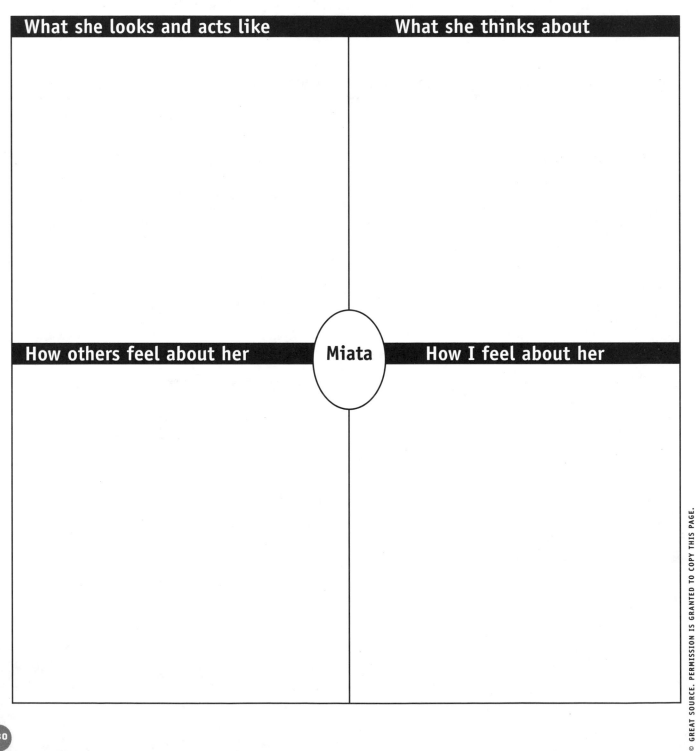

What she looks and acts like	What she thinks about

How others feel about her	Miata	How I feel about her

Name _____

WORD WORK

After Reading

DIRECTIONS Complete the web below by adding *some-* to the words in the box.

one	day	body	how	place	time

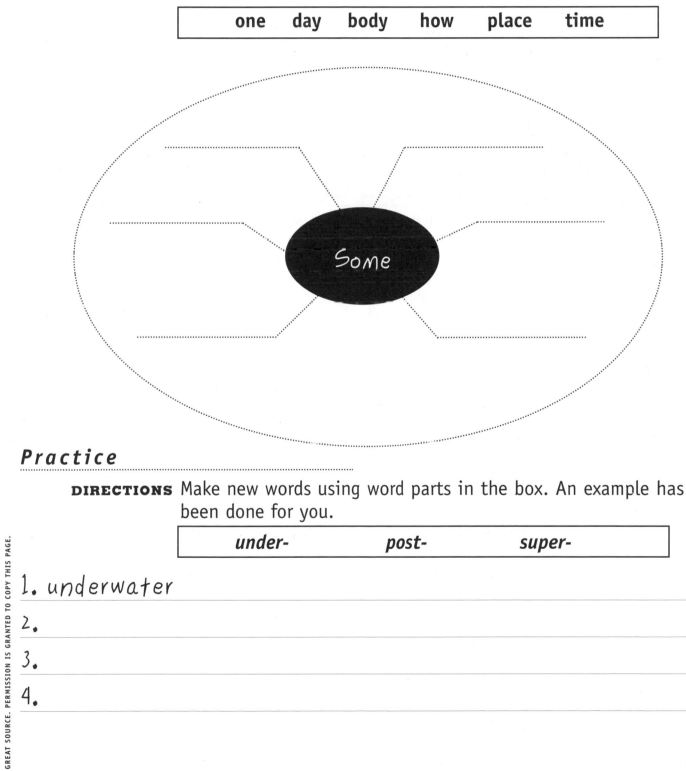

Some

Practice

DIRECTIONS Make new words using word parts in the box. An example has been done for you.

under-	*post-*	*super-*

1. underwater

2.

3.

4.

Name _____

GET READY TO WRITE

Writing a Narrative Paragraph

DIRECTIONS Follow these steps to write a narrative paragraph.

STEP 1 Write a topic sentence. Complete this sentence starter.

When I was _____ years old, I

_____ .

STEP 2 Organize details. Think of sensory words that can help your reader see, hear, and feel the event you describe.

When I made this mistake . . .
I saw . . .

I heard . . .

I felt . . .

STEP 3 Write your paragraph. Use notes from this page to help.

_____

_____

_____

_____

Name _____

LESSON TEST

Multiple-Choice

DIRECTIONS On the lines, write the letter of the best answer for each question.

_____ 1. What is Miata chasing at the beginning of the story?
A. her sister   C. the bus
B. a boy   D. a car

_____ 2. Miata needs the skirt for . . .
A. a special dance.   C. a play.
B. church.   D. to give to her mom.

_____ 3. Why is Miata always getting in trouble with her mother?
A. She is always late.   C. She argues with her.
B. She loses things.   D. She skips her homework.

_____ 4. How does Miata feel when she loses the skirt?
A. happy   C. relaxed
B. terrible   D. angry

_____ 5. Miata thinks she is a disappointment to her . . .
A. mother.   C. sister.
B. teacher.   D. friends.

Short Answer

What advice would you like to give Miata?

_____

_____

_____

Through Grandpa's Eyes

BACKGROUND

Patricia MacLachlan's *Through Grandpa's Eyes* tells the story of a gentle, observant boy named John who adores visiting his blind grandfather and watching the ways this plucky man "sees" and moves in the world. This award-winning book, which was first published in 1980, offers an engaging family story, as well as a fascinating glimpse of how the vision-impaired develop alternatives to sight. MacLachlan's musical tone and her flawless prose make this a book both children and adults can enjoy.

Patricia MacLachlan began writing at the age of thirty-five, after her three children were in school full time. She published her first work in 1977. Eight years later, she wrote what one critic calls "the simplest of love stories expressed in the simplest of prose." The best-selling *Sarah, Plain and Tall* earned MacLachlan a Newbery Medal a year later. It has since become a children's classic.

BIBLIOGRAPHY Check the school library for additional books by Patricia MacLachlan. Choose one of her more challenging books to read aloud to your students or recommend one of these titles for them to read on their own:

(Lexile 560)   (Lexile 500)   (Lexile 620)

How to Introduce the Reading

Open the lesson by reading aloud the introductory paragraph on page 119. Have students tell what they do to find their way in a completely dark room. What senses do they rely on when they can't use their sense of sight? Help students understand that all five senses can be used to "see." Your discussion will help students appreciate Grandpa and the delight he takes in using his senses.

Other Reading

Introduce students to authors they might like to read in their spare time. These three authors are favorites of children at a reading level comparable to that of *Through Grandpa's Eyes* (Lexile 560)

DREAM WOLF by Paul Goble

JUST LIKE EVERYONE ELSE by Eve Bunting

TOUCHDOWN FOR TOMMY by Matt Christopher

(Lexile 550)   (Lexile 560)   (Lexile 570)

Through Grandpa's Eyes

(STUDENT PAGES 119-130)

Skills and Strategies Overview

PREREADING	prediction
READING LEVEL	Lexile 560
RESPONSE	draw
VOCABULARY	✦ carved ✦ blind ✦ burrow ✦ banister ✦ protest
COMPREHENSION	retell
WORD WORK	multi-syllable words
PREWRITING	word web
WRITING	descriptive paragraph / homophones
ASSESSMENT	understanding

OTHER RESOURCES

The first **four** pages of this teacher's lesson describe Parts I–V of the lesson. Also included are these **six** blackline masters. Use them to reinforce key elements of the lesson.

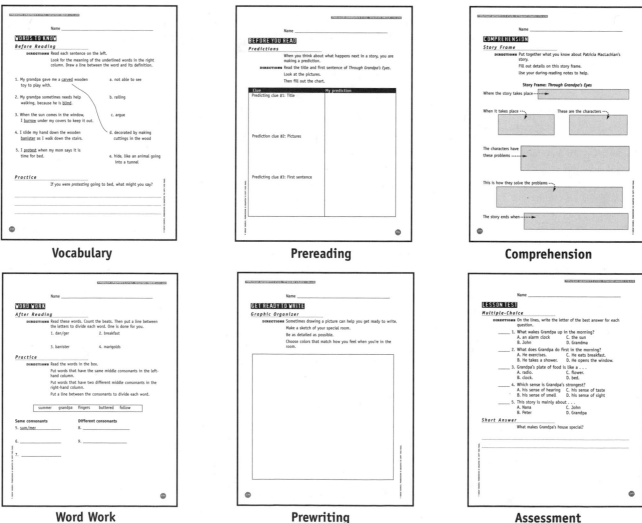

Vocabulary	Prereading	Comprehension
Word Work	**Prewriting**	**Assessment**

BEFORE YOU READ

Continue your discussion of using the other four senses to compensate when a fifth sense is not available (e.g., when in a dark room, when wearing headphones, and so on). Also have students say which sense they think they rely on the most, and then rank the other senses by use. Many will say that they rely on sight first, hearing next, then touch, taste, and smell. Have them think of scenarios in which one sense is more important than the others (for example, at dinner the sense of taste is most important, while in a car, the sense of sight is most important). When you've finished your discussion, turn students' attention to the prereading activity, a **prediction**. (Refer to the Strategy Handbook, page 49, for more help.)

Motivation Strategy

CONNECTING WITH STUDENTS Ask students to tell about friends or relatives who are vision- or hearing-impaired. How does this impairment affect their day-to-day life? Have students share stories that relate to the topic and theme of MacLachlan's story. Help them make a strong connection to the text even before they begin reading.

Words to Know

CONTEXT CLUES Use the **Words to Know** blackline master on page 190 as a way to troubleshoot vocabulary problems. After working through the page, you might decide to teach a short vocabulary lesson on using **context clues.**

Help students use context clues as they read to figure out the meanings of difficult words, especially the key vocabulary for this lesson: *carved, blind, burrow, banister,* and *protest.* Although the footnotes define these words, students should get into the habit of defining in context. This makes reading faster and more enjoyable. Model using context and then checking your ideas against the footnote: "I don't know the word *banister.* I see, however, that it has something to do with a staircase and that you can run your hand along it while going down the stairs. I hold onto the railing when I walk down stairs. Could *banister* be the same thing as 'railing'? I'll check the footnote to see if my prediction is correct."

Prereading Strategies

ANTICIPATION GUIDE As a prereading activity, students will complete an **anticipation guide.** Read aloud the four quotations on page 120 of the student book. Explain that you'd like students to work together to figure out the proper order of these statements. This brief activity introduces students to the plot of MacLachlan's story.

PREDICTION As a further prereading activity, ask students to make **predictions** about the reading. Remind the class that they can use the title, art, and first sentence of the work to help them form their predictions. Give students a moment or two to look at these elements.

Then, have them fill out the prediction organizer on the **Before You Read** blackline master on page 191.

MY PURPOSE Read aloud students' purpose for reading *Through Grandpa's Eyes*: Find out why Grandpa and his house are so special. Point out that the purpose for reading is twofold. It may help to list the two parts of the purpose statement on the board:

1. Find out about Grandpa.

2. Find out why John, the narrator, thinks a visit to Grandpa's house is so special.

II. READ

Response Strategy

FIRST READING An excellent option is to have students stay with their reading partners and do a shared reading of *Through Grandpa's Eyes*. Invite partners to read one page at a time, trading jobs at the end of every page. Students who are reading aloud should read with expression. Students who are listening should make a concerted effort to visualize the people and places the reader tells about. Each time they "see" something new, they should **draw** it in the Response Notes. Have pairs share their sketches when they've finished reading.

Comprehension Strategy

SECOND READING Be sure students understand that as they are reading MacLachlan's story, they will need to stop occasionally in order to **retell** the events described. Retelling a story can help readers make connections between the separate events of the plot. Retelling can also help readers clarify in their own minds exactly what the author or narrator is saying.

For more help with **Comprehension,** assign the blackline master on page 192.

Discussion Questions

COMPREHENSION 1. Who is the narrator of the story? *(John, the grandson)*

2. What comment does the narrator make about Peter and Maggie's houses? *(He likes these two houses, but he likes his grandfather's house better.)*

CRITICAL THINKING 3. What inferences can you make about John? *(Possible: He is loyal, loving, and observant.)*

4. What inferences can you make about Grandpa? *(Possible: He is smart, loving, and full of optimism. He takes pleasure in his life and enjoys having his grandson visit.)*

5. What is the significance of the title? *(Encourage students to discuss the play on words MacLachlan creates with her title. What does it mean to "see through Grandpa's eyes"?)*

Reread

THIRD READING The directions on page 125 ask students to reread MacLachlan's story, keeping a close eye on details that help them understand Grandpa and his house. To help reinforce the assignment, have students return to their reading purpose and read it one more time. On their final reading, students should ask themselves: "Have I met my reading purpose? Can I knowledgeably discuss the details of the story?"

Word Work

MULTI-SYLLABLE WORDS The Word Work lesson on page 126 may be a review for some students and fresh material for others. Show students how to clap the syllables of words, and then practice doing so with several **multi-syllable words.** Have students clap along with you until you are sure they can really "hear" how a word breaks.

For additional practice, see the **Word Work** blackline master on page 193.

III. GET READY TO WRITE

Prewriting Strategies

WEB To begin, students will complete a **web** that explores their five senses and their feelings about a special room in their house or school. Remind students that good writers try to make their descriptions as fresh and interesting as possible. They write words that can help their readers see, hear, smell, taste, and touch the thing they are describing. The web on page 127 offers students the chance to think about good, strong sensory words that they can use in their own writing.

Have students use the **Get Ready to Write** blackline master on page 194.

IV. WRITE

Be sure students understand that their assignment is to write a **descriptive paragraph** about their special place. Students should offer physical descriptions as well as information about how the room makes them feel. Stress the importance of creating a cohesive paragraph, with a beginning, a middle, and an end. The topic sentence belongs in the opening. Specific facts and details are discussed in the body. In the closing, students should reiterate how the place makes them feel and why they love it.

When students have finished drafting, have them double-check the structure of their paragraphs. Point out that rewriting is an important step in the writing process. Even the best writers do some rewriting before they turn over a final copy.

WRITING RUBRIC Use this rubric to help with a quick assessment of students' writing.

Do students' descriptive paragraphs

• open with a topic sentence that states the subject and focus of the paragraph?

• include three or more sensory details about their special place?

• close with a sentence that tells how the place makes the writer feel and why he or she loves it?

Grammar, Usage, and Mechanics

When students are ready to edit their work, refer them to the **Writers' Checklist.** Read aloud the question on the checklist and teach a review lesson on **homophones** if you think students need it.

V. LOOK BACK

Discuss with students their **understanding** of MacLachlan's story. Point out the **Readers' Checklist.** If students had trouble reading this selection, find out why. Use what you learn to help you plan strategies for future reading.

To test students' comprehension, use the **Lesson Test** blackline master on page 195.

Name _____

WORDS TO KNOW

Before Reading

DIRECTIONS Read each sentence in the left column.

Look for the meaning of the underlined words in the right column. Draw a line between the word and its definition.

1. My grandpa gave me a <u>carved</u> wooden toy to play with.

2. My grandpa sometimes needs help walking, because he is <u>blind</u>.

3. When the sun comes in the window, I <u>burrow</u> under my covers to keep it out.

4. I slide my hand down the wooden <u>banister</u> as I walk down the stairs.

5. I <u>protest</u> when my mom says it is time for bed.

a. not able to see

b. railing

c. argue

d. decorated by making cuttings in the wood

e. hide, like an animal going into a tunnel

Practice

If you were *protesting* going to bed, what might you say?

_____

_____

_____

Name _____

BEFORE YOU READ

Predictions

When you think about what happens next in a story, you are making a prediction.

DIRECTIONS Read the title and first sentence of *Through Grandpa's Eyes*.

Look at the pictures.

Then fill out the chart.

Clue	My prediction
Prediction Clue #1: Title	
Prediction Clue #2: Pictures	
Prediction Clue #3: First sentence	

Name _____

COMPREHENSION

Story Frame

DIRECTIONS Put together what you know about Patricia MacLachlan's story.

Fill out details on this story frame.

Use your during-reading notes to help.

Story Frame: *Through Grandpa's Eyes*

Where the story takes place • • • • • • ▶ [ ]

When it takes place • • • ▼ [ ]

These are the characters • • • ▼ [ ]

The characters have these problems • • • • • • ▶ [ ]

This is how they solve the problems • • • ▼ [ ]

The story ends when • • • • • • ▶ [ ]

Name _____

WORD WORK

After Reading

DIRECTIONS Read these words. Count the beats. Then put a line between the letters to divide each word. One is done for you.

1. dan/ger

2. breakfast

3. banister

4. marigolds

Practice

DIRECTIONS Read the words in the box.

Put words that have the same middle consonants in the left-hand column.

Put words that have two different middle consonants in the right-hand column.

Put a line between the consonants to divide each word.

| summer | grandpa | fingers | buttered | follow |

Same consonants

5. <u>sum/mer</u>

6. _____

7. _____

Different consonants

8. _____

9. _____

Name _____

GET READY TO WRITE

Graphic Organizer

DIRECTIONS Sometimes drawing a picture can help you get ready to write.

Make a sketch of your special room.

Be as detailed as possible.

Choose colors that match how you feel when you're in the room.

Name _____

LESSON TEST

Multiple-Choice

DIRECTIONS On the lines, write the letter of the best answer for each question.

_____ 1. What wakes Grandpa up in the morning?
A. an alarm clock   C. the sun
B. John   D. Grandma

_____ 2. What does Grandpa do first in the morning?
A. He exercises.   C. He eats breakfast.
B. He takes a shower.   D. He opens the window.

_____ 3. Grandpa's plate of food is like a . . .
A. radio.   C. flower.
B. clock.   D. bed.

_____ 4. Which sense is Grandpa's strongest?
A. his sense of hearing   C. his sense of taste
B. his sense of smell   D. his sense of sight

_____ 5. This story is mainly about . . .
A. Nana.   C. John.
B. Peter.   D. Grandpa.

Short Answer

What makes Grandpa's house special?

_____

_____

Me and My Shadow

BACKGROUND

In Arthur Dorros's *Me and My Shadow,* a group of children explain—in clear, straightforward language—the origins of shadows. In addition, they offer some basic information about day and night and the phases of the moon. Scattered throughout the text are simple activities that offer readers the chance to experiment a bit with light, shading, and shadows. Students who have ever wondered where shadows come from and how they are formed should find this an interesting and informative book. Your low-level readers will respond well to the kid-friendly style Dorros uses throughout.

Arthur Dorros is an award-winning author who has traveled much of the world in search of ideas for his writing. One of his more recent books, *Abuela,* enjoys a wide audience of children and adults alike. Dorros has written and illustrated other fiction and nonfiction books as well, including the popular *Radio Man.*

BIBLIOGRAPHY Students might enjoy reading another book by Arthur Dorros. Have them choose one of these titles. All three have a reading level close to that of *Me and My Shadow* (Lexile 560):

(Lexile 540)

(Lexile 550)

(Lexile 560)

How to Introduce the Reading

Have students read the introduction to the lesson on page 131. Then ask them to write or respond out loud to the questions on the page: "Was there a moon last night?" "What did it look like?" "What will it look like tomorrow?" Ask students to tell about full moons and "sliver" moons. Why does the moon appear to change size? Use your discussion to assess prior knowledge of the topic of the reading. If you feel students need more information, search for a video or book that explains the moon and its phases.

Other Reading

Encourage students to take an interest in reading nonfiction, especially books that relate to science. These three time-tested titles have proved popular in classrooms across the country:

(Lexile 560)   (Lexile 570)   (Lexile 570)

Me and My Shadow

Skills and Strategies Overview

PREREADING	anticipation guide
READING LEVEL	Lexile 560
RESPONSE	question
VOCABULARY	✧shadow ✧gigantic ✧shine ✧circles ✧sliver
COMPREHENSION	organize
WORD WORK	compound words
PREWRITING	main idea and supporting details
WRITING	poem / capitalization
ASSESSMENT	ease

OTHER RESOURCES

The first **four** pages of this teacher's lesson describe Parts I–V of the lesson. Also included are these **six** blackline masters. Use them to reinforce key elements of the lesson.

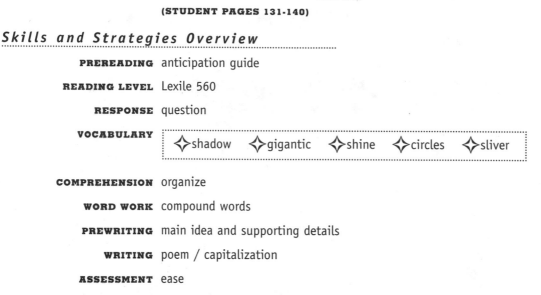

Vocabulary

Prereading

Comprehension

Word Work

Prewriting

Assessment

I. BEFORE YOU READ

Continue your discussion of the moon. Have students name their favorite books about the moon or movies they've seen in which phases of the moon play an important role. When you feel they are ready, ask students to work on the prereading activity, an **anticipation guide.** (Refer to the Strategy Handbook, page 48, for more help.)

Motivation Strategies

MOTIVATING STUDENTS Borrow a copy of *Me and My Shadow* from the library and ask students to do one of the shadow activities Dorros describes. Have them bring from home the necessary materials and spend half a class period making shadows, re-creating the moon with lights, and so on. These moon activities can be an interesting warm-up to the topic of the reading. They may also help to set at ease those students who are intimidated at the thought of reading nonfiction.

CONNECTING WITH STUDENTS Ask students to tell about a time they took a moonlit walk or sailed at night or did something else that relates to the moon. What words would they use to describe how the moon looked that night? Make a list of words on the board. Students may want to use some of these words later, when it comes time to write their poems.

Words to Know

CONTEXT CLUES Use the **Words to Know** blackline master on page 202 as a way to troubleshoot vocabulary problems. After working through the page, you might decide to teach a short vocabulary lesson on using **context clues.**

Context clues can be particularly helpful when reading a selection that includes scientific words or other specialized vocabulary. Although many of the words in Dorros's article are footnoted at the bottom of the page, students should try defining in context so that there's no need to interrupt the rhythm of their reading. Have students watch for key vocabulary words for this lesson: *shadow, gigantic, shine, circles,* and *sliver.* Ask them to define these words in context if possible and then make a note of the definitions of the words in the Response Notes.

Prereading Strategies

ANTICIPATION GUIDE As a prereading activity, students will complete an **anticipation guide.** Read aloud the four statements on page 132 of the student book. Point out the "Before" column and ask students to mark whether they agree or disagree with the statements. Then call on volunteers to explain their answers. If they disagreed with a statement, find out why. This quick oral activity will help you assess the level of students' prior knowledge about the topic. If you think they could use more information, offer additional background about the selection or the topic of shadows.

SKETCH As an additional prereading activity, have students keep a moon journal over the course of two or more weeks. Ask them to make a **sketch** of the moon each night and then write a sentence describing what the moon looks like (or why they are unable to see it on a particular night).

Use the **Before You Read** blackline master on page 203 to support this activity.

MY PURPOSE Students' purpose for reading *Me and My Shadow* is twofold. First, they'll read to figure out what shadows are. They'll also read to figure out what shadows have to do with the moon. If you prefer, have students concentrate on the first purpose on the first reading, and the second purpose as they are rereading.

II. READ

Response Strategy

FIRST READING After giving the reading assignment, discuss the strategy of **questioning** and the purpose it serves. Explain to the class that as they read, questions will naturally occur to them. An excellent strategy they can use to improve their reading skills is to note questions *as they come up,* instead of waiting until they've finished reading. Each time they think of a question, have them note it in the Response Notes, even if they think it will be answered later. Questions that remain unanswered at the end should be addressed by the group.

Comprehension Strategy

SECOND READING As they're reading Dorros's work, students will stop twice to **organize** what they've learned. In each case, students should say what they've learned from the reading. Students will need to refer to these notes later, when they're thinking about whether or not they've met their reading purpose.

For more help with **Comprehension,** assign the blackline master on page 204.

Discussion Questions

COMPREHENSION 1. In what ways is the earth like a big ball? *(It is round, and it spins and turns smoothly.)*

2. What happens to the side of the moon that is not facing the sun? *(It is shadowed.)*

CRITICAL THINKING 3. How do shadows change the appearance of the moon? *(They block a part of the moon from our vision. When the moon is a sliver, what we're seeing is a large part of the moon's shadow and just a tiny part of the moon itself.)*

4. What would you say is the main idea of Dorros's article? *(Possible: Shadows create night and day on earth, and light and darkness on the moon.)*

Reread

THIRD READING Before students return to the selection for an additional reading, have them mark the "After" column of the Anticipation Guide on page 132. This quick activity will show students how much they learned from their initial reading of Dorros's work. Then ask them to go back to the first page of the selection and begin rereading. Remind them of their reading purpose and have them concentrate on finding important details about shadows and their effect on the moon. Any additional notes they make about the topic will come in handy when it comes time to create their poems.

Word Work

COMPOUND WORDS The Word Work lesson offers a review of **compound words** and how they are formed. Give students a set of compounds and have them divide the words. Help them commit to memory the spelling of the longer words, such as *homework, sunrise, afternoon, maybe, underground, daytime, snowstorm, without,* and *folklore.*

For additional practice, see the **Word Work** blackline master on page 205.

III. GET READY TO WRITE

Prewriting Strategies

MAIN IDEA AND SUPPORTING DETAILS Students should know that all nonfiction writing has a **main idea.** The main idea is the central, or most important, idea. It is like the topic sentence of a paragraph, except that the main idea relates to the piece as a whole, instead of just a small part. Before they begin, work with students to come up with a main idea statement for the Dorros selection. Then have them turn to the prewriting diagram on page 137 to see if they understand this main idea statement. Finish the activity by having students come up with three additional **details** from the reading that support the main idea on the page.

Have students use the **Get Ready to Write** blackline master on page 206.

IV. WRITE

Read aloud the directions on page 139. Students should write a **poem** about shadows that incorporates some of the sensory words they came up with at the prewriting stage. Offer students the option of using the poem starters on page 139 or writing a poem completely on their own. If students seem unsure of how to begin, have them thumb through their *Sourcebook* and find poems they can read as examples. Students should feel free to model their style on one of these poets' styles.

WRITING RUBRIC Use this rubric to help with a quick assessment of students' writing.

Do the students' poems

• explore the subject of shadows?

• contain words that appeal to the five senses?

• follow proper poetic form: appropriate line breaks, first word of each line capitalized?

Grammar, Usage, and Mechanics

Refer the class to the **Writers' Checklist** and then teach a brief lesson on **capitalization** of important words in a title. Explain that words such as *and, or, the,* and *if* are not capitalized unless they are the first word of the title.

V. LOOK BACK

Point out the **Readers' Checklist** at the bottom of page 140. Discuss the **ease** or difficulty with which students read Dorros's article. Some might say the article was a challenge. If this is the case, ask them to explain what was hard. Was it the language, the subject matter, or something else?

To test students' comprehension, use the **Lesson Test** blackline master on page 207.

Name _____

WORDS TO KNOW

Before Reading

DIRECTIONS Look at the sentences under the picture. Use words from the word box to complete each sentence. Each word will be used only once.

shadow	gigantic	shine	circles	sliver

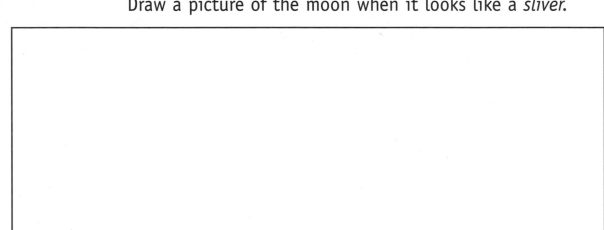

1. If you _____ a light on the earth or moon, a _____ is created.

2. A _____ shadow makes our days and nights.

3. When we can see a lot of the moon's shadow, the moon looks like a _____.

4. The earth _____ the sun.

Practice

Draw a picture of the moon when it looks like a *sliver*.

Name _____

BEFORE YOU READ

Sketch

DIRECTIONS Look at the moon every night for _____ nights.

Draw pictures of what you see.

Write words that describe what you have observed.

MY MOON JOURNAL

Date_____	Date_____	Date_____	Date_____
Date_____	Date_____	Date_____	Date_____
Date_____	Date_____	Date_____	Date_____

Name _____

COMPREHENSION
Chart

DIRECTIONS Write details of what you've learned on the chart.

Check your book if you need help.

Then answer a question about the article.

I've learned this about Earth . . .	I've learned this about the moon . . .	I've learned this about shadows . . .
	The moon circles the earth.	

What would you say is the main idea of *Me and My Shadow*?

_____

_____

_____

Name _____

WORD WORK

After Reading

DIRECTIONS Read the small words in the box. Put the words together to form compound words. Make as many compound words as you can.

snow	table	out	sea	food
see	well	field	over	flake
top	come	in	rain	fall

My Compound Words

1. _____   2. _____

3. _____   4. _____

5. _____   6. _____

7. _____   8. _____

9. _____   10. _____

Practice

DIRECTIONS Read these compound words. Put a line between the two small words. One has been done for you.

11. every/body

12. buttermilk

13. background

14. somehow

Name _____

GET READY TO WRITE

Writing a Poem

DIRECTIONS In the box, write some "shadow" words that rhyme.

Word Pairs That Rhyme

```
light / bright                    _____
_____                 _____
_____                 _____
```

DIRECTIONS Now write a title for your poem.

Then write the first two lines of your poem.

The last word of line 2 should rhyme with the last word of line 1.

Poem title: _____

line 1 _____

line 2 _____

Name _____

LESSON TEST

Multiple-Choice

DIRECTIONS On the lines, write the letter of the best answer for each question.

_____ 1. How does the earth move?
A. It spins.   C. It moves back and forth.
B. It doesn't move.   D. It moves up and down.

_____ 2. What happens when our part of the earth is in shadow?
A. We have rain.   C. We have night.
B. We have winter.   D. We have daytime.

_____ 3. What circles around the earth?
A. the other planets   C. the sun
B. the moon   D. nothing

_____ 4. Which moon shape shows the biggest shadow?
A. full moon   C. sliver moon
B. half moon   D. tiny moon

_____ 5. Another good title for this article might be . . .
A. *Shadows Are Funny*   C. *The Earth, Moon, and Shadows*
B. *Facts About the Moon*   D. *The Earth Rotates*

Short Answer

Why does the moon appear to change shape?

_____

_____

_____

Follow That Trash!

BACKGROUND

Francine Jacobs's *Follow That Trash!* is a young reader's introduction to recycling: how it works and why it is important. In her book, Jacobs presents the argument that recycling is the most viable solution to this country's trash problems. To support her thesis, Jacobs offers interesting trash facts and details about how recycling reduces the volume of trash in landfills.

In the opening of her book, Jacobs explores various trash disposal methods, including the use of landfills and burning. She points out the many problems associated with these methods and then explains to her readers that recycling is the best way to rid ourselves of the problem of too much trash. Jacobs's conversational writing style and simple language create a book about garbage and recycling that is entertaining, accessible, and inspiring to young people. Rather than simply complaining about the problem, Jacobs offers some very real solutions that most young children will embrace.

BIBLIOGRAPHY Offer additional background on the topic of garbage and recycling by having volunteers read and report on one of these books. All three have a Lexile level similar to that of *Follow That Trash!* (Lexile 570):

(Lexile 520)

(Lexile 560)

(Lexile 530)

How to Introduce the Reading

Before you begin the lesson, ask a group of students to keep a week-long record of the amount of trash thrown away in the lunchroom each day. If your lunchroom has a recycling program, have one group note what is recycled, while another group notes what is thrown away. Ask students to report their findings to the class. Is your school guilty of contributing to the mountain of trash that Francine Jacobs describes?

Other Reading

Ask students who seem intimidated by nonfiction to read and report on a high-interest nonfiction book. These titles might capture the interest of even your most reluctant readers:

(Lexile 580)   (Lexile 580)   (Lexile 580)

Follow That Trash!

(STUDENT PAGES 141-150)

Skills and Strategies Overview

PREREADING	think-pair-and-share
READING LEVEL	Lexile 570
RESPONSE	make clear
VOCABULARY	◇leak ◇poisons ◇pollute ◇incinerators ◇ashes
COMPREHENSION	double-entry journal
WORD WORK	suffixes with words that end in *y*
PREWRITING	opinion and supporting details
WRITING	paragraph of opinion / capitalization
ASSESSMENT	meaning

OTHER RESOURCES

The first **four** pages of this teacher's lesson describe Parts I–V of the lesson. Also included are these **six** blackline masters. Use them to reinforce key elements of the lesson.

Vocabulary

Prereading

Comprehension

Word Work

Prewriting

Assessment

BEFORE YOU READ

Read through the introduction on page 141 with students. Ask students to tell about recycling programs in their communities. What items are collected for recycling? What items must be thrown in the trash? Where does the trash then go? Help students make a connection to the topic of the article before they begin reading. Then assign the prereading activity, a **think-pair-and-share**. (Refer to the Strategy Handbook, page 50, for more help.)

Motivation Strategies

MOTIVATING STUDENTS   Invite someone from your community in to speak about trash collecting and recycling in your town or city. Ask a government or trash collection official or a parent who has an aggressive recycling program in his or her office to discuss the importance of recycling with your class. After your visitor leaves, encourage students to discuss what they've learned and say whether or not they agree with the speaker's ideas.

CONNECTING WITH STUDENTS   Ask students to tell about recycled items they use often. Some might know about playground equipment that is recycled from old tires, or paper products used at home that are recycled from old plastics or newspapers. Also have them discuss any "homemade" recycling projects, such as turning an old can into a pencil holder or a discarded box into a mini-storage shed.

Words to Know

SYNONYMS   Use the **Words to Know** blackline master on page 214 as a way to troubleshoot vocabulary problems. After working through the page, you might decide to teach a short vocabulary lesson on **synonyms.**

To begin, show students the five key vocabulary words in *Follow That Trash!*: *leak, poisons, pollute, incinerators,* and *ashes.* Ask students to say which words they've heard before, and in what context. Create a synonym chart on the board and ask students to suggest synonyms for each of the words. As you know, learning the synonym for a word can be a shortcut to learning the word's full definition. Your chart might look something like this:

Word	Where I've heard it before	Synonym
ashes	My mom talks about ashes in the fireplace.	soot

Prereading Strategies

THINK-PAIR-AND-SHARE   The **think-pair-and-share** on page 142 should be fun for students. Most of them will have had some exposure to this topic in school, which means that they should be able to make some educated true/false predictions. Encourage students to discuss or debate their answers with their reading partners. Explain that there are no wrong answers at this point, but that you'd like them to be able to tell why they made the choices they did.

GRAPHIC ORGANIZER   Ask students to keep a running record on a **graphic organizer** of the amount of after-lunch trash students and teachers throw away and recycle. At the end of the week, students should be able to form an opinion about their school's recycling habits.

Use the **Before You Read** blackline master on page 215 to support this activity.

MY PURPOSE   Read aloud the purpose statement on page 142. As they're reading, students will look for information about what happens to trash after it is thrown away.

II. READ

Response Strategy

FIRST READING Before students begin their first readings, explain the response strategy of **making things clear.** Students will mark important facts and details by underlining or highlighting, and then clarify what the facts and details mean in the Response Notes. Point out the sample response on page 143 and help students understand that this is an example of a comment one reader made to clarify what the author is saying.

Comprehension Strategy

SECOND READING As they are reading Jacobs's work, students should think carefully about the connections they can make to the activities described. To help, have students stop and reflect on what they're reading using the **double-entry journals** that are scattered throughout the text. Point out the first journal entry on page 144. Explain that students need to read the quote in the left-hand column and then respond to it in the right-hand column. Emphasize that their responses should be in the form of their thoughts and feelings.

For more help with **Comprehension,** assign the blackline master on page 216.

Discussion Questions

COMPREHENSION 1. How much trash do Americans throw away each year? *(180 million tons)*

2. What are some of the problems with landfills and incinerators? *(Landfills can be ugly, and they fill up rapidly. Incinerating sometimes results in poisonous smoke.)*

CRITICAL THINKING 3. What is Jacobs's main idea? *(Possible: Recycling can solve our trash problems.)*

4. Do you agree with her main idea? Explain why or why not. *(Answers will vary. Have students support their opinions with evidence from the text or their own lives.)*

5. Why do you think garbage is such a problem in the U.S.? *(Possible: The country is highly populated, which means a lot of trash. Plus, some Americans can be wasteful and indifferent to environmental concerns.)*

Reread

THIRD READING The directions on page 145 request that students reread the article with an eye to specific details about what happens to garbage after it is thrown out. Have students make additional comments of clarification in the Response Notes as they reread. They'll want to return to these comments later as they write their paragraphs of opinion.

Word Work

SUFFIXES The Word Work lesson on page 146 offers practice adding **suffixes** to words that end in a consonant plus a *y*. Remind students that the *y* in these words must be changed to an *i* before adding a suffix that starts with a vowel (e.g., *-ed, -es,* and *-est*).

For additional practice, see the **Word Work** blackline master on page 217.

III. GET READY TO WRITE

Prewriting Strategies

OPINION AND SUPPORTING DETAILS Students' writing assignment in **Part IV** is to write a paragraph of opinion. To help them get started, model how to find **support** for an **opinion**. Ask students to turn to the organizer on page 147 and tell them: "I need to find support for the opinion that it's important to recycle our trash. To find my support, I'll go back to the text and look for places that Jacobs discusses the trash problem in the U.S. The first detail I find is in the opening of the article. I see that Americans throw away 180 million tons of trash a year. That seems like a problem to me! I'll write that as my first supporting detail. I can rephrase what Jacobs says or quote her directly using quotation marks."

Have students use the **Get Ready to Write** blackline master on page 218.

IV. WRITE

Read aloud the directions on page 149. Students are asked to write a **paragraph of opinion.** If you feel students would benefit, review the characteristics of this type of writing. Explain that a paragraph of opinion states an opinion about something. Supporting details are used to prove that the opinion is correct.

Students should open their paragraphs with a strong opinion statement. (Have them use the one in the book or write one of their own.) Next, they will offer three to four details that support the opinion. The closing sentence should be a restatement of the opinion statement.

WRITING RUBRIC Use this rubric to help with a quick assessment of students' writing.

Do students' opinion paragraphs

• open with a clearly worded opinion statement?

• explain why they feel this way?

• use details from the reading and their own lives as support for the opinion?

Grammar, Usage, and Mechanics

When students are ready to edit their work, refer them to the **Writers' Checklist.** Teach a brief lesson on **capitalization** of geographical names.

V. LOOK BACK

Ask students to explain what *Follow That Trash!* **meant** to them personally. (Have them use the **Readers' Checklist** as a starting point for discussion.) Explain that it's always important to stop and think about what a reading taught you or made you think about.

To test students' comprehension, use the **Lesson Test** blackline master on page 219.

Name _____

WORDS TO KNOW

Before Reading

DIRECTIONS Read each sentence.

Tell what you think the underlined words mean.

If you don't know, make a prediction. Use the rest of the sentence to help you.

1. There was a <u>leak</u> in the milk carton, so milk spilled all over the floor.

I think leak means _____ .

2. There are <u>poisons</u> in the water that can make people sick.

I think poisons means _____ .

3. Garbage can <u>pollute</u> our water and air.

I think pollute means _____ .

4. The <u>incinerators</u> burn the trash and make <u>ashes</u>.

I think incinerators means _____ .

I think ashes means _____ .

Practice

Use the word *pollute* in a sentence. Your sentence should help readers understand what *pollute* means.

_____

_____

214

Name _____

BEFORE YOU READ

Graphic Organizer

DIRECTIONS Make a record of your school's lunchroom trash for one week. Watch what students and teachers throw away and recycle. Then form an opinion about your school's recycling habits.

Day	Items thrown in the garbage	Items recycled
Monday		
Tuesday		
Wednesday		
Thursday		
Friday		

(circle one)

My school recycles   not at all   some   a lot

Name _____

COMPREHENSION

Word Bank

Transitional words and phrases help readers move along from one sentence to the next in a piece of writing.

DIRECTIONS With a partner, make a list of transition words and phrases that you can use when writing a paragraph of opinion.

Write your words in the bank. Try to think of at least 10.

Word Bank

1. First,
2. To begin with,
3.
4.
5.
6.
7.
8.
9.
10.

Name _____

WORD WORK

After Reading

DIRECTIONS Add suffixes to these words to make new words. Write the new words on the lines.

1. carry + -ing = _____

2. scary + -est = _____

3. tiny + -er = _____

4. worry + -er = _____

5. happy + -est = _____

6. vary + -ing = _____

Practice

DIRECTIONS Circle the words in the box that end with a consonant and a *y*. Then add a suffix of your choice to each word.

dirty	joy	likely	city	try

7. _____

8. _____

9. _____

10. _____

Name _____

GET READY TO WRITE

Writing a Paragraph of Opinion

You can support an opinion with details from a book or from your own life.

DIRECTIONS Read the boxed opinion statement.

Fill in details from your own life in the boxes below.

Then use this organizer and the one on page 148 to help you write your paragraph of opinion.

Opinion Statement: It's important to recycle our trash.

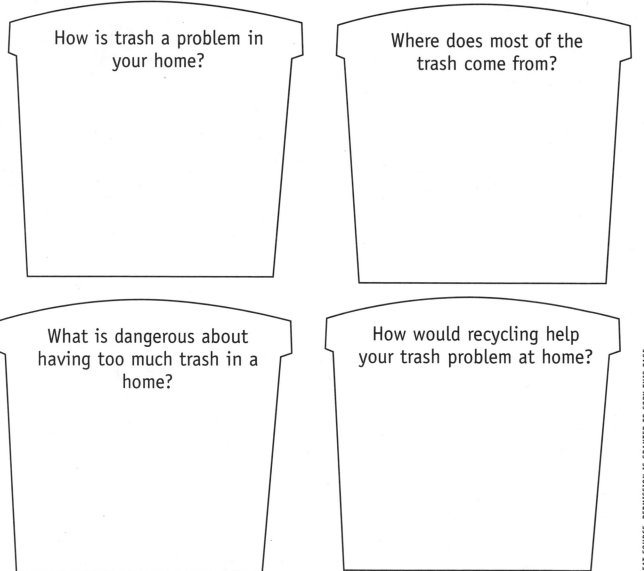

How is trash a problem in your home?

Where does most of the trash come from?

What is dangerous about having too much trash in a home?

How would recycling help your trash problem at home?

Name _____

LESSON TEST

Multiple-Choice

DIRECTIONS On the lines, write the letter of the best answer for each question.

_____ 1. How much trash do Americans throw away each day?
   A. 180 pounds   C. 180 tons
   B. 4 pounds   D. 4 tons

_____ 2. Most of our trash gets buried in . . .
   A. a garbage truck.   C. the ocean.
   B. a desert.   D. a landfill.

_____ 3. What can happen when you burn garbage?
   A. There are soot   C. The air becomes polluted.
      and ashes.
   B. There is smoke.   D. All of these answers

_____ 4. Jacobs says the best way to get rid of garbage is to . . .
   A. burn it.   C. recycle it.
   B. ignore it.   D. bury it.

_____ 5. Trash is a problem because . . .
   A. it can be poisonous.   C. there is not enough space
                               for it.
   B. it can smell bad.   D. All of these answers

Short Answer

What can *you* do to help with the trash problem?

_____

_____

Otherwise Known as Sheila the Great

BACKGROUND

Sheila Tubman, the ten-year-old protagonist of *Otherwise Known as Sheila the Great,* often feels like she has a split personality. Sometimes she is outgoing, witty, and totally self-confident. Other times, she's afraid of the dark, spiders, dogs, and deep water. When her family takes a summer home in Tarrytown, New York, Sheila must confront some of her fears and work to show others her best side. Anxious to make friends and impress the kids of Tarrytown, Sheila makes some major mistakes before finding the right path.

Like all of Blume's books, *Otherwise Known as Sheila the Great* is as humorous as it is poignant. Thanks to Blume's confidential, kid-friendly writing style, readers can't help but cringe when Sheila fails and cheer when she succeeds. This is a high-interest book that will capture the imaginations of girls and boys alike.

Judy Blume is the much-loved author of several funny and honest stories about children, preteens, and adolescents. Some of her more popular titles include *Superfudge, Fudge-a-mania,* and *Tales of a Fourth Grade Nothing.*

BIBLIOGRAPHY After they finish reading the excerpt from *Otherwise Known as Sheila the Great,* students might want to try an entire novel by Judy Blume. As they grow older, students can choose from among Blume's many pre-adolescent stories. Present these choices to the class. Ask volunteers to read and report on whichever they choose.

IGGIE'S HOUSE	ARE YOU THERE, GOD? IT'S ME, MARGARET	JUST AS LONG AS WE'RE TOGETHER
(Lexile 540)	(Lexile 590)	(Lexile 600)

How to Introduce the Reading

Borrow a copy of *Otherwise Known as Sheila the Great*. Begin the lesson by reading aloud the first few pages. Give students a chance to get to know Sheila and her family before they read the excerpt in the ***Sourcebook***. Use your voice to convey enthusiasm for the story and characters. This will help generate interest in the reading to come.

Other Reading

As children grow older, it becomes more and more difficult to decide which books are appropriate and interesting. These high-interest novels all have a Lexile level similar to that of *Otherwise Known as Sheila the Great* (Lexile 590):

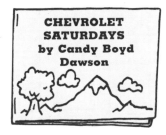

(Lexile 590)

(Lexile 590)

(Lexile 600)

Otherwise Known as Sheila the Great

(STUDENT PAGES 191–198)

Skills and Strategies Overview

PREREADING prediction

READING LEVEL Lexile 590

RESPONSE connect

VOCABULARY ◇sound ◇ceiling ◇phony ◇notice ◇baying

COMPREHENSION story chart

WORD WORK suffixes with words that end in a consonant

PREWRITING character map and story chart

WRITING narrative paragraph / apostrophes

ASSESSMENT ease

OTHER RESOURCES

The first **four** pages of this teacher's lesson describe Parts I–V of the lesson. Also included are these **six** blackline masters. Use them to reinforce key elements of the lesson.

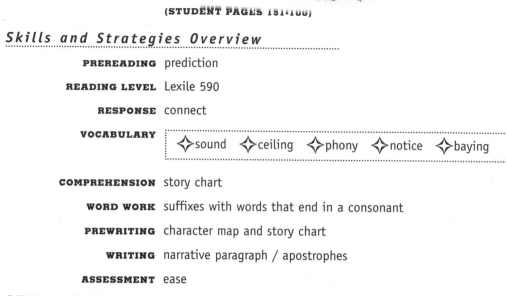

Vocabulary

Prereading

Comprehension

Word Work

Prewriting

Assessment

BEFORE YOU READ

Have a volunteer read aloud the opening paragraph on page 151. Ask students to tell about a time they comforted someone who was afraid of the dark. What did they do or say to allay this person's fears? Use this discussion to help students form an initial personal connection to the text. Then assign the prereading activity, making **predictions**. (Refer to the Strategy Handbook on page 48 for more help.)

Motivation Strategy

CONNECTING WITH STUDENTS   Ask students to comment on what frightened them when they were little. Which fears were the worst? Which were easily conquered? See if students can spot a trend in childhood fears. Make a list on the board and count how many students were afraid of the dark, spiders, snakes, or strange sounds. Help students feel they have something in common with Sheila. This will make her behavior in the story easier to understand and relate to.

Words to Know

CONTEXT CLUES   Use the **Words to Know** blackline master on page 226 as a way to troubleshoot vocabulary problems. After working through the page, you might decide to teach a short vocabulary lesson on using **context clues.**

Work with students to sharpen their ability to find context clues surrounding an unknown or a difficult word. This skill can be particularly useful when reading longer selections, such as the Blume excerpt reprinted in the *Sourcebook*. For practice, ask students to find context clues for these key vocabulary words: *sound* (as an adjective), *ceiling, phony, notice,* and *baying.*

Prereading Strategies

PREDICTION   As a prereading activity, students are asked to make **predictions** about the story. Making predictions about a text can help spark student interest while at the same time give readers a purpose for reading. Students will want to continue reading to find out if their predictions come true. As they're completing the activity on page 152, remind students that you're not concerned about "right" or "wrong" answers at this point. What you are interested in is some good, solid predictions about the story. Students will make their predictions after reordering the three quotations from the story.

ANTICIPATION GUIDE   As an additional prereading activity, have students complete an **anticipation guide**. Choose four or more quotations from the text and ask students to order them in a way that makes sense. Then have them make a prediction about the topic of the story. This activity also will help engage them in the reading.

See the **Before You Read** blackline master on page 227 for an anticipation guide.

MY PURPOSE   Students' purpose for reading the story is to find out what happens to Sheila and why she is scared. Remind them to watch carefully for character clues as they read. Ask them to write their inferences about Sheila and her parents in the Response Notes.

II. READ

Response Strategy

FIRST READING As they read, students should think about the ways in which the main character reminds them of themselves or someone they know. In addition, they should try to **connect** to the character's experiences. Students will do this naturally as they read, especially since Sheila's problem (being afraid) is universal. Each time they make a connection, they should jot it down in the Response Notes.

Comprehension Strategy

SECOND READING To aid in their comprehension of the reading (and the genre), students will fill out five separate **story charts** that explore the literary elements of setting, plot, character, conflict, and resolution. Remind students that the setting of a work is where and when the story takes place. The conflict is the chief problem the main character must face. In all good stories, the problem is resolved by the end of the story.

For more help with **Comprehension,** assign the blackline master on page 228.

Discussion Questions

COMPREHENSION 1. What are some of the things Sheila is afraid of? *(the dark, spiders, strange noises)*

2. What is the noise that frightens Sheila? *(The dog Jennifer is baying at the moon.)*

CRITICAL THINKING 3. How do Sheila's parents act toward her? *(Possible: They are irritated that she keeps waking them up, but they obviously care about her. They keep trying to put her fears to rest.)*

4. What kind of a girl is Sheila? *(Answers will vary. Students might conclude that she's a scaredy-cat, or at least very nervous.)*

5. What would you say is "great" about Sheila? *(Possible: She's funny and intelligent. Plus, she knows just the right way to get her parents to help her without them getting mad.)*

6. What themes does Blume explore in this story? *(Possible: fear and growing up; learning to be independent)*

Reread

THIRD READING Be sure students reread at least once before they begin the prewriting activity. Ask them to look carefully at the scary details they marked and the connections they noted in the Response Notes. Also have them return to the anticipation guide they completed on the **Before You Read** blackline master. Do they still hold the same opinions? Did their prediction about Sheila come true? Show students that anticipating this way can help them think critically about a text.

Word Work

SUFFIXES The Word Work lesson on page 164 affords you an excellent opportunity to review the spelling rules for adding a **suffix** to a one-syllable word that ends in a consonant. Tell students to double the final consonant when adding a suffix only if the suffix begins with a vowel.

For additional practice, see the **Word Work** blackline master on page 229.

III. GET READY TO WRITE

Prewriting Strategies

CHARACTER MAP AND STORY CHART Use the prewriting activity on page 165 to help prepare students to write a narrative paragraph about a time they were afraid. Begin by having students complete a **character map** that explores their inferences about Sheila. Remind the class that good writers never tell readers everything they need to know about a character. They offer clues and then leave it up to the reader to find the clues and decide what they mean. This is called *making inferences,* and it's something good readers do when they read.

Next, have students plan their own stories using the **story chart** on page 166. Notice that the chart is similar to the graphic organizers students completed as they were reading. In addition to planning the setting, problem, and resolution, have students plan which characters (besides themselves) will be included in the writing.

Have students use the **Get Ready to Write** blackline master on page 230.

IV. WRITE

Read aloud the directions on page 167 to help students understand the assignment. Remind them that their **narrative paragraph** should explore a time they were afraid. As always, students should open with a topic sentence that identifies the event to be described and says how it made them feel or what lesson it taught them.

WRITING RUBRIC Use this rubric to help with a quick assessment of students' writing.

Do students' narrative paragraphs

- open with a topic sentence that names the scary event and how it made them feel?

- contain interesting details about setting, character, conflict, and resolution?

- conclude with a sentence that tells what they learned or how they felt after the event was over?

Grammar, Usage, and Mechanics

When students are ready to edit their work, refer them to the **Writers' Checklist.** Teach a lesson on using **apostrophes** to show possession. Have them read aloud the question on the checklist and then apply what they've learned to their own writing.

V. LOOK BACK

Point out the **Readers' Checklist.** Discuss the **ease** or difficulty with which students read Blume's story. Do students find her writing style easy to understand? Did they find themselves involved in the story?

To test students' comprehension, use the **Lesson Test** blackline master on page 231.

Name _____

WORDS TO KNOW

Before Reading

DIRECTIONS Read this paragraph. Decide what you think the underlined words mean. Write their meanings on the lines.

> I was wide awake, but everyone else was <u>sound</u> asleep. I stared at a spider on the <u>ceiling</u>. It was real, not <u>phony</u> like the one I tricked my sister with. I always <u>notice</u> stuff in the dark. I listened to my dog <u>baying</u> at the moon.

1. I think <u>sound</u> means _____ .
2. I think <u>ceiling</u> means _____ .
3. I think <u>phony</u> means _____ .
4. I think <u>notice</u> means _____ .
5. I think <u>baying</u> means _____ .

Practice

Draw a picture of a dog *baying* at the moon.

Name _____

BEFORE YOU READ

Anticipation Guide

DIRECTIONS Read these sentences. Check "agree" or "disagree" for each. Then make a prediction about the main character of the story.

Anticipation Guide: *Otherwise Known as Sheila the Great*

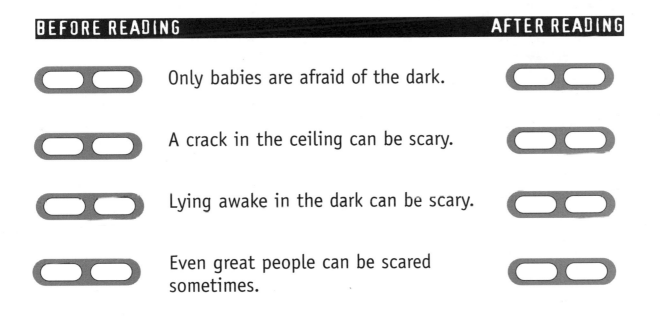

BEFORE READING		AFTER READING
⬭⬭	Only babies are afraid of the dark.	⬭⬭
⬭⬭	A crack in the ceiling can be scary.	⬭⬭
⬭⬭	Lying awake in the dark can be scary.	⬭⬭
⬭⬭	Even great people can be scared sometimes.	⬭⬭

What kind of person do you think Sheila the Great is?

_____

_____

_____

Return to this page after you finish reading. Check "agree" or "disagree" again. How have your opinions changed?

Name _____

COMPREHENSION

Story Chart

DIRECTIONS Write details about Sheila and her scary night on the chart.
Check your book if you need help remembering what happens.
Then answer a question about the story.

What Sheila sees	What Sheila hears	What Sheila feels
a spider creeping		

What do you think Sheila is really afraid of?

_____

_____

_____

_____

Name _____

WORD WORK

After Reading

DIRECTIONS Add suffixes to these words to make new words. Write the new words on the lines. One has been done for you.

1. set + -ing = _setting_
2. stop + -ing = _____
3. spot + -ed = _____
4. cut + -ing = _____
5. tip + -ing = _____
6. wrap + -ed = _____

Practice

DIRECTIONS Proofread this paragraph. Circle the misspelled words. Then rewrite them correctly.

I am wraping a gift for Sheila. Her mother spoted me and asked if I needded help. I said no, but I was hopping she would stay and talk. It's beter to have company when wrapping gifts!

_____
_____
_____

Name _____

GET READY TO WRITE

Writing a Narrative Paragraph

DIRECTIONS Complete this story frame. Tell about a time you were scared.

The event took place

_____ (when)

_____ (where)

_____ (who) was there when it happened.

_____ was also there.

I was _____ while the event was happening.

The main problem was _____

_____ .

The problem was solved when _____

_____ .

The whole thing ended when _____

_____ .

After it was over, I felt _____

_____ .

Name _____

LESSON TEST

Multiple-Choice

DIRECTIONS On the lines, write the letter of the best answer for each question.

_____ 1. In what season does this story take place?
A. winter   C. summer
B. spring   D. fall

_____ 2. What is Sheila's main problem?
A. She is lonely.   C. She is hungry.
B. She can't sleep.   D. She has the hiccups.

_____ 3. Sheila is afraid of . . .
A. a spider.   C. a scratching sound.
B. the wind howling.   D. the moon.

_____ 4. What is Jennifer doing?
A. walking around   C. sleeping
B. eating   D. baying at the moon

_____ 5. How does Sheila's dad feel when she wakes him up?
A. nervous   C. happy
B. sad   D. annoyed

Short Answer

What else could Sheila have done besides wake up her parents?

_____

_____

_____

Hawk, I'm Your Brother

BACKGROUND

In Byrd Baylor's narrative poem "Hawk, I'm Your Brother," Rudy Soto has just one dream: to fly like a hawk over Santos Mountain. To make his dream come true, Rudy captures a hawk in the hopes that this will also allow him to capture the hawk's ability to fly.

Byrd Baylor is the award-winning author of a variety of books for children. In much of her writing, Baylor explores the American Southwest, the desert in particular. In her poems and stories, Baylor sets a tone that reveals her reverence for the land and its people. Baylor keeps her writing style as simple as possible in order to draw attention to the things she describes, rather than the way she describes them. The result is stories that read like quiet poems, and poems that read like quiet stories.

BIBLIOGRAPHY Students might enjoy listening to you read aloud a storybook or book of poetry written by Byrd Baylor. After students complete the *Sourcebook* lesson, follow up on Rudy and the hawk by reading aloud the rest of "Hawk, I'm Your Brother." Or try one of these selections, all of which relate thematically and stylistically to the selection in the *Sourcebook:*

(Lexile 520)

(poetry)

(poetry)

How to Introduce the Reading

Give students a sense of the beauty of Byrd Baylor's writing style before they begin reading the **Sourcebook** selection. Borrow from your library an audiocassette of one of her works and play it for the class. (Some titles are read aloud by Baylor herself.) Invite students to listen with their eyes closed. Tell them you want them to get a feel for Baylor and what she "sounds" like.

Other Reading

Invite students to read other award-winning books about Native Americans. These titles are all popular with fourth-graders and at a reading level close to that of this selection (Lexile 600).

(Lexile 610)   (Lexile 590)   (Lexile 610)

Hawk, I'm Your Brother

(STUDENT PAGES 169-182)

Skills and Strategies Overview

PREREADING	preview
READING LEVEL	Lexile 600
RESPONSE	connect
VOCABULARY	✦float ✦soar ✦canyon ✦ flutters ✦whirlwind
COMPREHENSION	retell
WORD WORK	contractions
PREWRITING	web
WRITING	descriptive paragraph / apostrophes in plural nouns
ASSESSMENT	meaning

OTHER RESOURCES

The first **four** pages of this teacher's lesson describe Parts I–V of the lesson. Also included are these **six** blackline masters. Use them to reinforce key elements of the lesson.

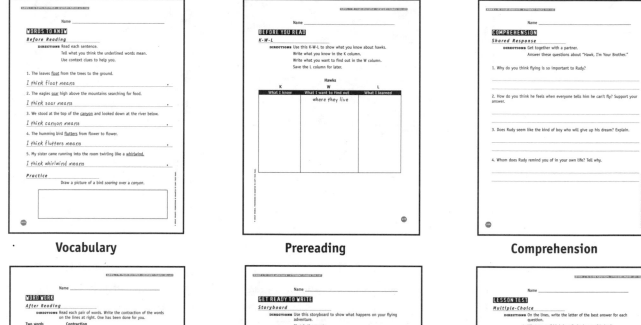

Vocabulary	**Prereading**	**Comprehension**
Word Work	**Prewriting**	**Assessment**

1. BEFORE YOU READ

Have students read the introduction to the unit on page 169. Ask them to picture themselves soaring like a bird above the treetops. What would they see, hear, and feel? Then assign the prereading activity, a **preview**. (Refer to the Strategy Handbook, page 49, for more help.) The previewing activity will help students consider the joy of flying.

Motivation Strategy

MOTIVATING STUDENTS   Read aloud a selection or two from *And It Is Still That Way,* Baylor's award-winning collection of legends told by Arizona Indian children. This book will serve as an excellent warm-up to the topic and theme of "Hawk, I'm Your Brother." Ask students to comment on the legends you read. What do they all have in common? What did the stories make them think about?

Words to Know

CONTEXT CLUES   Use the **Words to Know** blackline master on page 238 as a way to troubleshoot vocabulary problems. After working through the page, you might decide to teach a short vocabulary lesson on using **context clues.**

To begin, show students the key vocabulary words in "Hawk, I'm Your Brother": *float, soar, canyon, flutters, whirlwind.* Remind the class these (and other) words are defined at the bottom of the page, but that you'd like them to try to make predictions about the meanings of the words before they check the footnoted definitions. Model using context clues by saying: "I don't know the meaning of the word *flutters.* I see, however, that it is used to describe the movement of a light-winged bird. I also see that the word *flaps* appears right before that, and I can tell that *flaps* describes the movement of the bird's wings. Could *flutter* have something to do with the movement of the bird as it flies, or the way the bird's wings move as it flies? I'll check the footnoted definition to see if my prediction is correct."

Prereading Strategies

PREVIEW   Before they read, students will do a **preview** of Baylor's story. A preview is a helpful pre-reading strategy because it gives readers a glimpse of what's to come. Thumbing through the pages they are about to read can help students learn about the subject and anticipate any comprehension problems they might have. A preview is also a good way to ease reluctant readers into a long or complex text, or a text that doesn't follow the standard form, such as "Hawk, I'm Your Brother."

K-W-L   As an alternate or additional prereading strategy, have students create a **K-W-L** for hawks. Begin by asking a student to read aloud an encyclopedia entry on hawks. Then set up a K-W-L on the board. Have students make some "what they know" notes, as well as "what they want to find out" notes. When they've finished the story, ask them to return to the L column and say what they've learned. They might be surprised to see that their L columns turn out to be longer than their K columns.

To extend the activity, use the **Before You Read** blackline master on page 239.

MY PURPOSE   Students' purpose for reading "Hawk, I'm Your Brother" is twofold. Be sure students understand both parts of their purpose:

Find out what Rudy's dream of flying is like.

Find out why he wants to fly.

II. READ

Response Strategy

FIRST READING Explain how important it will be for students to make during-reading **connections** to the story. Encourage them to imagine themselves in Rudy's place. Have they ever felt the same kind of longing to fly? Or is there something else they've longed to do that adults told them couldn't be done? Students' comments in the Response Notes will help them become actively involved in the reading.

Comprehension Strategy

SECOND READING As they read "Hawk, I'm Your Brother," students will need to occasionally stop and **retell** the events of the story. In addition, they'll need to tell what they've learned about Rudy. Retelling is a particularly good strategy to use with longer selections such as Baylor's story. You can supplement the interrupters in the text by having students pause at the bottom of each page and tell what happens on that page.

For more help with **Comprehension,** assign the blackline master on page 240.

Discussion Questions

COMPREHENSION 1. Who is the main character of "Hawk, I'm Your Brother"? *(Rudy)*

2. What is Rudy's only dream? *(to fly)*

CRITICAL THINKING 3. Why do you think Rudy wants to fly? *(Have students support their ideas with evidence from the text.)*

4. What does Rudy imagine flying will be like? *(Ask students to quote parts of the text that reveal his thoughts about flying. What does this tell them about Rudy's personality?)*

5. What is the significance of the title? *(Possible: Rudy feels so passionate about flying that he imagines he is the bird—or at least the brother of the bird—that he most admires.)*

Reread

THIRD READING The directions on page 178 ask students to reread with an eye as to why Rudy would like to fly and what he thinks flying would be like. You may want students to reread in pairs, especially since this is a longer story.

Word Work

CONTRACTIONS The Word Work lesson on page 179 offers students some excellent practice on forming **contractions.** Before they begin, remind them that an apostrophe takes the place of the missing letter or letters when forming a contraction. In addition to the contractions on the page, you might have students practice forming contractions from *this will, they will, does not, had not, must not, that is, who is, one is,* and *who are.* These usually are the most troubling contractions for low-level readers and students who speak English as a second language.

For additional practice, see the **Word Work** blackline master on page 241.

III. GET READY TO WRITE

Prewriting Strategies

WEB Use the prewriting activity on page 180 to help prepare students to write a descriptive paragraph about a flying adventure. Point out the link between Baylor's story and the writing activity. Then have students complete the **web** about flying. Encourage them to think of sensory details that will help readers, see, hear, and feel the flying adventure described.

Supplement the activity in the book by having students write a topic sentence about how they will fly and where they will go. Remind students that their topic sentence should also tell how flying makes them feel. Post this equation on the board and have students use it to write their topic sentences:

my flight + how it makes me feel = my topic sentence

Have students use the **Get Ready to Write** blackline master on page 242.

IV. WRITE

The directions at the top of page 181 instruct students to write a **descriptive paragraph** about a flying adventure. Remind the class of the rule that a descriptive paragraph has a beginning (the introduction, which includes the topic sentence), a middle (body), and an end (concluding sentence).

WRITING RUBRIC Use this rubric to help with a quick assessment of students' writing.

Do students' descriptive paragraphs

- open with a topic sentence that names the flying adventure and how it makes the writer feel?

- offer three or more sensory details about the adventure?

- include a closing sentence that is a restatement of the topic sentence?

- stay focused on the topic of flying?

Grammar, Usage, and Mechanics

When students are ready to proofread their work, refer them to the **Writers' Checklist.** Read aloud the information about **apostrophes** in plural nouns. For practice, put some words on the board and have students make possessives out of each. These words might work well: *children, deer, ox,* and *women*.

V. LOOK BACK

Reflect with students on the **meaning** of "Hawk, I'm Your Brother." Refer them to the **Readers' Checklist** and help them express the connections they were able to make to the text as they were reading.

To test students' comprehension, use the **Lesson Test** blackline master on page 243.

Name _____ _____

WORDS TO KNOW

Before Reading

DIRECTIONS Read each sentence.

Tell what you think the underlined words mean.

Use context clues to help you.

1. The leaves <u>float</u> from the trees to the ground.

I think <u>float</u> means _____ .

2. The eagles <u>soar</u> high above the mountains searching for food.

I think <u>soar</u> means _____ .

3. We stood at the top of the <u>canyon</u> and looked down at the river below.

I think <u>canyon</u> means _____ .

4. The humming bird <u>flutters</u> from flower to flower.

I think <u>flutters</u> means _____ .

5. My sister came running into the room twirling like a <u>whirlwind.</u>

I think <u>whirlwind</u> means _____ .

Practice

Draw a picture of a bird *soaring* over a *canyon.*

_____

238

Name _____

BEFORE YOU READ

K-W-L

DIRECTIONS Use this K-W-L to show what you know about hawks.

Write what you know in the K column.

Write what you want to find out in the W column.

Save the L column for later.

Hawks

K What I know	W What I want to find out	L What I learned
	where they live	

Name _____

COMPREHENSION

Shared Response

DIRECTIONS Get together with a partner.

Answer these questions about "Hawk, I'm Your Brother."

1. Why do you think flying is so important to Rudy?

_____

_____

2. How do you think he feels when everyone tells him he can't fly? Support your answer.

_____

_____

3. Does Rudy seem like the kind of boy who will give up his dream? Explain.

_____

_____

4. Whom does Rudy remind you of in your own life? Tell why.

_____

_____

Name _____

WORD WORK

After Reading

DIRECTIONS Read each pair of words. Write the contraction of the words on the lines at right. One has been done for you.

Two words	Contraction
1. I am	I'm
2. should have	
3. was not	
4. I will	
5. are not	
6. can not	

Practice

DIRECTIONS Read the contractions in the box. Use each in a sentence that shows you know what the contraction means.

don't	weren't	that'll	she'll

7. _____

8. _____

9. _____

10. _____

Name _____

GET READY TO WRITE

Storyboard

DIRECTIONS Use this storyboard to show what happens on your flying adventure.

Sketch the events.

Write sentences underneath that describe what you drew.

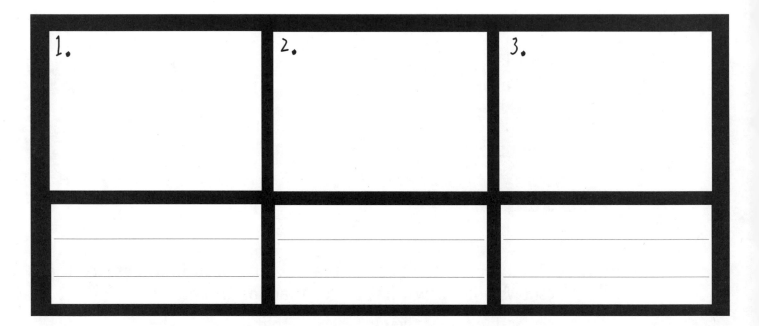

Name _____

LESSON TEST

Multiple-Choice

DIRECTIONS On the lines, write the letter of the best answer for each question.

_____ 1. What type of bird does Rudy dream of being?
A. a wren   C. a sparrow
B. a hawk   D. an eagle

_____ 2. When Rudy was born, he . . .
A. reached for the birds. C. began to fly.
B. went to sleep.   D. said the word "fly."

_____ 3. Where does Rudy play?
A. in the forest   C. in the desert
B. on a playground   D. on the mountainside

_____ 4. What was **not** one of Rudy's first words?
A. sky   C. flying
B. up there   D. bird

_____ 5. Whom does Rudy think might have the secret to flying?
A. children   C. old people
B. magic people   D. B. and C. only

Short Answer

Why do you think Rudy wants to fly?

_____

_____

_____

"Fun" and "By Myself"

BACKGROUND

Eloise Greenfield is the author of more than thirty children's books of fiction, poetry, and biography. Over the course of her career, Greenfield has received an incredible forty awards for her writing, including the prestigious Coretta Scott King Award for her book, *Africa Dream*.

As a poet, Greenfield has an uncanny ability to create images that are fresh and interesting. She seems to write with the reluctant reader in mind. Her poems are as fun as they are lyrical, and children of all ages respond well to them.

The two Eloise Greenfield poems reprinted in the **Sourcebook** are found in the collection of poetry *Honey, I Love*. In "Fun," Greenfield uses sensory language to tell about a squeaky school piano. In "By Myself," Greenfield celebrates the individual and reminds readers that the best thing to be is "what I care to be." Both poems exemplify the kind of effortless rhythm and rhyme schemes that have become a hallmark of Greenfield's poetic style.

BIBLIOGRAPHY Students might enjoy another work by Eloise Greenfield. Choose one of her poetry anthologies to read aloud, or invite students to do some reading on their own. Suggest they begin by checking out these titles:

(Lexile 620)   (Lexile 600)   (poetry)

How to Introduce the Reading

To help set the appropriate mood for the two poems in the ***Sourcebook***, read *Africa Dream* aloud to students. It has a poetic flavor that makes it the perfect accompaniment to "Fun" and "By Myself." After your read-aloud, discuss Greenfield's writing style: her word choices, tone, and mood. In this work and others, Greenfield celebrates the individual and explores the theme of pride in oneself.

As an alternate introductory activity, have students research Greenfield on the Internet. Students might be interested in reading the advice she offers young writers. Have them start with this website: http://teacher.scholastic.com/authorsandbooks/authors/egreen.

Other Reading

Encourage students to appreciate poetry. Work to foster in your students a lifelong love for the sounds and style of a good poem. To help, read aloud from one of these modern classics:

"Fun" and "By Myself"

(STUDENT PAGES 183-191)

Skills and Strategies Overview

PREREADING	web
READING LEVEL	NP*
RESPONSE	draw
VOCABULARY	◇pedal ◇dimple ◇gospel song ◇gong ◇turning
COMPREHENSION	double-entry journal
WORD WORK	consonants and consonant clusters
PREWRITING	brainstorm
WRITING	poem / apostrophes in plural nouns
ASSESSMENT	understanding

*NP=Not Prose and cannot be Lexiled

OTHER RESOURCES

The first **four** pages of this teacher's lesson describe Parts I–V of the lesson. Also included are these **six** blackline masters. Use them to reinforce key elements of the lesson.

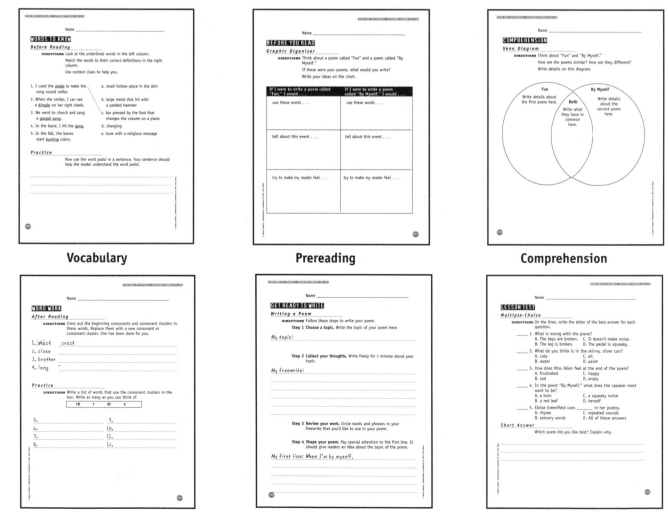

Vocabulary

Prereading

Comprehension

Word Work

Prewriting

Assessment

BEFORE YOU READ

Discuss mood with students. Mood is the atmosphere of a work of literature. It is the feeling the work arouses in a reader: happiness, sadness, peacefulness, and so on. For an example of mood, ask students to think of stories they've read that have easily identified moods. (Help them name scary or sad stories.) Point out the elements that create this mood: word choice, illustrations, tone, and so on. Then have students begin the prereading activity, a **web**. (Refer to the Strategy Handbook, page 51, for more help.)

Motivation Strategy

CONNECTING WITH STUDENTS
Help students connect to the topic of the poems before they begin reading. Have them say what they would write about if they were asked to create a poem called "Fun." Have them do the same with the poem "By Myself." Encourage students to name words, ideas, and images that come to mind when they hear these two titles. This short discussion will also reinforce your lesson on mood.

Words to Know

PRONUNCIATION
Use the **Words to Know** blackline master on page 250 as a way to troubleshoot vocabulary problems. After working through the page, you might decide to teach a short vocabulary lesson on pronounciation.

To begin, show students the key vocabulary words in the two Greenfield poems: *pedal, dimple, gospel song, gong,* and *turning.* As you know, knowing how to pronounce a new word is as important as knowing the word's definition. Write the following words and pronunciations on the board and ask students to practice pronouncing them:

pedal (PE duhl)   *dimple* (DIM pul)

Look for other words in the poems that may be a challenge for your students, such as *greasy* (GREE see) and *plinked* (PLINKD).

Prereading Strategies

WEB
As a prereading activity, students are asked to make a **web** that explores this topic: "What I'd like to be." Have students call on their own thoughts and feelings as they complete the web. This prereading activity will help you create another valuable link between student and text.

GRAPHIC ORGANIZER
As an additional prereading activity, have students make some before-reading connections to the subject matter (and mood) of the two Greenfield poems. Photocopy the **Before You Read** blackline master on page 251 and ask students to fill in the chart with thoughts and ideas that come to mind when they hear the two titles. Also ask them to list experiences or events. If they were to write a poem about "Fun," what event or experience from their own lives would they write about?

MY PURPOSE
Students' purpose for reading "Fun" and "By Myself" will be to find out what the poems say to them personally. Encourage students to make a personal connection to the words and lines in each poem. Also have them think about the mood of the two works. Mood can profoundly affect what a poem "says" to a reader.

II. READ

Response Strategy

FIRST READING When students are ready to read, remind them of the importance of visualizing as they read. Tell students to **draw** in the Response Notes and try to capture the feelings and actions that Greenfield describes. Each time students make a picture, they'll need to think carefully about what is being described in the text. This can greatly improve their comprehension of the two poems.

Comprehension Strategy

SECOND READING During their reading of "Fun" and "By Myself," students will need to pause at two different points and fill in **double-entry journals** that ask them to respond to a line from the poem with their own thoughts and feelings. Again, your purpose here is to help students make a personal connection to the reading. Students will find it easier to understand the mood and themes of the two works if they've made connections to their own lives along the way.

For more help with **Comprehension,** assign the blackline master on page 252.

Discussion Questions

COMPREHENSION 1. Who is having "fun" in "Fun"? *(the children, but not Miss Allen)*

2. How does the speaker of "By Myself" feel when she is alone? *(Possible: happy)*

CRITICAL THINKING 3. What is funny about "Fun"? *(Possible: Miss Allen is irritated.)*

4. What kind of a person is the speaker of "By Myself?" *(Possible: happy and self-confident)*

5. What is the mood of "Fun"? What is the mood of "By Myself"? *(Possible: Both have lighthearted, happy moods.)*

6. What do you notice about the style of the two poems? *(Possible: "By Myself" is rhymed verse, and "Fun" is unrhymed. Students might also notice that many of the words in "Fun" sound the same, due to alliteration. For example, point out repeated initial consonant sounds in plinked, piano, pushed, pedal.)*

Reread

THIRD READING Have students do a paired third reading of the two poems. Ask pairs to read aloud the poems to each other, using expression. Then have partners trade books to see the sketches the other has made. Students can add to their sketches at this point if they like.

Word Work

CONSONANTS AND CONSONANT CLUSTERS The Word Work lesson on page 188 offers additional practice on initial **consonants** and **consonant clusters.** Review the clusters used on the page (*pl, ch, dr*). Then write a list of other clusters on the board. Choose those that seem problematic to your students (e.g., *th, wh, th, scr*).

For additional practice, see the **Word Work** blackline master on page 253.

III. GET READY TO WRITE

Prewriting Strategies

BRAINSTORM As preparation for the writing assignment, students will **brainstorm** a list of eight or more ideas of what they would like to be. This activity can be done alone or in pairs, with pairs helping each other come up with ideas. When they've finished, have students circle the three or four ideas they like best. These should be the basis for the poem they write on page 189.

Have students use the **Get Ready to Write** blackline master on page 254.

IV. WRITE

On pages 190–191 students are asked to write a **poem** that explores the kind of person they'd like to be. Remind the class to use "By Myself" as a model for their work. Also remind them that their poems should open with the line starters on page 190. They should strive to use descriptive words and sensory language in their writing. As always, the amount students write is not nearly as important as the quality of the writing.

WRITING RUBRIC Use this writing rubric to help you quickly assess students work. Do students' poems

- begin with the appropriate opening lines?

- tell about what students would like to be?

- contain descriptive details and sensory language?

- seem similar in form and content to "By Myself"?

Grammar, Usage, and Mechanics

When students are ready to edit their work, refer them to the **Writers' Checklist.** Teach a short lesson on **apostrophes** in plural nouns. Focus on forming possessives from plural words that end in *s*. For practice, have students make possessives of these words and use the words in a sentence.

trees   The trees' leaves are changing color.

boys   The boys' sports equipment is in the shed.

V. LOOK BACK

At the end of the lesson, refer students to the **Readers' Checklist** and talk about their **understanding** of "Fun" and "By Myself." Remind the class that many times a poet's message or theme is whatever the reader takes away from the reading. It is not important to reach consensus on what a literary work means.

To test students' comprehension, use the **Lesson Test** blackline master on page 255.

Name _____

WORDS TO KNOW

Before Reading

DIRECTIONS Look at the underlined words in the left column.

Match the words to their correct definitions in the right column.

Use context clues to help you.

1. I used the <u>pedal</u> to make the song sound softer.

2. When she smiles, I can see a <u>dimple</u> on her right cheek.

3. We went to church and sang a <u>gospel song</u>.

4. In the band, I hit the <u>gong</u>.

5. In the fall, the leaves start <u>turning</u> colors.

a. small hollow place in the skin

b. large metal disk hit with a padded hammer

c. bar pressed by the foot that changes the volume on a piano

d. changing

e. tune with a religious message

Practice

Now use the word *pedal* in a sentence. Your sentence should help the reader understand the word *pedal*.

_____

_____

_____

Name _____

BEFORE YOU READ

Graphic Organizer

DIRECTIONS Think about a poem called "Fun" and a poem called "By Myself."

If these were your poems, what would you write?

Write your ideas on the chart.

If I were to write a poem called "Fun," I would . . .	If I were to write a poem called "By Myself," I would . . .
use these words . . .	use these words . . .
tell about this event . . .	tell about this event . . .
try to make my reader feel . . .	try to make my reader feel . . .

Name

COMPREHENSION

Venn Diagram

DIRECTIONS Think about "Fun" and "By Myself."

How are the poems similar? How are they different?

Write details on this diagram.

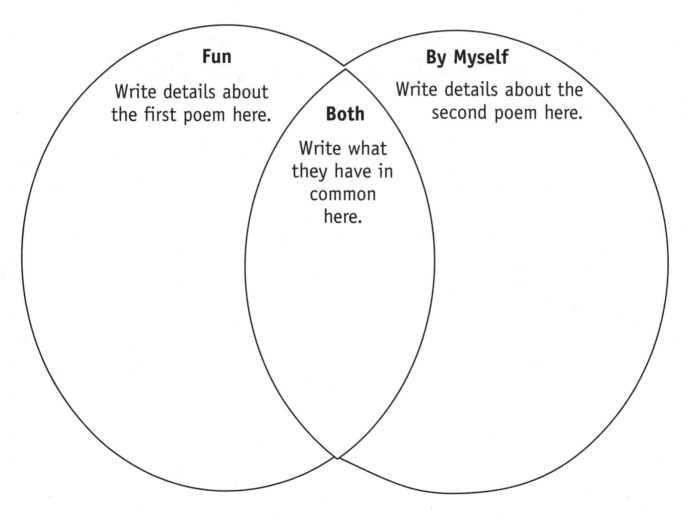

Fun

Write details about the first poem here.

Both

Write what they have in common here.

By Myself

Write details about the second poem here.

Name _____

WORD WORK

After Reading

DIRECTIONS Cross out the beginning consonants and consonant clusters in these words. Replace them with a new consonant or consonant cluster. One has been done for you.

1. ~~sh~~ack   crack _____

2. close _____

3. brother _____

4. long _____

Practice

DIRECTIONS Write a list of words that use the consonant clusters in the box. Write as many as you can think of.

ch	r	dr	s

5. _____   9. _____

6. _____   10. _____

7. _____   11. _____

8. _____   12. _____

Name _____

GET READY TO WRITE

Writing a Poem

DIRECTIONS Follow these steps to write your poem.

Step 1 Choose a topic. Write the topic of your poem here.

My topic: _____

Step 2 Collect your thoughts. Write freely for 1 minute about your topic.

My freewrite: _____

_____

_____

_____

_____

Step 3 Review your work. Circle words and phrases in your freewrite that you'd like to use in your poem.

Step 4 Shape your poem. Pay special attention to the first line. It should give readers an idea about the topic of the poem.

My first line: When I'm by myself,

_____

_____

Name _____

LESSON TEST

Multiple-Choice

DIRECTIONS On the lines, write the letter of the best answer for each question.

_____ 1. What is wrong with the piano?
   A. The keys are broken.   C. It doesn't make noise.
   B. The leg is broken.   D. The pedal is squeaky.

_____ 2. What do you think is in the skinny, silver can?
   A. cola   C. oil
   B. water   D. paint

_____ 3. How does Miss Allen feel at the end of the poem?
   A. frustrated   C. happy
   B. sad   D. angry

_____ 4. In the poem "By Myself," what does the speaker most want to be?
   A. a twin   C. a squeaky noise
   B. a red leaf   D. herself

_____ 5. Eloise Greenfield uses _____ in her poetry.
   A. rhyme   C. repeated sounds
   B. sensory words D. All of these answers

Short Answer

Which poem did you like best? Explain why.

_____

_____

_____

BOOKER T. WASHINGTON

II. Read

(Students' answers will vary.)

What was Booker T. Washington's home like?

(He lived in a shack on a Virginia plantation. The house had a dirt floor and a door that didn't shut well. The windows didn't have glass, and there were cracks in the walls. Booker didn't have a bed.)

What two jobs did Booker T. Washington have?

(He swatted flies away from the table during meals. He also took corn to the mill.)

Word Work

(Students' answers will vary.)

birthday	birth + day
fireplace	fire + place
mealtimes	meal + times
inside	in + side

TEACHER'S GUIDE ANSWERS

Words to Know

1. plantation
2. shack
3. ground
4. meal
5. master

Comprehension

smart — orphaned — poor — sickly — education — hard (Booker T. Washington)

Word Work

1. mealtimes
2. slowpoke
3. bookkeeper
4. sunlight
5. sometimes
6. teacher
7. body
8. paper
9. drop
10. out

Assessment

1. A
2. C
3. B
4. B
5. C

GLORIA'S WAY

II. Read

(Students' answers will vary.)

What You Think It Means

(If Gloria lets Julian do what he wants, he will think she is a good friend.)

What You Think It Means

(Gloria shouldn't think about her friendship too much. If someone has a good friend, the only thing that matters is that both people are happy. Happiness can't be measured by people.)

Word Work

Word	+ed	+ing
1. edge	edged	edging
2. like	liked	liking
3. measure	measured	measuring
4. suppose	supposed	supposing

TEACHER'S GUIDE ANSWERS

Words to Know

1. c
2. a
3. e
4. d
5. b

Comprehension

1. Gloria is upset that her friend Julian may not like her more than his other friends.
2. Answers will vary.
3. For Gloria, friendship is similar to a contest. Until she talks to her mom, she thinks it is something one wins and earns.
4. Answers will vary.

Word Work

1. fined
2. living
3. smiled
4. baker
5. voter
6. shame
7. scrape
8. time
9. write
10. mope

Assessment

1. B
2. B
3. A
4. A
5. C

TRAIN TO SOMEWHERE

II. Read

(Students' answers will vary.)

Why are the orphans going to the New West?

(There are a lot of people living there who want to adopt children.)

Why is Marianne worried?

(She doesn't think she's pretty, so she fears nobody will adopt her. Also, she's worried about being separated from Nora.)

Word Work

1. there
2. their
3. They're
4. their
5. There
6. they're

TEACHER'S GUIDE ANSWERS

Words to Know

1. conductor
2. bundles
3. aboard
4. coach
5. platform

Word Work

1. see
2. too
3. won
4. sea
5. two

they're — a word that shows ownership
there — a contraction for *they are*
their — a word that points out direction

Get Ready to Write

(Answers will vary.)

sight words
1. dirty glass
2. hair twirls and bright ringlets
3. grass rolling

sound words
1. gliding on tracks
2. wheels mumble
3. clickety-clack, clickety-clack

taste words
1. thick milk out of a can
2. fillings
3. sandwiches

touch words
1. clutches at my hand
2. hard seats
3. soft feather

smell words
1. medicine
2. new clothes
3. old clothes

Assessment

1. B
2. C
3. B
4. D
5. C

FIRST FLIGHT

II. Read

(Students' answers will vary.)
What You Think It Means
(The men looked different from Tom and his family, so he thought that they came from a different place.)
What You Think It Means
(The wind will make the first airplane fly.)

Word Work

1. I'm
2. it's
3. you've
4. you'll
5. don't
6. that's
7. they've

III. Get Ready to Write

(Students' answers will vary.)
Who: Orville and Wilbur Wright
What: They are testing their new invention.
When: 1902
Where: Kitty Hawk, North Carolina
Why: They have invented a machine that can fly on the wind.
Closing Sentence: Answers will vary.

TEACHER'S GUIDE ANSWERS

Words to Know

1. tent
2. beach
3. machine
4. windiest
5. imagining

Comprehension

1. Orv and Will Wright were brothers who built the first flying machine.
2. He is curious and wants to know how the machine will fly.
3. Flying machines are things that fly in the air like birds. They need wind and a certain balance of the wings to fly.
4. An important idea is to never underestimate things. Things that may seem impossible may actually be possible.

Word Work

1. we are
2. they have
3. is not
4. we would
5. do not
6. could not
7.–10. Answers will vary.

Assessment

1. D
2. C
3. C
4. B
5. A

A DROP OF BLOOD

II. Read

(Students' answers will vary.)

Where does blood go in your body?

(It moves through little tubes to the tips of your fingers, your head, your toes, and other places.)

Why is oxygen important to people?

(Your body needs oxygen in every part of your body all the time. Your lungs breathe oxygen, and blood carries it to the rest of your body.)

Word Work

parted

department

removed

movement

unmoveable

III. Get Ready to Write

1. carry oxygen to my brain so I can think
2. take oxygen from my lungs and carry it to every part of my body
3. carry oxygen to my bones so they are healthy
4. carry food to every part of my body
5. carry oxygen to my muscles so they are strong

TEACHER'S GUIDE ANSWERS

Words to Know

1. smallest and most basic units in a living thing
2. liquid that flows freely
3. organ into which food passes first
4. instrument that shows objects that can't be seen by the eye alone
5. organ into which food passes last

Comprehension

Blood Cells: red; tiny; donut-shaped

Blood: flows all over body; red; moving

Plasma: watery fluid;   carries blood cells

Word Work

1. trouble
2. govern
3. shake
4. smile
5. develop
6. knowing, knows
7. climbing, climbed, climbs
8. closing, closed, closes, closer, closest
9. moving, moved, mover, moves
10. changing, changed, changes

Get Ready to Write

1. You breathe oxygen into your lungs.
2. The red cells in your blood take the oxygen from your lungs.
3. Red cells carry the oxygen to every part of your body.

1. When you eat, food goes down to your stomach and intestines.
2. Food changes into fluid.
3. The fluid moves from your intestines into your blood.

Assessment

1. A
2. C
3. B
4. A
5. C

A RIVER DREAM

II. Read

(Students' answers will vary.)

Why should Mark keep watching the fly?
(He will not feel a fish on his line. He has to see it.)

What happened when Mark raised the rod?
(The line ran out as a trout jumped up out of the water.)

Word Work

The fishing rod had a <u>fly</u>. — small insect with wings

The <u>fly</u> buzzed by my nose. — kind of fish

The <u>rainbow</u> shone in the sky. — hook used to catch fish

The <u>rainbow</u> trout wiggled at the end of the fishing line. — colorful reflection of light that shines in the sky after a rainfall

TEACHER'S GUIDE ANSWERS

Words to Know

(Answers will vary.)
1. threw
2. staring with one's mouth open
3. jumped
4. strong
5. beautiful, fabulous

Word Work

1. bird
2. dark, sweet fruit
3. plans with a friend
4. jumped, moved toward
5. day, month, year
6.–7. Answers will vary.

Assessment

1. D
2. B
3. A
4. D
5. C

HOW WE LEARNED THE EARTH IS ROUND

II. Read

(Students' answers will vary.)

Why did people think the earth was flat?

(The earth looks flat because people are too small to see the curve of the ground.)

What made the Greeks wonder about the shape of the earth?

(They noticed that ships seemed to disappear as they sailed away.)

Word Work

Long Words Word	Prefix Suffix	Base
discovered	dis ed	cover
returning	re ing	turn
reopening	re ing	open
unlearned	un ed	learn

TEACHER'S GUIDE ANSWERS

Words to Know

1. hull
2. harbor
3. surface
4. disappears
5. prairie

Comprehension

1. The ancient Greeks were the first people to discover the earth was round.
2. They lived about 2,500 years ago.
3.–5. Answers will vary.

Word Work

1. appeared   appear
2. trusting   trust
3. guessed   guess
4. moving   move
5. stopped, stopping
6. untie, tied, retie
7. shutting
8. redo, undo, doing
9. replay, played, playing
10. retell, telling

Get Ready to Write

1. At first, the Greeks believed the earth was flat.
2. But certain Greeks thought hard and tried to explain things.
3. They asked themselves questions and thought some more.
4. Finally, they realized the earth curved in all directions.

Assessment

1. B
2. C
3. D
4. C
5. A

I AM ROSA PARKS

II. Read

(Students' answers will vary.)

Effect: (The black person could be arrested or killed.)

Effect: (The driver asks the black people to give their seats to the white man.)

Effect: (The driver calls two policemen to arrest Rosa.)

Word Work

(Students' answers will vary.)
1. back, black, track, tack
2. jail, mail, bail, tail, flail, trail
3. seat, meat, beat, treat
4. send, mend, bend, tend, blend, spend
5. park, mark, bark, spark

Get Ready to Write

How was she brave?	How was she peaceful?
She stayed in her seat when the bus driver told her to get up.	She did not start a fight with the bus driver.
How was she stubborn?	How was she fair?
She refused to give up up her seat.	She wanted to be treated equally.

Rosa

TEACHER'S GUIDE ANSWERS

Words to Know

(Answers will vary.)
1. places that charge people to eat
2. sent to jail
3. followed the rules
4. away
5. part

Word Work

(Answers will vary.)
1. tack
2. slot
3. day
4. came

Assessment

1. D
2. A
3. B
4. C
5. A

GERMS MAKE ME SICK!

II. Read

(Students' answers will vary.)

How are viruses different from bacteria?

(They are a lot smaller. They also come in different shapes.)

What 2 parts of the body help keep germs out of you?

(Skin, nose, mouth, and throat are all possible answers.)

What are 3 ways germs can get inside of you?

(You can breathe in germs when someone else sneezes. You can get germs in your stomach when you use a straw with germs on it. You can scrape your knee on the ground and let germs into your skin.)

Word Work

(Students' answers will vary.)

Compound Word	Small Word	Small Word
everywhere	every	where
everything	every	thing
inside	in	side
into	in	to

III. Get Ready to Write

1. What are germs?
(Germs are tiny living things.)

2. How do germs make me sick?
(Some bacteria and viruses slip inside us and make us sick.)

3. Why do germs make us sick?
(My body cannot fight off some harmful bacteria and viruses.)

4. Where are germs?
(Germs are found everywhere.)

5. Who can catch germs?
(Everyone can catch germs.)

TEACHER'S GUIDE ANSWERS

Words to Know

(Answers will vary.)

1. hurt
2. sicknesses
3. circular, coiled
4. dangerous

Before You Read

What are they? living things

Size very tiny

Place #1 air, food, water

germs

What do they look like? Bacteria look like little round balls, straight rods, or spirals. Viruses look like balls with spikes, loaves of bread, or metal screws with spider legs.

Where can you catch them?

Place #2 skin and everything you touch

Word Work

1. underwater
2. sickbed
3. cannot
4. fingernail
5. schoolteacher
6. stepmother
7. raincoat
8. backache
9. applesauce

Assessment

1. D
2. D
3. A
4. C
5. B

THE SKIRT

II. Read

(Students' answers will vary.)

Why is Miata worried?

(She left her skirt on the bus, and she needs it for her dance show. She doesn't want to be the only girl without a costume. Also, the skirt used to belong to her mother. Her mother always gets angry when Miata loses things.)

What do you think Miata should do? Why?

(She could call the bus company and see if the driver found her skirt. That way, she could get it back.)

Word Work

autograph
automobile
automotive
automated
automation

III. Get Ready to Write

(Students' answers will vary.)

Miata's mistake

(She forgets her skirt on the bus.)

When and where it took place

(on a city street after school)

What happens

2. (She can't catch the bus.)

3. (She catches a paper airplane, which is a math quiz with a perfect score.)

TEACHER'S GUIDE ANSWERS

Words to Know

(Answers will vary.)

1. speaking angrily
2. back
3. tiredness
4. group
5. old and worn

Comprehension

What she looks and acts like

She acts proud of her heritage and culture. She acts irresponsibly because she loses a lot of things.

What she thinks about

She thinks about the dance troupe and her parents' certain disappointment in her.

How others feel about her

Her parents are tired of her losing things.

How I feel about her

Answers will vary.

Word Work

Someone
Someday
Somebody
Somehow
Someplace
Sometime

1. underwater
2. postwar
3. supermarket
4. underwear

Assessment

1. C
2. A
3. B
4. B
5. A

THROUGH GRANDPA'S EYES

II. Read

(Students' answers will vary.)

How does the sun wake up Grandpa?

(It makes him warm.)

What does Grandpa teach John to do?

(Grandpa teaches John to close his eyes to hear where his Grandmother is.)

Word Work

Same Consonant Letters	Different Consonant Letters
bur/row	mor/ning
run/ning	break/fast
nod/ded	fin/ger
lad/der	

TEACHER'S GUIDE ANSWERS

Words to Know

1. d
2. a
3. e
4. b
5. c

Comprehension

The story takes place in Grandpa's house.

It takes place in present day.

The characters are Grandpa, Nana, and John.

The characters have these problems: Grandpa is blind and John doesn't understand what that's like.

This is how they solve the problems: Grandpa tells John to close his eyes and take in the sounds and smells of the house. John carefully observes Grandpa's morning routine.

The story ends when Nana, Grandpa, and John have breakfast. John understands Grandpa's life better than before.

Word Work

1. dan/ger
2. break/fast
3. ban/is/ter
4. mar/i/golds
5. sum/mer [left-hand column]
6. but/tered [left-hand column]
7. fol/low [left-hand column]
8. grand/pa [right-hand column]
9. fin/gers [right-hand column]

Assessment

1. C
2. A
3. B
4. B
5. D

ME AND MY SHADOW
II. Read

(Students' answers will vary.)
What things have you learned about day and night?
(When our side of the earth faces the sun, it is day. When the round earth rotates, we find ourselves in the shadow of night.)
What have you learned about the moon?
(The moon has a shadow. One side always faces the sun and is bright. The shadow side is always dark. The moon takes many days to circle the earth.)

Word Work

moonbeam
moonshine
moonrise
moonlight

III. Get Ready to Write

(Students' answers will vary.)
Detail #1
(When our part of the earth spins toward the sun, we have day.)
Detail #2
(When our part of the earth spins away from the sun, we have night.)
Detail #3
(One part of the moon is always dark.)
Detail #4
(Each night we see different amounts of the moon's shadow.)

TEACHER'S GUIDE ANSWERS
Words to Know

1. shine, shadow
2. gigantic
3. sliver
4. circles

Word Work

1. snowflake
2. tabletop
3. outcome
4. outfield
5. oversee
6. seafood
7. infield
8. income
9. snowfall
10. rainfall

11. every/body
12. butter/milk
13. back/ground
14. some/how

Assessment

1. A
2. C
3. B
4. C
5. C

FOLLOW THAT TRASH

II. Read

(Students' answers will vary.)

My Thoughts About It

(Students may mention that they don't want to see landfills or have one in their neighborhood.)

My Thoughts About It

(Students will probably say that they do not want incinerators where they live.)

Word Work

dry	drier	driest
easy	easier	easiest
noisy	noisier	noisiest
busy	busier	busiest
creepy	creepier	creepiest

III. Get Ready to Write

(Students' answers will vary.)

How much trash is there?

(180 million tons every year from Americans)

What are the dangers of too much trash?

(We don't know where to put the trash. Landfills and incinerators have dangers. Landfills can leak poison into water, and incinerators make posion air.)

Why is recycling good?

(If people recycle, there is less trash.)

What are the dangers of burning trash?

(Some of the smoke is poisonous. It also makes soot and ash.)

TEACHER'S GUIDE ANSWERS

Words to Know

(Answers will vary.)
1. hole
2. toxins
3. poison
4. trash burners, dust

Word Work

1. carrying
2. scariest
3. tinier
4. worrier
5. happiest
6. varying
7.–10. Answers will vary
[Circle dirty, likely, city, try.]
7. dirtier
8. liking
9. cities
10. tried

Assessment

1. C
2. D
3. D
4. C
5. D

OTHERWISE KNOWN AS SHEILA THE GREAT

II. Read

(Students' answers will vary.)

What is the setting of the story?

Where? (Sheila's bedroom)

When? (Late at night)

What 2 things have happened up to this point?

1. (Sheila has had trouble sleeping in her new room.)
2. (Sheila sees a spider and gets scared.)

Who are 2 characters in the story? What have you learned about each one?

1. (Sheila is afraid of the dark.)
2. (Sheila's father helps her even though he's tired.)

What is Sheila's problem? How is it solved?

1. (She sees a spider.)
2. (She gets her father to kill it.)

What 3 things happened after Sheila's dad killed the spider? Put the events in order in the storyboard boxes.

1. (Sheila hears a noise outside and gets scared.)
2. (She wakes up her mother.)
3. (Sheila's mom doesn't like the noise either, but when she looks outside, she laughs.)

Word Work

1. running
2. sitting
3. batted
4. putting
5. bigger
6. ripped

III. Get Ready to Write

(Students' answers will vary.)

How was she imaginative?

(She imagines bad things when she sees the spider and hears the noise. She thinks the spider will come get her, and she thinks there is a ghost outside.)

How was she a troublemaker?

(She keeps waking up her parents.)

Why didn't she give up?

(She's too scared to sleep.)

TEACHER'S GUIDE ANSWERS

Words to Know

(Answers will vary.)

1. deeply
2. the inside upper surface of a room
3. fake
4. see
5. howling

Comprehension

What Sheila sees	What Sheila hears	What Sheila feels
a spider creeping	a scary noise	scared, worried

Word Work

1. setting
2. stopping
3. spotted
4. cutting
5. tipping
6. wrapped

I am wraping a gift for Sheila. Her mother spoted me and asked if I needded help. I said no, but I was hopping she would stay and talk. It's beter to have company when wrapping gifts!

wrapping, spotted, needed, hoping, better

Assessment

1. C
2. B
3. A
4. D
5. D

HAWK I'M YOUR BROTHER

II. Read

(Students' answers will vary.)

What does Rudy Soto dream of doing and being?

(He wants to fly like a hawk.)

What is so hard about Rudy Soto's only wish?

(Humans can't fly.)

What are 3 things you have learned about Rudy Soto?

(Students might mention that he wants to fly, that he always wanted to be a bird when he was little, and that he believes that some humans can secretly fly.)

Word Work

that's
won't
he'd
they'd
don't

TEACHER'S GUIDE ANSWERS

Words to Know

(Answers will vary.)
1. fall gently
2. fly
3. deep valley
4. flies
5. tornado

Word Work

1. I'm
2. should've
3. wasn't
4. I'll
5. aren't
6. can't
7.–10. Answers will vary.

Assessment

1. B
2. A
3. D
4. A
5. D

FUN AND BY MYSELF

II. Read

(Students' answers will vary.)

What You Think This Means

(Students might mention that the music teacher may not be happy that the piano is still broken, and that's why she doesn't laugh with the class.)

What You Think This Means

(Students might mention that the speaker would rather be him/herself than any of those other objects that he/she imagines.)

Word Work

(Students' answers will vary.)
chin, grin, bin, tin
red, bed, fed, wed
drink, brink, pink, link
sing, bring, ring, cling

TEACHER'S GUIDE ANSWERS

Words to Know

1. c
2. a
3. e
4. b
5. d

Comprehension

Fun
music, piano, squeaky sounds, singing, laughter with other people

Both poems
music, squeaky sounds, song

By Myself
being alone

Word Work

(Answers will vary.)
1. crack
2. pose
3. mother
4. gong
5.–12. Answers will vary.

Assessment

1. D
2. C
3. A
4. D
5. D

PE signals a pupil's edition page number.

TG signals a teacher's guide page number.